Law and the Shaping of the
American Labor Movement

D0095960

Law and the Shaping of the American Labor Movement

William E. Forbath

Harvard University Press
Cambridge, Massachusetts
London, England
1991

K H

An earlier version of this work appeared in the *Harvard Law Review* 102, no. 6 (April 1989).

This book is printed on acid-free paper, and its binding materials
have been chosen for strength and durability.

Library of Congress Cataloging-in-Publication Data

Forbath, William E., 1952–
    Law and the shaping of the American labor movement / William E. Forbath.
        p. cm.
    Includes bibliographical references and index.
    ISBN 0-674-51781-4 (alk. paper).—ISBN 0-674-51782-2 (pbk.)
    1. Trade-unions—United States—Political activity—History. 2. Working class—
United States—Political activity—History. 3. Labor disputes—United States—History. I. Title.
HD6510.F67 1991
322′.2′0973—dc20   90-49662
                                                                                      CIP

12/23/05

To my parents,
Thomas and Pauline Forbath

Contents

Preface

Like all historical scholarship, this work is a conversation with persons long gone—a conversation, in this case, about the development of American labor law and the American labor movement. It is also the product of conversations with persons present, many of whom I thank in the acknowledgments, both about American labor history and about the broader themes of law, politics, and society. Here I briefly describe that broader conversation, which has involved scholars in diverse disciplines over the past several years, for it reveals the theoretical issues that concerned me during the research and writing of this book. The description is here separated out, because, like most histories, the one that follows leaves many of its theoretical arguments implicit, woven into narrative. For some readers that style of argument will seem appropriate, but others will want a more explicit theoretical discussion.

My first concern lies in the question of how far the legal order has had an autonomous role in social and political development. A great many legal scholars and legal historians insist upon the lesson of Legal Realism: that law almost always plays a derivative role in human affairs. Given the prominence of law in American culture and society, this denial of its relatively independent power to shape social life is surprising. Some critics depict the denial as a flight by lawyers from responsibility for the substantial power they wield. Perhaps the denial springs, instead, from disillusionment regarding law's efficacy as a vehicle of reform.

Whatever may inspire it, however, the view of law as epiphenomenon shaped the reactions of my own law teachers to this historical project when it first occurred to me, almost a decade ago. They told me it was folly, and no doubt that had much to do with my deciding to pursue the subject. It was folly, they said, because the research would be terribly time-consuming (on that they were right), and because it simply would show that the notorious Lochner Era judiciary and the infamous labor injunction made no big difference in American labor history. The era's courts and judge-made law reflected more fundamental conflicts and developments. What happened would have happened, whatever the courts had done.

I was vexed; all the more so because, as I show in the text, my mentors' view proved also to be the prevailing one among labor historians. That cannot be because the historians have a stake in what may be a collective denial on the part of legal academics. Rather, I think, the denial partakes of broader currents of modern social thought, which have tended to see the realm of the social and economic as determining, and the realm of law and politics as derivative. Among historians and social and political scientists as with law professors, scholarship about law and society has emphasized the ways that the interests of social groups shape the law; it has slighted the ways that law shapes the very interests that play upon it.

Of late, this view of law as epiphenomenon or "superstructure" has been subject to a growing battery of criticisms, most insightfully, I think, by critical legal scholars like Robert Gordon.[1] However, the argument for viewing law as "constitutive" rather than "reflective" of the social world has been made largely on the plane of theory. One aim of this book is to offer a more empirically grounded case for the constitutive power of law. Thus, in my research, I tried to probe the limitations of the prevailing model, and to explore how the specific structures and traditions of American law contributed toward shaping the labor movement's and its members' identities, material interests, and capacities for collective action.

---

1. See, especially, Gordon, "Critical Legal Histories," 36 *Stanf. L. Rev.* 57 (1984).

To inquire into the shaping influence of law requires a view of *how* law may have influenced social actors; that is the second main theoretical concern animating the book. Two general views have proved fruitful. The first is associated with social choice theory. This view focuses upon the material constraints and inducements which any institutional order creates for social actors. It posits that social actors make "rational choices" among alternative courses of action. But, in the version of the theory that interests me, it also underscores that such choices are always contextually constrained, and however rational in the short term, often yield a long-term irrationality. Thus, the constraints on action forged by the legal order may render rational the pursuit of a narrow trade union strategy: yet this strategy may yield a weakened labor movement in the long run. That is what Joel Rogers has found in applying this model of social action to the unions and labor law of the post-World-War II era.[2] The model also proved useful in analyzing the constraints and inducements which courts created for earlier trade unionists who were making strategic choices about politics and organizing in the Gilded Age. Therefore, although it does not use the vocabulary of social choice theory, my narrative is informed by some of its basic insights. I have tried to show how American trade unionists made many hard-nosed choices that importantly narrowed their political and industrial paths as a result of harsh constraints and significant incentives forged by the nation's courts.

At least in the law schools, proponents of this theoretical approach insist that it exhausts the explanatory significance of law for social action. In particular, they insist that attending to the ideological, discursive, and symbolic dimensions of law adds precious little to an understanding of the historical conduct of subordinate groups such as labor.

I disagree. First, material constraints and inducements, and calculations of group self-interest, do not present themselves in transparent, nonideological terms. They are always imbued with ideo-

---

2. See Rogers, "Divide and Conquer: Further 'Reflections on the Distinctive Character of American Labor Law,' " 1990 *Wisc. L. Rev.* 1.

logical significance. Subordinate groups encounter an enormous array of coercions and constraints. Some they defy, even in the face of state violence; some they seek to alter in various ways; others they simply take for granted and may not even recognize as constraints. These individual and collective responses go a long way toward defining the political outlook of a social movement such as labor. In the case of no group or movement with which I am familiar can one derive these choices simply on the basis of an "objective" calculus of material costs and benefits. For culture and ideology also profoundly affect the responses, fostering particular forms of political creativity and bravery, and, at the same time, obscuring or condemning other possible avenues of change and resistance.

Of course, one could concede that culture and ideology shape the ways that people experience and respond to material constraints and constellations of social power; and still one could object that the language and imagery of *law* play a negligible part in this. How far the discourse of law enters ordinary people's social experience is, largely, an empirical question, and the answer may vary greatly across different groups and different time periods. In the case of the group and era studied here, I will show that the penetration was great. Late-nineteenth- and early-twentieth-century trade unionists encountered the language of judge-made law everywhere, setting many of the key terms of public discourse and debate. They wrestled with it, and it entered deeply into their own language of protest and reform.

A last question remains, one much discussed by social and cultural as well as legal thinkers. How ought we to characterize the influence of legal discourse or "rights talk" upon the consciousness and aspirations of subordinate social groups? Many scholars characterize "rights talk" as profoundly confining, as silencing the authentic aspirations of subordinate groups; others insist that the language of law supplies invaluable rhetorical resources for articulating those aspirations. In the Conclusion I return to this debate and offer some insights that emerge from this work. It is sufficient here to note that, as with the theme of law's "constitutive" power, much of the writing on this topic has a decidedly abstract air. I think we do well to address it in a less abstract fashion, by attending in some detail to the specific and intricately intertwined experiences of such groups with law as language, as discourse, on one hand, and, on the other, law as institutional practices, constraints, and legitimated violence. That too is my aim.

Acknowledgments

I began the research on which this book rests while a Samuel I. Golieb Fellow in Legal History at New York University School of Law. I thank William E. Nelson and John Reid who preside over the fellowship and all other aspects of legal history at N.Y.U. for generously sharing their knowledge and enthusiasms. Most of the financial support for my work has come from the UCLA Academic Senate and Institute for Industrial Relations and from the UCLA School of Law Dean's Fund. However, Dean Susan Prager has done much more than sign checks; her support is deeply appreciated.

Jacqueline Braitman, Julia Jimmerson, Louis Karlin, Mark Palley, and, especially, Margaret Talbot provided expert research assistance.

Various portions of this book were first presented as papers at a number of venues: the M.I.T. Industrial Relations Symposium; the Harvard/M.I.T. Colloquium on Society and Politics; the Workshop in Critical Perspectives on the History of American Labor Law, Georgetown Law School, June 1987; "Historical Perspectives on American Labor: An Interdisciplinary Approach," New York State School of Industrial and Labor Relations, Cornell University, April 1988; Organization of American Historians, Annual Conference, 1988; Law and Society Association Annual Conference, 1988. My thanks to the commentators and participants at these events. I hope they will note that I have tried hard to respond to their many keen criticisms and suggestions.

As the various papers found their way into a single, unwieldy manuscript, many friends and colleagues generously contributed substantive ideas and criticisms as well as stern editorial advice. I would like especially to thank Richard Abel, Jean-Christophe Agnew, Alison Anderson, Peter Arenella, James Atleson, Craig Becker, David Brion Davis, Carole Goldberg-Ambrose, Dirk Hartog, Sanford Jacoby, Kenneth Karst, Daniel Lowenstein, Staughton Lynd, Martha Minow, Gary Nash, Karen Orren, Steven Ross, Steven Shiffrin, Theda Skocpol, Katherine Stone, Chris Tomlins, John Wiley, and Stephen Yeazell. In addition, two fellow historians, David Scobey and Allan Steinberg, offered solidarity and hours of conversation.

Improved by all their efforts, this work first appeared as a long article in *Harvard Law Review* where it benefited from the editing of Warrington Parker and Robert Townsend.

Then, as I was turning to other tasks Aida Donald of Harvard University Press generously invited me to publish the long article as a short book. Neither of us, it turned out, wanted to see the article simply reprinted, and so began a process of modest revision and expansion. These modest improvements might have continued indefinitely, but for the editor's wise nudging. Rita Saavedra shared what turned out to be some onerous technical chores involved in turning article into book.

Throughout, Joel Handler was there with unflagging support and shrewd criticisms. Robert Goldstein supplied wonderfully lucid readings and rereadings and always buoyed my spirits. Zoey and Aaron Forbath, for their parts, provided enormous joy. Judy Coffin's love, humor, patience, and impatience saw me through.

Law and the Shaping of the
American Labor Movement

Introduction

America's labor laws provide far fewer protections against exploi-
tation, injury, illness, and unemployment than the laws of the dozen
other leading Western industrial nations. Our laws also exclude more
workers from their crabbed coverage.[1] A key reason for the paltriness
of American labor law and social provision lies in the fact that
American workers never forged a class-based political movement to
press for more generous and inclusive protections. Elsewhere, in the
decades around the turn of the century, labor's national organizations
embraced broad, class-based programs of reform and redistribution,
but the American Federation of Labor spurned them, with the lasting
effects that countless scholars have chronicled.[2] How does one explain this; how account for organized labor's historical devotion to
voluntarism?[3] And what part did the legal order itself play in the
story?

1. See Bok, "Reflections on the Distinctive Character of American Labor Law," 84
Harv. L. Rev. 1394, 1417–20, 1459–60 (1971); Rogers, "Divide and Conquer: Further
'Reflections on the Distinctive Character of American Labor Law,'" 1990 *Wisconsin
Law Review 1*; Shalev, "Class Politics and the Western Welfare State," in *Social Policy
Evaluation: Social and Political Perspectives* (S. Spiro & E. Yuchtman-Yaar, eds., 1983).
In the recent past attacks on the welfare state appear to have swept through several of
these other nations. Yet even today the relative paltriness of American labor law and
social provision is remarkable. See Rogers, supra.

2. See Bok, supra note 1; Rogers, supra note 1.

3. "Voluntarism" is the political philosophy that predominated in the American labor
movement from the 1890s through the 1920s and continues to color organized labor's
outlook today. It stands for a staunch commitment to the "private" ordering of industrial

The problem of explaining American labor's distinctive politics has a traditional answer, one that suggests that the legal order's role in shaping labor's politics was a minor and derivative one. American workers and the American labor movement have always been conservative and hostile to broad visions of reform and redistribution. The unique social context of the United States produced a working class that lacked "class consciousness." Instead, American workers have been wedded to individualistic strategies for bettering their lot, and the American labor movement has generally scorned class-based reform efforts. American trade unionists have been "pragmatists," not "class conscious" but "job conscious."[4] This particular union vision, the tale continues, sprang from various structural features of American society. Social mobility, ethnic and racial divisions among workers, and a pervasive individualism undermined the cohesiveness and class-based politics that apparently characterized Europe's working classes.

Traditional accounts do not fail to note how courts loomed large in late-nineteenth-century labor conflicts, enjoining strikes and voiding reforms. Indeed, the first great labor historians in the early twentieth century, those whom I will call the classics, paid much greater attention to the role of law and government in labor history than do current accounts. Even in the classic accounts, however, the law's role emerges as derivative—a reflection of "deeper" social forces including the same individualism that shaped the labor movement itself. These deeper structural forces shaped labor's politics. Experiences and struggles in the actual arenas of law and government

relations between unions and employers. Voluntarism teaches that workers should pursue improvements in their living and working conditions through collective bargaining and concerted action in the private sphere rather than through public political action and legislation. Thus voluntarism is labor's version of laissez-faire, an anti-statist philosophy that says that the "best thing the State can do for Labor is to leave Labor alone." Gompers, "Judicial Vindication of Labor's Claims," 7 *Am. Federationist* 283, 284 (1901). In truth, even in the Gompers era, voluntarism never meant abstention from politics. Rather, as we shall see, voluntarism meant spurning broad "positive" state regulation of industrial life, such as maximum-hours laws for all workers or state-based social insurance.

4. The phrases are from Selig Perlman's classic, *A Theory of the Labor Movement* (1923). On Perlman see infra Chap. 1, notes 1 and 2 and accompanying text.

tend to be mere epiphenomena, determining nothing essential about organized workers' political identities and aspirations.

As we shall see, today's labor historians reject the classic view that workers and the labor movement in nineteenth-century America were conservative compared to their European counterparts.[5] Yet they share with the classics a picture of the law as derivative. Indeed, they tend to rely on an old-fashioned Marxist model of the state as "superstructure," and the state and legal order are abstract and scantily examined in their work.

Although deeply indebted to the pioneers of American labor history and also to the labor historians of today, this book suggests that some of their key common assumptions about law's role in that history are wrong. It argues that during the late nineteenth and early twentieth centuries, courts, legal doctrine and language, and legal violence played a crucial, irreducible part in shaping the modern American labor movement, a part that repays closer scrutiny.

Contemporary labor historians have redrawn the classic picture of the nineteenth-century labor movement. The American labor movement, these scholars have shown, was *not* born with a voluntarist perspective. In the Gilded Age, from the 1870s through the 1890s, most American trade unionists embraced broad and radical reform ambitions. They did not shun politics in favor of pure and simple trade unionism, but rather put great faith in the ballot and in reforming industry through legislation.[6] What now demands analysis is the way in which labor's broader vision of reform was dethroned by the rise of Samuel Gompers's "pure and simple"[7] trade unionism. What requires explanation are not the mythical "permanent" structures of American labor history but its significant ruptures.

Paradoxically, the "new *social* history of American workers," as the work of these historians is often called, invites renewed attention to the role of the state and the polity in shaping the American

5. See infra pp. 11–15.
6. See infra Chap. 1, notes 6–14 and accompanying text.
7. 1. S. Gompers, *Seventy Years of Life and Labour* 385 (complete repr. ed. 1967) [hereinafter S. Gompers, *Seventy Years*].

labor movement.[8] Their groundbreaking studies undermine the view that social factors can adequately account for the distinctive character of American labor politics. But as yet they have forged no new account, partly, I think, because their dedication to rewriting history "from the bottom up" has led most of these historians away from the centers of public power and the making and workings of state policy. Yet the logic of their discoveries compels one to ask: what lessons from the arenas of politics, làwmaking, and social reform, and what engagements with state policy and state power inspired labor voluntarism?

8. The great innovation of the new social history of American workers as compared to the work of the field's founders has been the new history's expansion of the realms of research beyond the institutional history of trade unions. Thus labor historians now focus on the workplace and the community as well as the union, the rank and file as well as the leaders, the unorganized as well as the organized, and the cultural as well as the institutional life of workers. They have transformed our understanding of the American working class in the nineteenth century. See infra pp. 11–15, 18–23; see also Brody, "The Old Labor History and the New: In Search of an American Working Class," 20 *Lab. Hist.* 111 (1979); Montgomery, "To Study the People: The American Working Class," 21 *Lab. Hist.* 485 (1980); Veysey, "The 'New' Social History in the Context of American Historical Writing," 7 *Rev. Am. Hist.* 1 (1979).

Lately, labor historians have called for renewed attention to the roles of state and polity in shaping working-class life. See generally Bernstein, "Expanding the Boundaries of the Political: Workers and Political Change in the Nineteenth Century," 32 *Int'l Lab. and Working-Class Hist.* 59 (1987). Some splendid recent work has been done on labor, local politics, and political parties. See, e.g., A. Bridges, *City of the Republic: Antebellum New York and the Origins of Machine Politics* (1984); S. Wilentz, *Chants Democratic: New York City and the Rise of the American Working Class, 1788–1850* (1984). Despite wide acknowledgment of its significance, however, the "state" remains abstract and scantily examined in recent labor history. David Montgomery's magisterial *The Fall of the House of Labor: The Workplace, the State, and American Labor Activism, 1865–1925* (1987) [hereinafter D. Montgomery, *Fall of the House of Labor*] is a case in point. Montgomery underscores the significance of state repression—the use of federal and state troops and local police against strikers. He makes passing reference to the labor injunction. But, despite the presence of the "state" in his subtitle, Montgomery's account of the state is thin compared to the empirical richness and careful analysis that characterize his book's other dimensions. Although he offers superb structural accounts of the economy and the workplace, he leaves the state's structure unanalyzed. He neglects the court's active policymaking and ignores the chronic battles for policymaking initiative between courts and legislatures. Finally, Montgomery also passes over the labor movement's mounting preoccupation and engagements with judge-made law. He asserts that the judiciary's role was unimportant. See id. at 271. I aim, by emulating Montgomery's craftsmanship, to show that he is mistaken.

These questions, and especially labor's experiences with the legal order, have received little sustained scrutiny since the work of the classics in the early part of the century.[9] Many historians have remarked that it is time to revisit these domains. That is what I do here, but I have tried to employ a multiple vision. I look at contests and developments in the centers of public authority and public discourse; but, at the same time, I also examine this history "from the

9. Many scholars have written insightful legal and intellectual histories of substantive due process and the law of the labor injunction; these were indispensable to this book. But precious few have tried to capture the law's historical significance for the development of the American labor movement. Among the legal histories I found most useful were J. Commons, *The Legal Foundations of Capitalism* (1930); A. Paul, *Conservative Crisis and the Rule of Law: Attitudes of Bar and Bench, 1887–1895* (1960); Hovenkamp, "The Political Economy of Substantive Due Process," 40 *Stanf. L. Rev.* 379 (1988); Soifer, "The Paradox of Paternalism and Laissez-faire Constitutionalism: United States Supreme Court, 1888–1921," 5 *Law and Hist. Rev.* 249 (1987); Nelles, "A Strike and Its Legal Consequences," 40 *Yale L. J.* 507 (1931).

Most valuable among the few sustained discussions of law's role in labor history were C. Tomlins, *The State and the Unions: Labor Relations, Law, and the Organized Labor Movement in America, 1880–1960* (1985); G. Eggert, *Railroad Labor Disputes: The Beginnings of Federal Strike Policy* (1967); and I. Bernstein, *The Lean Years: A History of the American Worker, 1920–1933*, at 190–244, 391–415 (1960) [hereinafter I. Bernstein, *The Lean Years*]. These pioneering books provided invaluable insights and points of departure. I first learned about the anti-injunction movement from a paper by my friend and law school classmate Christopher Stone, now of the Vera Foundation in New York. I also have benefited greatly from the recent work of two historians who have been exploring some similar terrain. See Fink, "Labor, Liberty, and the Law: Trade Unionism and the Problem of the American Constitutional Order," 74 *J. Am. Hist.* 904 (1987); Ernst, "The Yellow-Dog Contract and Liberal Reform, 1917–1932," 30 *Lab. Hist.* 251 (1989); Ernst, "The Woodtrim War: A Case Study in the History of Labor Activism, Antitrust Litigation, and Legal Culture, 1910–1917" (Working Paper, Institute for Legal Studies, Univ. of Wisconsin, Madison, 1988).

Two books from the injunction era were indispensable: Felix Frankfurter and Nathan Greene's famous *The Labor Injunction* (1930), with its detailed account of the doctrinal evolution and procedural enormities of that instrument and its survey of legislative efforts at reforming judicial practices; and Edwin Witte's *The Government in Labor Disputes* (1930), which examines many dimensions of local, state, and federal government involvement in strikes.

Only recently have I read the Ph.D. dissertation of Victoria Hattam, a historically minded political scientist. Although methodologically rather different, it pursues some of the same questions as this book. V. Hattam, "Unions and Politics: The Courts and American Labor" (Ph.D. diss., Massachusetts Institute of Technology, 1987). I discuss Hattam's work in 16 *Law and Social Inquiry* (Winter 1991).

bottom up.'' My aim is to reconstruct the links between these events at the centers of power and the language and experiences of labor in local contexts and conflicts.

The project seems overdue in light of law's central place in the historical experience of American labor. Nowhere else among industrial nations did the judiciary hold such sway over labor relations as in nineteenth- and early-twentieth-century America. Nowhere else did trade unionists contend so constantly with judge-made law.

By examining organized workers' actual encounters with courts and judge-made law, this book uncovers the legal construction of a particular form of labor consciousness. Using not only judicial opinions and other traditional legal materials but also labor and local newspapers, early labor law journals, state and federal legislative and commission hearings, and publications of employers' associations and reformers, the book explores a broad sampling of the diverse ways in which trade unionists encountered judges' words and deeds.[10] At the same time, it describes the main lines of legal development, examining how courts fashioned their preeminent role in the fields of labor relations and industrial strife. Drawing these two inquiries together, the book examines how this long era of judicial ascendancy shaped labor's vision and strategies.

During the decades bracketing the turn of the century, courts exacted from labor many key strategic and ideological accommo-

10. I have studied organized workers' experiences with courts and law in two major industrial cities, New York and Chicago, and in four major industries (throughout the country), railroads, coal mining, machine-making, and garment-making. The sources I relied on included: (1) *National Labor Tribune* (Pittsburgh, 1872 through the 1890s); *John Swinton's Paper* (New York, 1883–1887); *Knights of Labor* (Chicago, 1886–1887); *Journal of the Knights of Labor* (Washington, D.C., 1880–1897); *United Mine Workers Journal* (1896–1932); *American Federationist* (1894–1932); *The Advance* (New York, 1917–1932); *Justice* (New York, 1915–1932); *Chicago Federation News* (1919–1930); *Illinois State Federation of Labor Weekly Newsletter* (Chicago, 1915–1929); (2) *The New York Times*; *The Chicago Daily News*; *The Chicago Inter-Ocean*; and *The Chicago Tribune*; (3) *The American Federation of Labor Records: The Samuel Gompers Era, 1877–1937*, which reproduce on microfilm the correspondence of the AFL president's office, executive council vote books, speech files, a circular and neostyle file, and voluminous material gathered in ''reference material'' and ''scrapbook files''; (4) the volumes of testimony gathered around the country by the federal Industrial Relations Commission of 1898 to 1901, U.S. Congress, House of Representatives, *Industrial*

dations, changing trade unionists' views of what was possible and desirable in politics and industry. Judicial review and administration of labor legislation helped make broad legal reforms seem futile. Similarly, the courts' harshly repressive law of industrial conflict helped make broad, inclusive unionism seem too costly and a more cautious, narrower unionism essential.

Courts shaped labor's strategic calculus; in more subtle ways, law also altered labor's ideology. Freedom of combination and collective action, freedom to strike and boycott, these seemed indispensable to the very existence of trade unions. Thus while broad, positive reforms came to seem futile, the proliferation of anti-strike and anti-boycott decrees riveted trade unionists' political energies on re-pealing this judge-made regime. The goal of industrial liberty—negative and anti-statist—became the heart of labor politics for several crucial decades. During them the burdens and indignities of semioutlawry made challenging judge-made labor law a constant endeavor in the courts, in legislatures, and in the public sphere. At the same time, the courts' very sway made common law and constitutional discourse beckon as the surest framework within which to contend for legitimacy and relief. Thus, labor leaders at all levels began to speak and think more and more in the language of the law. As a language of protest and reform, law proved Janus-faced—at once enabling and confining. Common law doctrine was open-ended

Commission Reports, vols. 1–19, H.R. Doc. no. 380, 57th Cong., 1st Sess. (1902); and the federal Commission on Industrial Relations during the Wilson era, S. Doc. no. 415, 64th Cong., 1st Sess. (1912–1916); (5) the volumes of testimony taken at hearings conducted by the United States House and Senate Judiciary Committees on the major anti-injunction bills, see *Injunctions, Hearings on H.R. 55 and Other Bills before the House Committee on the Judiciary*, 62d Cong., 2d Sess. (1912); *Hearings before a Subcommittee of the Senate Committee on the Judiciary on H.R. 23635*, 62d Cong., 2d Sess. (1912); *Limiting Scope of Injunctions in Labor Disputes, Hearings before the Subcommittee of the Senate Committee on the Judiciary*, 70th Cong., 1st Sess. (1928); *Committee Substitute to Bill Limiting Scope of Injunctions in Labor Disputes, Hearings before the Subcommittee of the Senate Committee on the Judiciary*, 71st Cong., 2d Sess. (1930); (6) the following reform publications: *The Survey* (East Stroudsburg, 1897–1932), and *The American Labor Legislation Review* (New York, 1911–1932); and (7) the following employers' associations' publications: *Law and Labor* (1919–1932; published by the American Anti-Boycott Association, renamed the League for Industrial Rights in 1919); *Iron Age*; and *Railroad Age*.

enough to enable labor's self-taught jurists to construct alternative interpretations of labor's collective liberties, and those interpretations found encouragement from a handful of dissenting jurists. Moreover, constitutional tradition carried recessive radical strains, from which workers created an eloquent case for defying judge-made law and demanding recognition of their suppressed "rights." On the other hand, labor's embrace of a law-inspired, laissez-faire rights talk displaced a more radical vocabulary of reform. In this fashion, mingling coercion and consent, the legal order encouraged a reshaping of the labor movement's dominant ideology.

This book presents its argument in five parts. Chapter 1 sets the stage, providing a brief consideration of the relevant historiography, a guide to the courts' central and distinctive place in the nineteenth-century American state, and a recasting of the old question of the peculiarity of American labor politics. Chapter 2 recounts the history of judicial review of labor's late nineteenth-century efforts to promote change through reform legislation and describes how judicial hostility to those efforts influenced labor's political culture.

Chapter 3 explores how courts also intervened in the "private" realm of market relations, a realm to which labor leaders increasingly turned as they abandoned broader legislative reform ambitions. Throughout the nineteenth and early twentieth centuries, the judiciary defined the relatively narrow and unchanging bounds of allowable collective action. Beginning in the 1880s, however, courts vastly enlarged their role in regulating and policing industrial conflict. This expansion occurred through the vehicle of the labor injunction, and Chapter 3 examines the rise of "government by injunction" in the context of the Gilded Age's tumultuous boycotts and railway strikes. Finally, Chapter 3 examines the way that suppression of these new forms of labor protest affected the evolution of union strategy and outlook.

The American Federation of Labor's (AFL's) gradual relinquishing of many broad-gauged weapons did not end its preoccupation with the courts, because those weapons hardly exhausted the kinds of vital strike goals and activities that the courts would continue to assail from the turn of the century through the 1920s. Chapter 4 describes the continued, indeed increasing, experience of "government by injunction," building up a thick description of how courts and court-minted ideology figured in the varieties of state violence that early-twentieth-century trade unionists encountered. Chapter 4 also completes a neglected chapter in the history of American federalism, showing how judges repeatedly removed from local officials critical bits of authority over labor protest and mutual aid. By way of counterpoint, Chapter 4 concludes by exploring how some strikes flourished despite judicial condemnation and how a handful of unions even turned to the courts for injunctions against truculent employers.

Chapter 5 turns to the AFL's anti-injunction campaigns and labor's broader struggle for legitimacy in a court-dominated era. It reveals that labor's leading spokesmen recast an older republican "rights talk" into the common law's liberal mold, relinquishing a vision of law actively reconstructing the industrial world. Law reshaped labor's language and outlook in conservative directions, but labor also eventually reshaped the law. Chapter 5 shows how organized workers built on the antislavery legacy and created an alternative constitutional vision. It argues that industrial "disorder" and workers' massive yet articulate defiance of judge-made law gradually persuaded state and national lawmakers and political elites that the old legal order was untenable and that labor's exiled constitutional claims demanded recognition.

1 | Broad Contexts

Recasting American Exceptionalism

The picture of the American labor movement as one that was born with a "pragmatic," voluntarist perspective was first drawn in scholarly fashion by the founders of American labor history, John Commons, his colleagues at the University of Wisconsin, and particularly his brilliant student Selig Perlman.[1] Commons, Perlman, and generations of scholars after them have sought to explain this phenomenon, widely known as American "exceptionalism," American workers' apparent deviance from other countries' working-class history, their supposed lack of class consciousness. Some scholars have emphasized the privileged economic condition of American workers in the nineteenth and twentieth centuries: their affluence and mobility. Others have singled out the unique ethnic and religious divisions within the American working class. Generally, accounts of American "exceptionalism" have underscored both these factors and also pointed to the unusual pervasiveness of liberalism and individualism in American life, to America's tenacious two-party system, and to its distinctly "weak" and fragmented liberal state.[2]

1. See J. Commons, S. Perlman, et al., *History of Labour in the United States*, 4 vols. (1918–26); S. Perlman, *A Theory of the Labor Movement* (1928). See also the classic study by a German sociologist, W. Sombart, *Why Is There No Socialism in America?* (1905).

2. A recent effort by a leading student of American political development to identify and assess all the theories and factors that have been put forth is Lipset, "Why No

However, by reexamining nineteenth-century working-class life and politics in unprecedented detail, the "new labor historians" have transformed our understanding of American labor's historical experience.

First, the new labor historians have undermined the traditional assumption that American workers were more individualistic and less disposed than their English or European counterparts to turn to collective action as a way to better their lot. Through careful quantitative work and fine-grained case studies, they have rediscovered that the history of the workplace in industrializing America is a history of recurring militancy and class-based, as well as shop- and craft-based, collective action.[3] Measured by the frequency and duration of strikes, and by the number of "days lost" due to strikes per thousand workers, workers' disposition toward collective action was greater in the United States than in most European nations, and considerably greater than in England, during the late nineteenth and early twentieth centuries.[4]

Socialism in the United States," in *Sources of Contemporary Radicalism* (S. Bialer and S. Sluzar, eds., 1977). Lipset overlooks constitutional structure and the judiciary as factors. Another recent contribution is a rich collection of essays by both European and American scholars: J. Heffer and J. Rovet, eds., *Why Is There No Socialism in the United States?* (1988).

Among the classics, Sombart underscored social and geographical mobility and ethnic divisions, as well as the early enfranchisement of the American working class, as the keys to understanding American labor's "individualism," its lack of "class consciousness," and its voluntarist politics. So too did John Commons and the Wisconsin School founders of American labor history—and their heirs: P. Taft, *The AFL in the Time of Gompers* (1957); G. Grob, *Workers and Utopia* (1961); N. Fine, *Labor and Farmer Parties in the United States* (1961). Of the founders, Perlman was most sensitive to state- and polity-based sources of American labor politics. See *A Theory of the Labor Movement* at 61–64, 156–70. Perlman emphasized the role of judicial review in accounting for the AFL's "stubborn 'economism'." Id. at 170.

3. See P. Edwards, *Strikes in the United States, 1881–1974* (1982); Montgomery, "Strikes in the Nineteenth Century," 4 *Soc. Sci. Hist.* 81 (1980); J. Brecher, *Strike!* (1972). On the cultural sources of this militancy and mutualism, see Herbert Gutman's pioneering essays in H. Gutman, *Work, Culture and Society in Industrializing America* (1976).

4. See P. Edwards, supra Chap. 1, note 3, at 219–20; Korpi and Shalev, "Strikes, Industrial Relations, and Class Conflict in Capitalist Societies," 30 *Brit. J. of Soc.* 164 (1979).

The new labor history undermines another old assumption by showing that the mutualism that organized workers displayed at work frequently carried over into their communities and their political lives. In the older accounts of the nineteenth-century labor movement, the voices of radical politics and broad reform ambitions are those of meddling middle-class politicians, marginal intellectuals, and professional reformers and "agitators."[5] The bulk of real trade unionists, so the story goes, were committed to "trade unionism pure and simple." In actuality, however, most Gilded Age trade unionists were steeped in labor politics and reform, and most reformers were active trade unionists.[6] The Gilded Age's leading labor journalist, John Swinton, expressed a majority view when he proclaimed, "there is a world in the belly of the ballot." "All the enginery of power" lies there.[7]

The largest and most influential of Gilded Age labor organizations was the Knights of Labor, whose active membership in the 1880s numbered almost one million.[8] The Knights exemplified Gilded Age workers' melding of trade union and political endeavors as well as

5. See, e.g., S. Perlman, *A Theory of the Labor Movement;* S. Perlman, *The History of Trade Unionism in the United States* (1922); 2 J. Commons et al., *History of Labour in the United States* (1935); G. Grob, *Workers and Utopia* (1961).

6. See D. Montgomery, *Beyond Equality: Labor and the Radical Republicans, 1862–1873* (1967); L. Fink, *Workingmen's Democracy: The Knights of Labor and American Politics* (1983) [hereinafter, L. Fink, *Workingmen's Democracy*]; S. Ross, *Workers on the Edge: Class, Community, and Politics in Cincinnati* (1986); F. Couvares, *The Remaking of Pittsburgh* (1984). Indeed, as Leon Fink has recently reminded us, many native and foreign observers at the time believed that the trade unionists of Chicago, New York, and other American cities were *more*, not less, wedded to political radicalism than their English, French, and German counterparts. L. Fink, *Workingmen's Democracy* 12. See also R. L. Moore, *European Socialism and the American Promised Land* (1970); E. and E. Marx-Aveling, *The Working Class Movement in America* (1888); H. Pelling, *The Origins of the Labor Party* (1965); Pelling, "Knights of Labor in Britain, 1880–1901" 9 *Econ. Hist. Rev.* 313 (1956).

7. J. Swinton, *Striking for Life* 358 (1894).

8. See L. Fink, *Workingmen's Democracy*, supra Chap. 1, note 6; Forbath, "The Ambiguities of Free Labor: Labor and the Law in the Gilded Age," 1985 *Wis. L. Rev.* 767, 809 (citation omitted) [hereinafter Forbath, "Ambiguities of Free Labor"]. "Perhaps, no other voluntary institution in America, except churches, touched the lives of as many people as did the Knights of Labor." Montgomery, "Labor in the Industrial Era," in *A History of the American Worker* 107–08 (R. Morris, ed., 1983).

their radical social and political vision. Appealing to the "laboring classes" as both producers and citizens, the Knights reached out from a base among coal miners and artisans to a constituency that embraced the burgeoning new factory proletariat—and included new immigrants, blacks, and women alongside old immigrants and old-stock Americans—as well as small shopkeepers and even a few manufacturers.[9] As we shall see, the Knights waged strikes and boycotts, but they also created labor parties, ran candidates in thirty-four of the country's thirty-five states, and elected members to city and state governments. They founded factory cooperatives and established a panoply of cultural associations. Unifying all these activities was the project of preparing the "toiling classes" for republican self-rule.[10] The Knights hewed to a working-class version of traditional republican ideas about law and rights. They held that republican government rested on a virtuous and independent citizenry; and that citizens' political and economic independence were intertwined, both requiring a rough measure of economic equality. In keeping with traditional republicanism, they saw as law's chief aim not the security of private rights but the preservation of the social conditions necessary for such a self-governing citizenry. Workers read these traditional principles to mean that in an industrial society the very survival of republican government demanded the use of governmental power to quell the "tyranny" of corporations and capital.[11] Toppling "corporate tyranny" entailed hosts of legislative reforms: hours laws and other workplace regulations, the abolition of private banking, public funding for worker-owned industry, and the nationalization of monopolies.[12]

9. See L. Fink, *Workingmen's Democracy*, supra Chap. 1, note 6, at 219–33; F. Couvares, supra Chap. 1, note 6, at 9–30; P. Rachleff, *Black Labor in the South: Richmond, Virginia, 1865–1890*, at 109–78 (1984).

10. See Forbath, "Ambiguities of Free Labor," supra Chap. 1, note 8, at 809. The Knights' classwide, indeed cross-class, appeal enabled them to aspire toward a political and cultural alternative to the mass political parties and corporations. See Fink, "The New Labor History and the Powers of Historical Pessimism: Consensus, Hegemony, and the Case of the Knights of Labor," 75 *J. Am. Hist.* 115, 119 (1988).

11. For a more detailed account of this working-class republicanism, see Forbath, "Ambiguities of Free Labor," supra Chap. 1, note 8, at 806–17. See also infra Chap. 5.

12. See Forbath, "Ambiguities of Free Labor," supra Chap. 1, note 8, at 807–09.

The Knights' dedication to such wide-ranging reform ambitions was sure evidence, to the classic historians, of their "middle class" orientation. Whereas the Knights of Labor was born in 1869, the AFL only emerged in the early 1880s; the Wisconsin School historians insisted that the AFL trade unions tended to shun the Knights' "impractical" radicalism. But that was to assume that the Sam Gompers of the 1870s and the 1880s thought along the same lines as the Gompers of the 1910s and 1920s. It was to read into the outlook of the AFL founders too much of the narrower, anti-statist business unionism of many trade unions of Commons's and Perlman's own day.

In fact, even Gompers may have been a "two-card man" in the early 1880s, belonging to both the Cigarmakers and the Knights of Labor.[13] In any case, the typical Gilded Age AFL activist shared the Knights' radical reform ambitions and their faith in lawmaking and the ballot as ways of ending the "tyranny of capital." In a plebiscite vote in 1894, a majority of the AFL's constituent unions endorsed a socialist platform that called for "independent labor politics" and an eleven-point legislative program including not only workplace regulation and a universal eight-hour day but also cooperative, municipal, or national ownership of industry.[14]

Gompers assailed the program.[15] Throughout the era, he had been the preeminent spokesman for a somewhat narrower trade union philosophy and a more cautious conception of labor's possibilities. How-

13. See Shefter, "Trade Unions and Political Machines: The Organization and Disorganization of the American Working Class in the Nineteenth Century," in *Working-Class Formation* (I. Katznelson and A. Zolberg, eds., 1986) at 223.

14. The program met ultimate defeat at the 1894 Convention, although virtually all accounts agree that the defeat resulted from the "parliamentary sleight-of-hand" of Gompers and other leaders of the federation. See Shefter, supra Chap. 1, note 13, at 257; see also J. Rayback, *A History of American Labor* 198 (1959). For a more general portrait of the Convention, see 2 J. Commons, et al., *History of Labour in the United States*, supra Chap. 1, note 5, at 511–13.

15. He and his craft-union allies argued that independent labor politics were too divisive in a movement with so many members who were diehard Democrats and Republicans. See 2 J. Commons et al., *History of Labour in the United States*, supra Chap. 1, note 5, at 514. Moreover, they insisted, broad, class-based legislative reforms like eight-hour-day laws were hopeless because the nation's courts would not condone them. See infra pp. 42–57.

ever, during the Gilded Age the outlook associated with Gompers and his allies was far less distinct than it later became from the competing vision of broad unionism and radical reform ambitions. In the 1880s and early 1890s, those who shared Gompers's views often did not spurn such ambitions; rather they insisted that labor's first task lay in building disciplined, well-administered, and "businesslike" craft unions. This aim did not seem antithetical to the goals of building a political movement, organizing the unskilled into more inclusive unions, or hailing "labor's final emancipation" and the "abolition of the wages system"—those broader goals still resonated through the rhetoric and actions of many of Gompers's closest associates.[16]

By the end of the 1890s, however, the AFL's spokesmen had ceased talking about labor's "final emancipation." The Knights of Labor were defunct, and the AFL was the nation's leading labor organization. Government bludgeoning of one major strike after another had left the AFL leadership markedly wary of inclusive unionism and broad-based sympathetic actions. In the boom years after the 1890s depression, AFL unions' membership doubled. AFL leaders strove to weld their craft unions into more centralized, bureaucratic organizations—not only capable of wielding greater power through national coordination and mutual support, but also more restrained in their strike policies. Not "final emancipation" from the "wages system" but collective bargaining was the AFL's goal— to make workers (at least the minority of organized, skilled workers) an "equal partner" with capital.

State repression of strikes and labor protest drove many of Europe's labor organizations toward more radical and more statist politics. Some in the American labor movement shared this reaction, but the dominant unions in the AFL responded differently. By the century's end the AFL leadership sought to censor talk of "inde-

16. Indeed, many whom Gompers counted as sharing his "trades union philosophy"— men like P. J. McGuire and Karl Lendall—remained active political radicals. See R. Christie, *Empire in Wood, A History of the Carpenters' Union* 334–37 (1956) (discussing the union philosophy of Peter McGuire). For others, including Gompers, more sweeping social change was a goal deferred, but not yet disdained. See S. Kaufman, *Samuel Gompers and the Origins of the American Federation of Labor, 1848–1896* (1973).

pendent labor politics.'' And by the end of the next decade, the AFL actively assailed many kinds of protective legislation, social insurance, and other industrial and welfare reforms championed by labor movements in the rest of the world. The republican rights talk of the Gilded Age movement gave way to a liberal, laissez-faire language of protest and reform.

This new anti-statist outlook did not preclude involvement in national as well as state politics. To the contrary, the AFL became increasingly involved in electioneering and lobbying at both state and national levels. But the AFL turned to politics chiefly for *voluntarist ends*—above all, to halt hostile judicial interventions in labor disputes. During the half-century under study, the high point of labor influence in national politics came during the Wilson years (1912–1920); the landmark labor legislation of those years, the Clayton Act[17] and the Seamen's Act,[18] were laws that sought to revise hostile judge-made law. Through them and comparable state legislation, the AFL hoped to diminish, not extend, the scope of government regulation of industrial relations.[19]

In addition to freedom from court injunctions and relief from antitrust suits, the AFL's other main national legislative goal was restriction of immigration.[20] By stemming the flow of ''cheap'' new immigrant labor, the AFL strove to defend what it styled the ''American'' wage. Like labor's anti-injunction bills, immigration restriction represented an effort to alter the terms of industrial relations in organized labor's favor—without government intervention in the industrial arena.[21]

17. 38 Stat. 730 (1914) (codified as amended at 15 U.S.C. §§12–27, 44 (1982)). The Clayton Act's labor provisions sought to immunize from federal injunctions many strike and boycott activities and objectives.

18. 38 Stat. 1164 (1915) (codified as amended at 22 U.S.C. §258; 33 U.S.C. §§365–366; 46 U.S.C. §§222, 481, 569, 596, 597, 599, 601, 656, 660–1, 672–673, 683, 688, 701, 703, 712, 713 (1982)).

19. On the AFL campaign leading up to the Clayton Act, the Act's passage, and the fate of its labor provisions, see infra Chapter 5.

20. See G. Mink, *Old Labor and New Immigrants in American Political Development, 1890–1930* 30–73, 117–49 (1986).

21. Id.

At the state level, AFL voluntarism did not mean abandoning all forms of protective legislation. For example, most early-twentieth-century state Federations of Labor actively sought hours and wages laws for women. This kind of protective legislation, like immigration restriction and child labor laws, was the visible hand of voluntarism. The AFL sought such measures to put a floor under wage competition, to keep "cheap labor" out of the labor markets in which its unions would then rely on voluntarist means, on contracts and collective action, to work out their fortunes. Ironically, as we shall see, most AFL unions came to see women workers in the same light as the courts which upheld gender-based protective legislation—as a "dependent class," which could not weather the voluntarist world of free contract. Thus the kinds of protective legislation that the early-twentieth-century AFL unions continued to champion often came to signify the movement's narrowness; while the broader reform measures that it assailed frequently seemed the only plausible means for bettering the fortunes of the masses of unorganized, unskilled, and recent immigrant workers whom most unions spurned.

This narrower, more conservative and defensive trade union philosophy never enjoyed unchallenged dominion over the labor movement from 1900 to the 1920s. The Knights' anti-capitalist republicanism and their broad reform vision were carried into the twentieth century by the Socialist Party and others. Socialist labor leaders remained prominent in many important AFL unions throughout the period, and within and without the AFL, radicals continued to champion industrial unionism and independent labor politics. Moreover, the relative autonomy of state federations meant that broad reform politics held sway in some important industrial states and were not so thoroughly or uniformly vanquished elsewhere. Nevertheless, industrial unionists, progressives, and state-level radicals remained a minority, opposing, sometimes modifying, but never displacing the policies framed by the dominant outlook.[22]

22. Broad-social-reform-minded trade unionists and political radicals gained vastly increased sway during the New Deal, both with the forming of the Congress of Industrial Organizations and within the New Deal administration and the Democratic Party. Yet

In retrospect it is clear that the decades bracketing the turn of the century marked a sea change in the history of the American labor movement. They marked the unraveling of what David Montgomery has called the "moral universality" of the Gilded Age labor movement, the emergence of sharp, enduring divisions over industrial and political strategy and vision, and the consolidation of a dominant leadership that set its face against the kinds of broader reform politics and inclusive unionism that English and European labor elites were embracing.[23]

In light of the work of Montgomery and others, the old story line is no longer plausible. The voluntarist outlook that came to predominate in the early-twentieth-century AFL no longer seems to have sprung from a timeless bias among American trade unionists against broad reforms and radical visions of the uses of law and state power. The new question that the work of the new labor historians poses but has yet to answer is how that outlook and bias became dominant by the early twentieth century. Of course, the old sociological factors

the legacies of the preceding half-century continued to influence the bounds of labor's political and industrial opportunities and aspirations in the decades that followed. "It did not appear beyond reason," at the close of World War II, to anticipate for American unions "a role comparable to that played by the labor movement in British political life." Instead, however, as the leading historian of the twentieth-century labor movement has observed: "Insofar as it was its own master, insofar as the labor movement had choices to make," the course it took in political action derived from the voluntarist heritage "deeply rooted in the American trade-union past . . . if one listened closely, Gompers's words could be heard echoing long decades after his death." See "The Uses of Power II: Political Action," in D. Brody, *Workers in Industrial America: Essays on the Twentieth-Century Struggle* 215–57 (1985).

23. For an account of English developments over this period (and the courts' and state's parts therein), see Forbath, " 'In the Mother Country' Law Is Unprotected from the 'Gusty Passions' of Politics: Courts and Labor Politics in England and America, 1870–1930," 16 *Law and Social Inquiry* (Winter 1991) [hereinafter Forbath, " 'In the Mother Country' "]; see also A. Clegg, A. Fox, and A. Thompson, *A History of British Trade Unions Since 1889* (1964); H. Pell, *Origins of the Labour Party* (1965). For an account of French developments, see B. Moss, *The Origins of the French Labor Movement, 1830–1914* (1978); M. Perrot, *Workers on Strike: France, 1871–1890* (C. Turner, trans., 1987); and Scott, "Social History and the History of Socialism: French Socialist Municipalities in the 1890s," 111 *Le Mouvement Social* 145 (1979). For an account of German developments, see M. Nolan, *Social Democracy and Society: Working-Class Radicalism in Dusseldorf, 1890–1920* (1981).

still beckon as potential answers. But recent labor and social historical research also undermines much of their plausibility.

For example, the view that American workers enjoyed unparalleled opportunities to rise into the middle class figures prominently in most traditional explanations for American "exceptionalism." One can imagine the same view incorporated into an account of the demise of class-based reform politics. However, the mobility story's empirical foundations have proven shaky. Sophisticated recent quantitative histories have shown that the bulk of America's working class was no more mobile into the middle class than England's. Nor did any significant portion of the nineteenth-century industrial working class actually ever "go West" from urban shops and factories into farming, as traditional accounts from Engels to Sombart to Perlman and others have assumed. Even mobility *within* the American working class (from unskilled to skilled work) was far more varied and uneven than has been thought.[24]

Lively debate continues among historians over how far the experience of various groups of skilled workers bears out the assumption that upward mobility was not uncommon. It is no longer disputed, however, that mobility meant many divergent things, and, more often than not, something different from what the classic accounts assume. The typical forms of social mobility for nineteenth-century American workers, as well as their typical *aspirations* for it, were not incompatible with seeking material gains for oneself and one's fellow workers *as workers*—rather than as the individualistic incipient entrepreneurs that the mobility story describes.[25] For

24. See P. Kights, *The Plain People of Boston* (1971); P. Shergold, *Working-Class Life: The "American Standard" in Comparative Perspective* (1982); Holt, "Trade Unionism in the British and U.S. Steel Industries, 1880–1914: A Comparative Study," 18 *Lab. Hist.* 5 (1977).

25. The Irish immigrant laborer, for example, seemed typically to define "success" not in terms of rising into the middle class but rather in terms of apprenticing his son in a skilled trade; the Italian hod-carrier, in terms of earning enough to buy property back in the home country; and the Yankee skilled worker, most often, in terms of buying a home—not rising above the ranks of the working classes. See Henretta, "The Study of Social Mobility: Ideological Assumptions and Conceptual Biases," 18 *Lab. Hist.* 165 (1977); Chudacoff, "Success and Security: The Meaning of Social Mobility in America,"

these reasons, upward mobility probably must relinquish its place as a key factor accounting for the peculiarities of American labor politics.

Similarly, many scholars continue to assume that unionism was far less widespread among American than English or European workers around the turn of the century. On this assumption, some historians have argued, even quite recently, that the chief reason that the bulk of the labor movement abandoned broad ambitions for reform lay in the fact that organized labor in the United States was a distinctly minority movement. The slight proportion of organized labor during these years led Gompers and most other labor leaders to move toward ''pure and simple trade unionism'' and minimalist politics.[26] The difficulty with this view lies, again, in its shaky empirical assumptions. Late-nineteenth- and early-twentieth-century unions claimed a greater, not a lesser, portion of the industrial labor force in the United States than in some European countries well known for their radical labor politics.

France is a good example. Around 1910 unions claimed 15 percent of the manufacturing labor force in France, while they claimed almost 25 percent in the United States.[27] Apparently, its status as a ''minority movement,'' its slightness in relation to the whole working class, did not deter the French workers' movement from adopting an ambitious political agenda.[28]

10 *Rev. Am. Hist.* 101 (1982); Conk, ''Social Mobility in Historical Perspective,'' 3 *Marxist Persp.* 52 (1978).

26. See, e.g., N. Salvatore, *Samuel Gompers* (1990).

27. See A. Zolberg, ''How Many Exceptionalisms?'' in I. Katznelson and A. Zolberg, eds., *Working-Class Formation: Nineteenth-Century Patterns in Western Europe and the United States* 397, 398, 426 (1987).

28. See id. at 418–25. See also B. Moss, *The Origins of the French Labor Movement: The Socialism of Skilled Workers, 1830–1914* (1976); Scott, ''Social History and the History of Socialism,'' 111 *Le Mouvement Social* 145 (1979).

It is worth noting that, like the United States, France retained a significant portion of agricultural and other nonindustrial workers throughout the nineteenth and early twentieth century; it never became an industrial society to the same degree as England. See infra Chap. 1, note 30. The percentage of the French labor force employed in the secondary or industrial sector in 1910 was 33%, roughly the same as the American figure of 32%. See Zolberg, supra Chap. 1, note 27, at 438. Thus neither slightness as a proportion of the entire industrial working class nor slightness as a proportion of the overall population

England was doubtless the nation with the highest proportion of unionized industrial workers during this era. Yet even England's unions, according to one comparative study, enjoyed "not such different organizational strength" from America's as is often assumed; rather, "the percentages of the labor force unionized were comparable" during this period.[29] In the early years of the century when the American labor movement claimed 20–25 percent of industrial workers, the English movement claimed 30–35 percent of that country's manufacturing labor force. It too was a "minority movement," even within the nation's working class.[30] Moreover, American trade unionists formed most of their political goals and strategies, and learned many of their political lessons, in state and local arenas. It is significant, then, that levels of unionization in the major industrial states were substantially higher than levels in the nation as whole. When one compares union density in Massachusetts or Illinois in the period 1890–1910 with union density in England, the American figures emerge as much more similar to the English ones.[31] For these reasons, union density, like workers' mobility, cannot bear any great explanatory burden in accounting for why most American trade unionists diverged from the political trail they had begun to blaze with their English and European counterparts.

More salient than union density per se may have been the ability of English trade unions to maintain strongholds in certain key

prompted the French labor movement to adopt a minimalist politics à la Gompers and the AFL. The CGT, France's leading labor organization, regarded as its American cousin the Knights of Labor—which espoused broad politics and inclusive unionism and was Gompers's and the AFL's great Gilded Age foe. On the CGT and their affinities with the Knights, see G. Friedman, "The State and the Making of a Working Class: The United States and France" (paper prepared for Social Science History Conference, St. Louis, Mo., Oct. 1986).

29. Orloff and Skocpol, " 'Why Not Equal Protection?' Explaining the Politics of Public Social Spending in Britain, 1900–1911, and the United States, 1880s–1920," 49 *Am. Soc. Rev.* 726 (1984).

30. On the other hand, the industrial working class as a whole constituted a significantly larger proportion of England's population, 52% in 1910, than of America's, 31% in that year. See Zolberg, supra Chap. 1, note 27, at 438. As significant as these demographic figures, however, were the ways that the American party and electoral system refracted them.

31. See Orloff and Skocpol, supra Chap. 1, note 29, at 736.

twentieth-century industries such as steel. In the United States, employers drove the craft unions out of steel and prevented their establishing themselves in some other central industries. English employers in these industries envied their American counterparts' ability to free themselves of the vexing craft unions. But the American employers enjoyed two strategic advantages that the English firms lacked.

First was the American state. As we are about to see, its structure and traditions lent themselves to anti-union endeavors, supplying far greater leverage to labor's foes than did the English state. Second was the fact that English employers frequently were smaller than their American counterparts. England saw nothing comparable to the merger movement in the United States. Small and family-run firms persisted for at least half a century longer in Britain, and there were virtually no giant firms like U.S. Steel, with unparalleled resources for introducing new technologies and asserting managerial control over production. The persistence of an older, fragmented industrial structure helped the English craft unions weather the transition, for example, from the iron to the steel industry—a transition that saw the smashing of trade unionism in that industry in the United States.[32] The lack of a strong union presence in such industries as steel surely may have diminished American labor's political clout. However, the notoriety of U.S. Steel's successful attack on unionism should not lead one to assume that concentration or "trustification" in American industries always spelled the demise of unionism. As researchers for the turn-of-the-century federal Industrial Commission found, trustification often had happier implications for trade unionists: trusts and cartels could develop mutually advantageous relations with unions, for unionism frequently proved a useful means of stabilizing labor costs.[33]

32. See Elbaum and Wilkinson, "Industrial Relations and Uneven Development: A Comparative Study of the American and British Steel Industries," 3 *Camb. J. of Ec.* 275, 301 (1979). See also Holt, "Trade Unionism in the British and U.S. Steel Industries, 1888–1912: A Comparative Study," 18 *Lab. Hist.* 5 (1977).

33. See Furner, "Knowing Capitalism: Public Investigation and the Labor Question in the Long Progressive Era," in *The State and Economic Knowledge* 241, 271–74

Ethnic division is the other principle factor in the traditional exceptionalism story. In any revised account, ethnic and racial cleavages will surely remain central. However, the new labor historians have discovered that ethnic identities and affiliations were not as corrosive of class-based identities and actions as we tend to assume. As Wilentz observes in surveying the literature, "the familiar arguments that American exceptionalism arose from some unique divisions within the American working class are no longer as compelling as they once were."[34] Indeed, the new labor history demonstrates that in many contexts "ethnicity could be more of a reinforcement to class solidarity than a distraction from class antagonisms."[35]

As I have noted, ethnic divisions did not prevent the creation of the broad class-based organizational solidarities that characterized the Knights of Labor. On the Gilded Age railways, for example, tens of thousands of old-stock, native-born skilled workers enlisted in the Knights of Labor railway branches and in locals of Eugene Debs's American Railway Union, merging their craft-based solidarities with the Knights' and ARU's more radical goals and more inclusive unionism. In so doing, the old-stock railway workers threw in their lot with the railroads' new immigrant semiskilled and unskilled workers. Nor did ethnic antagonisms bring about the demise of these vigorous, class-based organizations.

Rather, as we shall see in Chapter 3, it was the courts' outlawing of sympathy strikes and boycotts, and the mass imprisonments and glint of bayonets behind the court decrees, that destroyed the ARU

(M. Furner and B. Supple, eds., 1990). See also P. Edwards, *supra* Chap. 1, note 3, at 129–33.

34. "Against Exceptionalism," 26 *Int'l. Labor and Working Class Hist.* 1, 5 (1984). "Comparative study of specific industries," Wilentz continues, "has shown that the supposedly distinctive splits among American workers sometimes have been exaggerated, and do little to explain the timing and underlying causes of important events."

35. Id. See also Foner, "Class, Ethnicity, and Radicalism in the Gilded Age," 2 *Marxist Persp.* 6 (1978); H. Gutman, *Work, Culture, and Society in Industrializing America* 234–60 (1976); V. Greene, *The Slavic Community on Strike: Immigrant Labor in Pennsylvania Anthracite* 207–15 (1968); Freeman, "Catholics, Communists, and Republicans: Irish Workers and the Organization of the Transport Workers Union," in *Working-Class America* (M. Frisch and D. Walkowitz, eds., 1983).

and the railway chapters of the Knights of Labor.[36] The outlawing of these forms of collective action would lead to the scrapping of the only weapons by which broad organizations of railroad men had been able to assert the rights of the skilled and unskilled alike.[37] At the same time, the courts made clear their readiness to defend, rather than repress, trade unionism on the railroads, as long as the old craft brotherhoods observed the courts' bars on sympathetic actions and abandoned class-based unionism.[38]

Chapter 3 will also suggest how the experience of late-nineteenth-century railway men paralleled experiences in other industries. Old-stock workers tended to respond warmly to the promise of class-based, ethnically inclusive labor organizations. And the class-wide nature of the constituency of these Gilded Age organizations made pursuing a class-based political agenda seem both possible and compelling. But legal repression destroyed the momentum of these organizations. Only in the shadow of hundreds of such broken big strikes did old-stock skilled workers withdraw from these Gilded Age organizations in favor of more restricted spheres of action and more exclusive organizations.[39]

The fact remains, however, that ethnic divisions—new immigrants versus old ones—often tracked the divisions between skilled and unskilled workers and helped make those differences antagonistic ones. If the antagonisms were often overcome, they also often impeded the creation of class-based alliances in both industrial and political contexts.[40] The greater complexity and open-endedness that the new social history has found regarding these matters do not imply that these social divisions were not significant. Rather they suggest that, by themselves, these divisions hardly account for the sharp narrowing of American labor politics.[41]

36. See infra. 68–79, 94–97.
37. Id.
38. See infra. 70 (quoting then Circuit Court Judge William Howard Taft).
39. See infra 94–97.
40. See G. Mink, *Old Labor and New Immigrants in American Political Development, 1890–1930* (1986).
41. See generally id. (arguing that it was the interaction of ethnic cleavages with distinctive features of the American state that molded AFL politics.)

We often forget that in the nineteenth century the industrial working classes of most of Western Europe included significant immigrant
groups and had deep ethnic rifts. Overall, as the new historians have
compared their investigations with the work of contemporary European labor and social historians, they have found that the political
cultures and social experiences of organized workers in the United
States and abroad in the second half of the nineteenth century resembled one another far more than the classic historians suspected.[42]
By showing that the values, dispositions, and social divisions of the
American working class were not so "exceptional," the new labor
history prompts one to ask whether the decisive differences in the
formation of American labor politics must not be located elsewhere,
not in the character of the working class or the labor movement so
much as in the character of the state and polity—less, that is, in
labor and more in the arenas in which labor made and remade its
strategies and visions.

The State of Courts and Parties

The courts were one of these arenas; they were a critical—perhaps
the critical—politics-shaping aspect of the nation's Constitution,
but they did not operate in a vacuum. In a longer work I aim to
show how nineteenth-century America's entire, complicated constitutional form of government molded the country's labor politics,[43]
but it will be useful here to note some of the other central features
of the nation's state and polity. Three seem central for our purposes:
federalism, the nature and role of political parties, and the absence
of an administrative state elite (or, what is the other side of the same
coin, the judiciary's role as the era's sole state elite). In the rest of

42. For a well-argued and amply supported presentation of this comparative view,
see S. Wilentz, "Against Exceptionalism: Class Consciousness and the American Labor
Movement, 1790–1920," 26 *International Labor and Working Class History* 1 (1984).
Another valuable treatment is E. Foner, "Why Is There No Socialism in the United
States?" 17 *History Workshop* 57 (1984). See also L. Fink, *Workingmen's Democracy,*
supra Chap. 1, note 6; I. Katznelson, *Working Class Formations* (1987); Zolberg, "How
Many Exceptionalisms?" supra Chap. 1, note 27.

43. W. Forbath, "Law, Labor and Democracy in America" (work-in-progress).

this book, we will glimpse these other aspects of state and polity in play, frequently reinforcing the influence of the country's courts. Many historians and political scientists have drawn a picture of the nineteenth-century American state that resembles the classic portrait of labor's "natural individualism" described in the preceding section. This picture of the nineteenth-century state employs the image of the "night watchman" or the concept of a laissez-faire regime. Compared to governments elsewhere, these authors proclaim, the "night watchman state" of nineteenth-century America had little impact on social developments, including the relations between labor and capital. But this comparison conceals as much as it reveals. True, the domain of the American state as a whole was far narrower than that of contemporary European counterparts. Within that narrower domain, however, the state intervened actively and frequently against workers. One misses this intervention if one focuses on legislative and executive actions; if one includes judicial actions and the roles of legal discourse and judge-made state policy, the picture changes dramatically. This section sketches the emergence of the peculiarly court-centered American state, and briefly draws in these three other aspects of the state and polity.

Generally, social historians and political scientists have not yet assimilated the perspectives that emerge from the work of many legal historians—particularly, the remarkable extent to which common law judges proved vigorous and self-conscious policymakers, presiding over social and economic development for much of the nineteenth century.[44] One political scientist, Stephen Skowronek, is on the mark, however, when he describes the nineteenth-century American state as the "state of courts and parties."[45] He reminds

44. See M. Horwitz, *The Transformation of American Law, 1780–1860* (1977); J. Hurst, *Law and the Conditions of Freedom* (1956); L. Levy, *The Law of the Commonwealth and Chief Justice Shaw* (1957); R. Newmeyer, *Supreme Court Justice Joseph Story* (1985).

45. S. Skowronek, *Building a New American State* 24 (1982). Skowronek actually devotes little attention to the operations or influences of the courts on social and political developments. Because his book concerns the efforts of reformers to supplant courts (and party politicians) with administrative agencies and a professional state elite, it treats the courts chiefly as obstacles and opponents to the building of this new state structure.

us that the "United States was born in a war that rejected the organizational qualities of the state as they had been evolving in Europe over the eighteenth century",[46] that is, toward an increasingly concentrated and centralized executive authority and an expanding administrative apparatus.[47] The radical republican American state governments of 1776 through 1787 embodied the revolutionary rejection of the emerging European organization of state power; they invested sovereignty in thirteen separate state legislatures. The framers, in turn, supplanted this radical design with a conservative one, but one that continued to reject the European trend and continued to legitimate itself in the revolutionary language of popular sovereignty. Their inspired yet clumsy federal frame of government had advertent ambiguities and institutional conflicts. It was calculated to resist domination not only by any single governmental institution but also by any social or sectional faction.

As Madison's *Federalist* no. 10 illustrates, the framers were haunted by the specter of enduring political "factions" based on economic condition—above all factions based on propertylessness. A poor or propertyless faction could well constitute a voting majority and seek to use the state to despoil the propertied or shirk its own economic obligations. Already, the framers had seen it happen in the new state republics. Partly to avert such politics, they created a constitutional scheme that treated the sphere of common law rights of contract and property as a suprapolitical realm of private right. As far as market and property and, therefore, class relations were concerned, the rules of the game were presumptively matters of law and not politics, matters for courts, not legislatures.[48]

Thus the framers' ambivalence toward centralized state authority, their aversion to factions, and their tenderness for property rights combined to create the conceptual and institutional space in which

46. Id. at 20.
47. See id. at 47–55.
48. See *The Federalist* nos. 10, 38 (J. Madison); *The Federalist* no. 70 (A. Hamilton); D. McCoy, *The Elusive Republic* (1980); G. Wood, *Creation of the Republic*, part 4 (1969); Nedelsky, "Confining Democratic Politics," 96 *Harv. L. Rev.* 340 (1982); J. Nedelsky, *Private Property and the Limits of American Constitutionalism* (forthcoming 1990).

a legal and judicial state elite could emerge—and fashion for itself a uniquely prominent role in setting social and economic policy. As Skowronek states, "[a]fter the bewildering interactions of legislative, executive, and juridical prerogatives . . . only the law itself emerged as a substantive referent of state direction."[49] At the level of both state and national government it fell to the courts "to nurture, protect, interpret, and invoke the state's prerogatives over economy and society as expressed in law."[50]

The framers hoped that the far-flung and federal nature of their new republic would also help avoid the formation of a class-based political "faction" of have-nots in the national arena.[51] Their hope was realized.

By the 1830s the United States had become the world's first nation with a mass franchise. By that decade, virtually all white adult males enjoyed the vote. Thus throughout the era of industrialization propertyless male industrial workers were voters. Yet, as Ira Katznelson has recently reminded us, the "diffuse federal organizational structure of the United States" helped take much of the charge out of the issue of franchise extension, "for there was no unitary state to defend or transform."[52] The federal structure of government meant that American labor reformers had to contend with multiple and competing tiers of policymaking authority. This structural exigency raised the costs and reduced the efficacy of labor reforms.[53] So doing, it strengthened the case for voluntarism.

The English state, by contrast, was unitary. During the nineteenth century, as England became an industrial nation, the making of public policies toward industrial workers happened increasingly at the center of government, as did the administration of those poli-

49. S. Skowronek, supra Chap. 1, note 45, at 22.

50. Id. at 27.

51. See *The Federalist* no. 10 (J. Madison).

52. Katznelson, "Working-Class Formation and the State," in P. Evans, D. Rueschmeyer, and T. Skocpol, eds., *Bringing the State Back In* 257, 273 (1985).

53. See J. R. Commons and J. B. Andrews, *Principles of Labor Legislation* 48–63 (1936); F. Kelley, *Some Ethical Gains through Legislation* (1921); Commission on Industrial Relations, *Final Report* (1915). But cf. R. Vallelly, *Radicalism in the States: The Minnesota Farmer-Labor Party and the American Political Economy* (1989).

cies.[54] The structure of government enabled the country's dispersed and localized unions and labor reform associations to meld and concentrate their political claims.

Just as the United States was the first nation with a mass franchise, so the nineteenth-century American political party was the world's first mass-based party. If the nineteenth-century courts supplied the bulk of substantive policy regarding government's relations to economy and society, it was this mass-based party that lent the new nation-state procedural and operational coherence. The framers' expectations were otherwise. They envisioned the emergence of a national governing elite of enlightened leaders whose common bonds would yield consensus and coherence.[55] But their vision rested on a politics of deference, and the polity was in fact growing significantly more democratic. Instead of forging a working national state apparatus, the combination of the Constitution's disjointed framework and the democratic upheavals of the late Jeffersonian era left the national government unhinged virtually to the point of disintegration. Quite beyond the framers' contemplation, constituent political parties arose to supply functional coherence to the state machinery.[56] Hence Skowronek's apt phrase for characterizing a state whose constituent elements and key actors were courts and parties.

In the United States, as opposed to Europe, the enfranchisement and political incorporation of workingmen into mass-based constituent parties occurred before the full-blown emergence of industrial capitalism. Party leaders formed ties with workers chiefly through particularistic appeals that revolved around patronage, ethnicity, and neighborhood affairs—not class-based visions or programs.[57] Class-

54. The Public Health, Factory, and Mine Acts passed from mid-century onward engendered a dramatic growth of England's central government. See G. Sutherland, *Studies in the Growth of Nineteenth-Century Government* (1972); P. Thane, *Origins of the Welfare State* (1986).

55. See R. Wiebe, *The Opening of American Society* 12–14, 35–66 (1984).

56. See R. McCormick, *The Party Period and Public Policy* 143–96 (1986); M. McGerr, *The Rise and Fall of Popular Politics* (1987); R. Wiebe, supra Chap. 1, note 55, at 177–80.

57. As some historians put it, American workers were "deprived" of the experiences of exclusion from and struggle for enfranchisement as a class. See, e.g., A. Dawley,

based appeals were hardly to be expected from parties that strove for and depended on cross-class coalitions. Thus, throughout the century, non-class-based ties of neighborhood and ethnicity remained the dominant way that political parties formed attachments with successive generations of new immigrant, and old-stock American, working-class voters.[58] Though not immutable, these particularistic party loyalties did have staying power, as did the political identities that crystallized around them.[59]

In 1894 the head of the Tailors' Union, John Lennon, put it this way, arguing against the prospects of independent labor politics in the United States: "We have in this country conditions that do not exist in Great Britain. We have the 'spoils' system which is something almost unknown in Great Britain and on account of it we cannot

Class and Community: The Industrial Revolution in Lynn (1976). Put differently, in countries where enfranchisement happened after the formation of an industrial working class, new and old parties alike found themselves competing for the allegiance of the new working-class voters on the basis of class-based, programmatic appeals. On these differences between American and European political parties and their relations with industrial workers, see Shefter, supra Chap. 1, note 13; Orloff and Skocpol, supra Chap. 1, note 29; and Zolberg, supra Chap. 1, note 27.

58. See P. Kleppner, *The Third Electoral System, 1853–1892* (1979); P. Kleppner, *The Cross of Culture: A Social Analysis of Midwestern Politics, 1850–1900* (1970); Oestreicher, "Urban Working-Class Political Behavior and Theories of American Electoral Politics, 1870–1940," 74 *J. Am. Hist.* 1257 (1988); Shefter, supra Chap. 1, note 13. At the same time, the "old parties" proved ever eager to recruit labor leaders into the ranks of professional politicians and placemen. As Richard Oestreicher points out: "The kinds of talented and ambitious working class personalities who were struggling [in the 1880s] to establish the Social Democratic parties of the Second International were by then successful machine politicians in the United States . . . Any effort to mobilize workers [on a class] basis . . . independent of, or against, existing party organizations faced not only . . . bourgeois resistance . . . but also the implacable opposition of armies of working-class and lower middle-class political professionals who correctly viewed [such] attempts as threats to their livelihoods." Oestreicher, supra, at 1272; see also D. Montgomery, *Beyond Equality*, supra Chap. 1, note 6, at 387–424. Similarly, the "old parties" proved ready to embrace significant portions of labor's legislative goals. See infra pp. 37–58, 147–51, 177–91, 199–203.

59. This was the lesson that Gompers and a majority of trade unionists drew from the defeats and disappointments that attended the majority of local efforts during the early 1890s to build a strong base for the People's Party upon trade unions and city and state labor federations. See S. Ross, supra Chap. 1, note 6; E. Staley, *The History of the Illinois State Federation of Labor* (1930); Shefter, supra Chap. 1, note 13.

afford to try at this time to start a political party as an adjunct with [our] unions."[60]

However, the "spoils" system and workers' attachments to the old party structures can only partly account for organized labor's disillusionment with broad reform ambitions. Likewise, the old parties' relative lack of interest in class-based reform programs tells only part of the story. These hurdles might have seemed and proven less daunting had there been a different state structure waiting to be gained—if courts had not been the principal state actors interpreting and administering labor laws. Labor reformers looked longingly at England, where Parliament's law trumped the courts' and not vice versa.

Also, in contrast to the United States, nineteenth-century England saw the development of a powerful, nonjudicial state elite—a substantial group of high-placed policymakers with institutional autonomy, permanence of office, and interests and traditions of their own. By the late nineteenth and early twentieth centuries many of these professional policymakers and administrative state-builders had grown extremely reform-minded—they were the architects of the early English welfare state—and they allied with labor against judicial restraints on collective action and in favor of broad class-based, state-administered social programs. Indeed, they actively wooed England's trade unions to win their support for social insurance and expanded industrial regulation; as a result, key reform proposals were designed to involve the unions in their administration. In the process, among turn-of-the-century English trade unionists,

60. *A Verbatum [sic] Report of the Discussion on the Political Programme at the Denver Convention of the AFL*, December 14, 15, 1894, at 8 (1895) [hereinafter *Verbatum Report*]. Local patronage, what Lennon called the spoils system, might also have supplied England's political parties with a way of drawing in the mass of working-class voters when that country's male workers gained suffrage. But the currency of patronage was no longer available to those parties by the time most of England's male workers were enfranchised; for prior to that time England had already undertaken major civil service reforms and bureaucratized government work. Accordingly, the Liberals and Conservatives in England leaned toward class-based programmatic appeals to workers in a way that the Democrats and Republicans in the United States did not. This leaning strengthened the hand of the English trade unionists who championed broad reformism. See Forbath, " 'In the Mother Country,' " supra Chap. 1, note 23.

the idea of national government as a vehicle of broad class-based social reform gained plausibility and appeal.

Nineteenth-century and early-twentieth-century America had no professional civil service and no comparable alternate state elite vying with the courts for primacy in regulating industry. There was no lack of reform-minded professionals eager to do similar government work. But the institutional—and constitutional—space for an organizationally autonomous administrative state elite was lacking. So the champions of broad reform in the U.S. labor movement had no such powerful allies in the corridors of state power, and the idea of a national government won over to broad reforms seemed a good deal more utopian.[61]

This lack of a competing state elite, as well as the particularistic, patronage, and procedural cast of the nineteenth-century parties, may have helped America's legal and judicial elite sustain the role Tocqueville designated as the nation's "high political class." In any case, they seized the opportunities that the eighteenth-century frameworks lent them to make the common law, rather than legislatures' statutes or administrators' edicts, the premier source of state policy respecting social development in general and labor affairs in particular. Nowhere else among industrializing nations did the judiciary and judge-made law so fully define state policy toward industrial relations throughout the nineteenth century.[62] Nor did the American judicial elite lack a will to intervene. In the late nineteenth and early twentieth centuries they regulated workers' marketplace freedom far more broadly and vigorously than did the English or French states.[63]

---

61. See Forbath, " 'In the Mother Country,' " supra Chap. 1, note 23.

62. See A. Fox, *History and Heritage: The Social Origins of the British Industrial Relations System* (1984) (emphasizing the importance of an active tradition of statutory, as against judicial, regulation); see also O. Kahn-Freund, *Labor Law: Old Traditions and New Developments* (1968) (same). For France's regulation of industrial conflict, in which legislation and administrative policymaking were vastly more central than courts, see M. Perrot, supra Chap. 1, note 23; E. Shorter and C. Tilly, *Strikes in France, 1820–1968* (1974); and for the experiences of Germany and other European nations, see *The Making of Labour Law in Europe* (B. Hepple, ed., 1986).

63. See Forbath, " 'In the Mother Country,' " supra Chap. 1, note 23; A. Fox, *History and Heritage*, supra Chap. 1, note 62; E. Shorter and C. Tilly, *Strikes in France*, supra Chap. 1, note 62.

In contrast to England's common law courts, they were unhindered by parliamentary supremacy or a strong countervailing tradition of statutory regulation. Instead, the Gilded Age legal and judicial elite strove to uphold the austere liberal social vision that they identified with the common law and the Constitution.[64] High regard for their institutional prerogatives combined with genuine dismay at what they saw as the faction-driven, class-bound character of labor law reforms led them to see much of the era's most important labor legislation as ill-considered, illegitimate tinkering with the common law. And, as we will see, they treated it accordingly.[65]

The great majority of federal judges in the late nineteenth and early twentieth centuries were Republicans, and the proportion grew ever greater.[66] Their pre-judicial occupations, wealth, as well as their ties of family and friendship placed 98 percent of these Republican gentlemen in positions at the very top of the nation's class and status hierarchies.[67] Small wonder that one finds no great diversity in their opinions affecting labor. But what about the state judges? They, after all, were mostly elected officials, subject to periodic reelection, and in at least some important industrial states, many of them were bound to be Democrats.[68] Yet state courts were no less prone than federal courts to strike down labor laws, and even slightly more prone to issue sweeping antistrike decrees.[69] If organized labor could pass legislation, why could it not ensure the election of pro-labor judges?

64. See Gordon, "Legal Thought and Legal Practice in the Age of American Enterprise, 1870–1920," in *The New High Priests* 70–139 (G. Gewalt, ed., 1984); Forbath, "Ambiguities of Free Labor," supra Chap. 1, note 8.

65. See infra pp. 37–58, 150–58.

66. See Hall, "Children of the Cabins: The Lower Federal Judiciary, Modernization, and the Political Culture," 75 *Nw. U. L. Rev.* 423, 447–48 (1980).

67. See id. at 436. As their collective biographer remarks, "the [lower federal court] judges increasingly, although incompletely, resembled a dominant ruling class." Id.

68. See J. Hurst, *The Growth of American Law: The Law Makers* 122–43 (1950); Jacob, "The Courts as Political Agencies: An Historical Analysis," in *Studies in Judicial Politics* 18–21 (K. Vines and H. Jacob, eds., 1962); see also E. Haynes, *The Selection and Tenure of Judges* (1944).

69. See Petro, "Injunctions and Labor-Disputes, 1880–1932," 14 *Wake Forest L. Rev.* 341, 461–63 (1978); infra pp. 37–58 (discussing laws); infra pp. 193–98 (discussing anti-strike decrees).

No one has reconstructed late-nineteenth- or early-twentieth-century organized labor's efforts to affect nominations and elections to state judiciaries,[70] but what we do know of those selection processes may suggest why labor's efforts bore little fruit. Although remembered as a radical Jacksonian reform, in fact the popular election of state judges was championed by moderate mid-nineteenth-century lawyers and judges who sought not to curb the courts but to enhance their power and legitimacy by putting them on a par with the other branches of government. The experiment succeeded. The judiciary wielded more power, and the bar and its increasingly well organized professional associations enjoyed decisive influence over judicial selection.[71] As a consequence, the machinery of judicial selection—election versus appointment—did little to alter the social identities and identifications of judges.[72]

70. Anecdotal evidence makes it clear that labor often *tried* to elect anti-injunction judges, and that it occasionally succeeded. See, e.g., "Anti-Injunction Judge Re-Elected," *New Majority*, Nov. 22, 1924, at 7, col. 1; "Oppose Injunctions," *The Federation News*, Oct. 18, 1924, at 7, col. 1 (candidate for Ohio Supreme Court appealing to union voters by promising "statewide attack on . . . government by injunction"). *See generally* E. Witte, *The Government in Labor Disputes*, supra Intro., note 9, at 125–27 (citing examples of judicial elections in industrial cities in which injunction policies figured prominently).

71. See Hall, "Progressive Reform and the Decline of Democratic Accountability: The Popular Election of State Supreme Court Judges, 1850–1920," 1984 *Am. B. Found. Res. J.* 345, 349 [hereinafter Hall, "Progressive Reform"]. The famous English observer of turn-of-the-century American law and politics, James Bryce, found that "party leaders" generally deferred to the leaders of the bar in the selection of "competent" nominees for judicial office. See id. at 348 (citing J. Bryce, *The American Commonwealth* 353 (1906)). To be sure, turn-of-the-century labor and others demanded that the courts be rendered more "accountable." Yet Progressives and legal reformers devised a series of reforms that had the opposite effect—or rather altered the meaning of the term, from democratic to professional accountability. Some of the Progressive reforms were aimed specifically at judicial elections, others were more broad-gauged, such as direct primaries, scheduling the election of judges apart from other elections, and removing party identifications from the names of judicial candidates on the ballot. In the name of "accountability" and taking matters out of the hands of the "party bosses," these reforms vested judicial nominations ever more firmly in the "competent" hands of the legal elites. See id. at 368–69.

72. See Hall, "Constitutional Machinery and Judicial Professionalism: The Careers of Midwestern State Appellate Court Judges, 1861–1899," in *The New High Priests*, supra, Chap. 1, note 64, at 29–49. "The social composition of the judiciary had little

Astute observers of the American legal elite, from Tocqueville in the 1830s[73] to Bryce in the 1890s and early 1900s,[74] underscored that elite's remarkable sway in state and national polities. They also emphasized how the Constitution enabled lawyers and judges to fuse institutional power and prerogative with high duty. Constitutional discourse treated the common law rights of contract and property as a suprapolitical realm. From this Chief Justice Marshall and the founding generation of Federalist jurists forged a role for the judiciary as guarantor of private rights against the gusty passions of "turbulent majorities."[75] In the legal and judicial elite Tocqueville discovered the indispensable conservative "counterpoise" to democracy in America, a popularly legitimated governmental mainstay against the tyranny of popular majorities.[76]

Madison and other framers had anticipated the inevitable expansion of "manufacturing interests"—and the likelihood that they would create a vast propertyless class of citizens. They hoped to project a future free of what the nineteenth century would call the "politics of class feeling," a polity with no enduring "party of the working classes."[77] In the chapters that follow we examine how the neofederalist judges of the late nineteenth and early twentieth centuries helped fulfill this anxious aspiration.

In the 1950s through the 1970s, the Federalist legacy would prove an invaluable resource for the black civil rights movement. In its landmark civil rights cases, the Supreme Court drew upon the tradition of a staunch, counter-majoritarian federal judiciary defending minority rights against invidious group-based legislation. In the name of minority rights, the federal judiciary struck down such legislation

relationship to the method of selection . . . Paradoxically, popular election slightly more frequently tapped judges of elite social class origins . . . than did the appointive method." Id. at 38–40.

73. See 1 A. de Tocqueville, *Democracy in America* 282–90 (P. Bradley, ed., 1945).

74. See J. Bryce, *The American Commonwealth* 353 (1906).

75. See *The Federalist* no. 10, at 133–34 (J. Madison). See, e.g., Dartmouth College v. Woodward, 17 U.S. (4 Wheat.) 518 (1819); Fletcher v. Peck, 10 U.S. (6 Cranch) 87 (1810).

76. See 1 A. de Tocqueville, supra Chap. 1, note 73, at 102–07, 282–90.

77. Forbath, "Ambiguities of Free Labor," supra Chap. 1, note 8, at 787–88.

and also issued broad injunctions against local elected officials and local government policies. It is a rich irony that the strongest precedents for those interventions would spring from the uses that the federal courts had made of the Federalist legacy and the fourteenth amendment a half-century earlier against the labor movement and its allies.

Judicial Review in Labor's Political Culture | 2

The labor movement of the 1880s and early 1890s embraced what was, by contemporary standards, a bold program for government regulation of the wage contract and working conditions.[1] Its central goal was to legislate a shorter workday.[2] Core demands also included legislation curtailing the sweated trades by banning manufacturing in tenement dwellings; wage laws abolishing payment by scrip or the truck-store system and requiring regular payment schemes; laws prohibiting anti-union discrimination by employers; and laws regulating the determination of coal miners' pay, particularly how, when, and by whom coal was weighed.[3] These reform campaigns were testing grounds for the proposition that workers could use the

1. See J. Viau, *Hours and Wages in American Organized Labor* 24–37 (1939); see also 2 J. Commons and D. Saposs, *History of Labour in the United States*, supra Chap. 1, note 1, at 509–11 (describing the political programs of the AFL in the early 1890s).

2. See D. Rodgers, *The Work Ethic in Industrial America* 156–60 (1974) (stating that "shorter hours . . . crusades [were] unsurpassed . . . by any other of the era's labor issues"); Forbath, "Ambiguities of Free Labor," supra Chap. 1, note 8, at 809–12; Shefter, supra Chap. 1, note 13, at 263 (noting that the eight-hour day "was the central demand of the American labor movement during the half century following the Civil War"); cf. D. Montgomery, *Beyond Equality*, supra Chap. 1, note 6, at 259–60 (discussing Ira Steward's arguments for a shorter working day).

3. See James, "Recent Labor Legislation," in *The Labor Movement: The Problem of Today* 45–66 (G. McNeill, ed., 1891); see also M. Carroll, *Labor and Politics* 56 (1923) (noting that hours and wage laws abolishing payment by scrip and the truck or company-store system, and regulating timing of pay, were "planks in the platform of the earlier [Gilded Age AFL] when more emphasis was laid on the solution of labor's problems through legislation").

ballot to " 'engraft republican principles' " on property and industry.[4] At issue was whether, as the Chicago Trade and Labor Assembly
resolved in 1888,

> [B]y the simple exercise of the duties of citizenship by the . . . work-
> ers, laws can be made and enforced that will regulate wages, hours,
> conditions of employment, and so change the relationship of employer
> and employee that an equitable distribution of the products of labor
> will be secured and the dangerous power of a few monopolists to
> legally rob the millions of workers of the results of their toil, will be
> abolished.[5]

Although substantial legislative success seemed to vindicate this
vision, Gilded Age labor also discovered that it was the courts that
principally determined how labor legislation, once passed, would
fare. Judicial review was the most visible and dramatic fashion in
which courts curtailed labor's ability to use laws to redress asymmetries of power in the employment relationship. By the turn of the
century state and federal courts had invalidated roughly sixty labor
laws.[6] During the 1880s and 1890s courts were far more likely than
not to strike down the very laws that labor sought most avidly.[7] For
workers, judicial review—the invalidation of labor laws under the
language of "liberty of contract" and "property rights"—became

4. McNeill, "The Problem of To-day," in *The Labor Movement*, supra Chap. 2, note
3, at 460.
5. T. C. Bigham, "The Chicago Federation of Labor," at 99 (Master's thesis, University of Chicago, 1924).
6. See infra Appendix A.
7. See infra Appendix A. Between 1885 and 1900, one law proscribing tenement
labor was struck down; none were upheld. Five prohibiting discrimination against union
members were invalidated; none were upheld. Five regulating the weighing of coal at
mines were voided; one was upheld. Four fixing the time of payment of wages were also
voided; none were upheld. Four prohibiting or regulating company stores were voided;
none were upheld. Three proscribing payment in scrip were invalidated; two were upheld.
Six hours laws of various sorts were struck down; three were upheld. Finally, seven laws
restricting labor injunctions were struck down or vitiated in explicitly constitutional terms;
none were upheld or enforced. Although both state and federal constitutional standards
were somewhat liberalized after the turn of the century, by 1920 courts had struck down
roughly three hundred labor laws. The cases, organized by categories of legislation, and
listed separately for the pre- and post-1900 eras, are found in Appendix A.

both evidence and symbol of the intractability of the American state from the perspective of labor reform.[8]

Samuel Gompers and *In re Jacobs*

The decision of the New York Court of Appeals in *In re Jacobs*,[9] the first high court decision to strike down a piece of labor legislation for infringing a workingman's constitutional liberty, is a landmark in the history of "laissez-faire constitutionalism." Invalidating an 1884 statute prohibiting the manufacture of cigars in tenement dwellings,[10] *Jacobs* is an eloquent, if ironic, statement of the Gilded Age courts' vision of "free labor" and workers' dignity and independence. The court envisioned each sweated outworker as a self-employed artisan "who carr[ies] on a perfectly lawful trade in his own home."[11] The inequitable statute hinders the artisan "in the application of his industry." It "deprives him of his property" in the disposition of his labor and skills and "of his personal liberty"

8. Elsewhere I have described the world view and political and cultural perspectives of the late-nineteenth-century judges who struck down these labor laws. See Forbath, "Ambiguities of Free Labor," supra Chap. 1, note 8. These high state and federal judges believed that the laws they struck down signified labor's turn toward a treacherous class-based politics. The judges were, for the most part, Republicans. Like most middle- and upper-class Republicans of the 1880s and 1890s, they had come to see Reconstruction as a divisive and doomed experiment in government intervention and regulation on behalf of black labor in the South. Equally disturbing was the fact that the labor movement in the North, like the agrarian movement in the West, had embraced this same flawed Reconstruction theory of government: an active democratic state reforming the social order to benefit a downtrodden class. All three movements—"black Republicans" in the South, labor in the North, and agrarians in the West—seemed driven by violent class feelings and hatreds; all three threatened the constitutional values of limited government and respect for the rights of property. The jurists struck down state labor and agrarian laws in the same spirit in which they nullified the more extreme federal civil rights legislation. All three kinds of laws were invidious class legislation. They sought not equality but group advantage, and it was the constitutional duty of the courts to strike down such faction-driven "unequal" laws.

9. 98 N.Y. 98 (1885). For a discussion of the ideological context and doctrinal history of *Jacobs*, see Forbath, "Ambiguities of Free Labor," supra Chap. 1, note 8, at 772–86.

10. See 98 N.Y. at 115.

11. Id. at 104.

by driving him out of his own shop to work in a factory "upon such terms as, under . . . the inexorable laws of supply and demand, he may be able to obtain from his employer."[12] The opinion is an unconscious parody of the values and fears of mid-nineteenth-century artisans. In fact, the income and working conditions of homeworkers in the sweated trades like cigarmaking were significantly worse than those of factory workers in the same industries, and rarely was the homeworker actually self-employed. Nonetheless, a judge reared on Lincoln's "Free Labor" ideology readily could have construed the homeworker's circumstances in that fashion. The homeworker was striving upward, hoping to become a propertied citizen and an entrepreneur. By the same Lincolnian lights, the anti-tenement law represented a tyrannical effort to hold Mr. Jacobs down, to reduce him to a factory wage-earner and a cog in the union's and manufacturer's big machines.[13] This view of labor legislation as a tyrannical or paternalistic insult to "Free Labor" resonates throughout Gilded Age opinions,[14] and *Jacobs* served as a leading precedent in substantive due process cases respecting labor laws through the rest of the century.[15]

Jacobs also figured as a landmark in Samuel Gompers's political evolution. In the late 1870s and early 1880s, Gompers was a vice-president of the Cigarmakers International Union and a leader of that union's large New York local. In those years Gompers still had strong ties to the Marxist branch of the first International. A pioneer in union administration, Gompers bitterly opposed the Lassallean socialists who disparaged trade unionism in favor of political engagement, but he remained open to political radicalism. He manifested little of his later rigid antipathy toward legislative intervention to reform labor conditions.[16] Indeed, he spearheaded the New York

12. Id. at 104–06.

13. See Forbath, "Ambiguities of Free Labor," supra Chap. 1, note 8, at 796.

14. See id. at 769, 772–800 (analyzing cases).

15. See C. Jacobs, *Law Writers and the Courts* 50–55 (1954); B. Twiss, *Lawyers and the Constitution* 99–101 (1942); Forbath, "Ambiguities of Free Labor," supra Chap. 1, note 8, at 795–96.

16. See Shefter, supra Chap. 1, note 13, at 222–24 (stating that in the early 1880s Gompers supported labor reform both through lobbying and legislation and through craft unionism); S. Kaufman, supra Chap. 1, note 16.

Cigarmakers' drive to secure legislation—ultimately invalidated in *Jacobs*—to halt tenement production in his trade.[17]

Gompers' autobiography[18] is a partial but revealing source on the formation of the trade union philosophy of the early twentieth century's preeminent American labor leader. In a chapter called *Learning Something of Legislation*, Gompers recalls the Cigarmakers' great expectations regarding workers' abilities to enlist the government and law to reform industry.[19] He describes his union's "years of educational work"[20] on the consequences of tenement manufacturing for both workers and consumers. At one point, Gompers even disguised himself as a book salesman and, like the Progressive social reformers he would later spurn, gathered survey material on life and work in the "Bohemian tenements."[21] Gompers lobbied and electioneered on behalf of the tenement-house bill. The bill passed, was signed, and a "jubilee demonstration" was held at Cooper Union, "a tremendous, inspiring success."[22]

But Gompers soon learned that, in an age of judicial supremacy, "[s]ecuring the enactment of a law does not mean the solution of the problem." "The power of the courts to pass upon constitutionality of law so complicate[d] reform by legislation as to seriously restrict the effectiveness of that method."[23] The tenement cigar manufacturers sought test cases and succeeded in winning opinions from the state's high court striking down two successive versions of the antisweating legislation.[24] *Jacobs*, the culmination of the second

17. At the time New York City had some 70,000 workers in the cigarmaking industry. Roughly one-seventh of them toiled in tenements; the rest worked in shops and factories. See H. Hurwitz, *Theodore Roosevelt and Labor in New York State, 1880–1900*, at 79 (1943). The city's cigarmakers' unions championed the law to halt the transformation of their craft into a sweated trade. On the rise of sweated labor or the "sweating system" in New York City's cigarmaking industry, see Schneider, "The New York Cigarmakers' Strike of 1877", 26 *Lab. Hist.* 325 (1985); for a brief account of the cigarmakers' union's anti-sweating campaign, see H. Hurwitz, supra, at 79–88.

18. See 1 S. Gompers, *Seventy Years*, supra Intro., note 7.

19. See id. at 183–98.

20. Id. at 186.

21. See id. at 187.

22. Id. at 194.

23. Id.

24. See H. Hurwitz, supra Chap. 2, note 17, at 83–86.

round of litigation, persuaded Gompers that this particular strategy was hopeless. "We found our work was nullified."[25] Gompers and the Cigarmakers considered whether to return to the political-legislative fray but decided instead that they would henceforth pursue their ends solely through "strikes and agitation."[26] In that fashion, the autobiography reports, they forced the manufacturers "to abandon the tenement manufacturing system and carry on the industry in factories under decent conditions. Thus we accomplished through economic power what we had failed to achieve through legislation."[27] In retrospect the experience became a nice text on the wisdom of voluntarism.[28]

By the end of the century, Gompers's and the Cigarmakers' experience with reform by legislation in the era of rising judicial supremacy had been repeated roughly sixty times and shared by trade unionists in almost every industrial state.[29] Maximum-hours laws were the Gilded Age labor movement's major legislative goal.[30] Therefore, we ought to examine the odysseys of those prized reforms in the courts.

25. 1 S. Gompers, *Seventy Years*, supra Intro., note 7, at 196.

26. Id. at 197.

27. Id.

28. The bakers' union of New York had a similar experience to the cigarmakers when the U.S. Supreme Court in *Lochner v. New York*, 198 U.S. 45 (1905), struck down a ten-hour law for which the bakers had long campaigned. In a speech to the cigarmakers in 1906, Gompers pointed to *Lochner* as teaching their comrades in the bakers' union the same lesson *Jacobs* had taught them. Through strikes and collective bargaining, he declared, "[t]he bakers [have now] secured the ten hour work day—the union men—to a large extent; but they have given up the fight for the ten hour law. That is not the way victories are won for labor." Transcript of Speech to Quarterly Meeting of Cigarmakers' Union No. 144, New York, April 26, 1906, p. 23. Reel 110, AFL Records: The Samuel Gompers Era (microfilm edition, 1979).

29. For a compilation of the labor laws struck down between 1885 and 1900 as well as a comparison of the proportion of central categories of labor laws that were invalidated versus those that were upheld, see intra Appendix A.

30. Why this was so and what significance attached to the struggles for shorter hours is well treated in D. Rodgers, supra Chap. 2, note 2, at 155–60; J. Viau, supra Chap. 2, note 1, at 46–50.

Hours Laws in Illinois

The Chicago Trade and Labor Assembly, renamed the Chicago Federation of Labor in 1893, wrote the ringing 1888 resolution on using the ballot and lawmaking to abolish the power of tyrannical capitalists.[31] Both the Illinois Federation of Labor and the Chicago Federation stood among the majority of AFL affiliates that put great faith and energy in reform by legislation.[32] The two federations were instrumental in the years of "unremitting agitation"[33] that preceded the passage in 1893 of an eight-hour law covering women and children in Illinois factories, mines, and mills.[34] In lobbying for the law, the federations joined forces with a coalition of working- and middle-class women reformers called the Illinois Women's Alliance. The leading lobbyist and drafter of the bill was Florence Kelley, a socialist lawyer, and a prominent figure among both Chicago's women reformers and the city's labor radicals.[35] Felix Frankfurter regarded Kelley as the reformer with the "largest single share" in promoting and securing labor legislation in the United States "during the first thirty years of this century";[36] although she remained indefatigable, Kelley's interventionist mission was repeatedly frustrated by the courts.

Both Kelley and the Chicago Federation envisioned the 1893 bill strategically, as an entering wedge for broader hours legislation that would ultimately cover men as well as women.[37] They also anticipated that in many workplaces men's hours would be "determined

31. See supra p. 38.

32. See supra pp. 12–14; see also E. Staley, *The History of the Illinois State Federation of Labor* 145–70 (1930) (describing the platforms and legislative proposals of the Illinois State Federation of Labor from 1884 to 1897).

33. *Final Report of the Commission on Industrial Relations* 42 (1915) [hereinafter *Final Report*].

34. See generally E. Beckner, *A History of Illinois Labor Legislation* 153–54 (1929) (describing the Sweat-Shop Act of 1893).

35. For an account of Kelley, 1890s Chicago, and the links between women and labor reformers campaigning for labor legislation, see Sklar, "Hull House in the 1890s: A Community of Women Reformers," 10 *Signs* 658 (1985).

36. Id. at 658.

37. See id. at 668–77.

by the length of the workday of the women and girls whose work interlocks with their own.''[38] The bill created a new state Department of Factory Inspection, and labor-backed Governor Altgeld named Kelley its chief.[39]

Despite opposition, the statute was vigorously enforced for two years until 1895, when the Illinois Supreme Court declared the eight-hour law an unconstitutional infringement on women's liberty of contract in *Ritchie v. People*.[40] According to Kelley and others, *Ritchie* short-circuited the progress of hours legislation as well as other labor reforms in Illinois and elsewhere for over a decade.[41] By 1905 Illinois's labor reformers had achieved not "universal hours legislation" but merely a restriction on the work of little boys at night in glassworks.[42] Finally, in 1910, the Illinois Supreme Court upheld a ten-hour law covering women in certain manufacturing occupations.[43] After almost two decades of delay, the slow work of state-building—developing adequate modes of enforcement, a work-

38. F. Kelley, *Some Ethical Gains through Legislation* 144 (1905).

39. See Sklar, supra Chap. 2, note 35, at 670. Among the deputy inspectors Altgeld appointed to assist Kelley was Abraham Bisno, a Russian-Jewish garment worker, union leader, and, like Kelley, a socialist. Bisno has left us a vivid account of the pioneering efforts of these radical reformers in office. "In those years," Bisno writes, "labor legislation was looked on . . . mainly as political fodder." A. Bisno, *Union Pioneer* 149 (1967). Where provision for state enforcement existed at all, prosecutors scoffed at unions' demands for enforcement; "it was left to our department to set the example of rigid enforcement of labor laws." Id. at 148–49. "[A]lso [we] educate[d] the parents who sent their children to work, and the employers of these children, the women who were employed longer than eight hours a day, and their employers." Id. at 149. Experience had taught all of them a "contempt for politician-made laws," which these new radical officers of the state strove to overcome. See id. They issued stern warnings, methodically built up cases of repeated violations, and brought their strongest cases to the courts. Bisno notes that "Governor Altgeld was overwhelmed with protests both against Mrs. Kelley and myself." Id. at 151.

40. 155 Ill. 98, 40 N.E. 454 (1895).

41. See F. Kelley, supra Chap. 2, note 38, at 145; Brandeis, "Women's Hour Legislation," in 3 D. Lescohier and E. Brandeis, *History of Labour in the United States, 1896–1932*, at 476 (1935); 7 *Report of the Industrial Commission on the Relations and Conditions of Capital and Labor, Hearings before the Industrial Commission on the Mining Industry*, H. R. Doc. No. 181, 57th Cong., 1st Sess. 254–55 (1900) (testimony of F. Kelley) [hereinafter *Industrial Commission Report on Capital and Labor*].

42. See F. Kelley, supra Chap. 2, note 38, at 43–57.

43. See Ritchie and Co. v. Wayman, 244 Ill. 509, 91 N.E. 695 (1910).

able and legitimated division of tasks between administrators and courts, and a competent and recognized corps of officials—had, at last, resumed.[44]

Hours Laws in Colorado

"The history of Colorado," in Kelley's words, "repeat[ed] in spectacular manner the experience of Illinois."[45] The opposition that labor reform met in courts and polity was more adamant, and so too was labor's reaction. In Illinois the courts slowed and diminished the accomplishments and constituency of labor radicals.[46] But in Colorado the courts and polity did much to elicit a change in the very character of that state's labor radicalism—from a populist and socialist faith in the ability of a democratic state to reconstruct industry and economic life to a syndicalist conviction of the state's capacity to work nothing but harm. As in Illinois, hours laws proved a critical arena in which Colorado's labor movement tested the limits of reform by the ballot and legislation. Beginning in the mid-1880s, Colorado labor's chief political demand was the eight-hour day. Indeed, it was the primary objective in the formation of the Colorado State Federation of Labor. The Populist ferment of the early 1890s helped galvanize the forces in the federation that favored broad political ambitions.[47] As one labor editor expressed the movement's commitment to reform through legislation: " 'what has been gained through the strength and force of organized labor must be bulwarked by proper legislation.' "[48]

44. See Brandeis, "Women's Hour Legislation," supra Chap. 2, note 41, at 476.

45. F. Kelley, supra Chap. 2, note 38, at 161–62.

46. See, e.g., Valesh, *Labor Legislation(?)*, 2 *Am. Federationist* 26, (1895). Valesh recounts an AFL leader's experiences with Illinois courts to show "how limited is the practical good that trade unions attain through legislation"; even laws on the books are illusory, for the state will not "compel the employer to do something . . . which a union" cannot enforce. Id. at 27.

47. To the eight-hour day they added nationalization of the telephone, telegraph, and railroads, state ownership of the mines, utilities, and coal yards, as well as state-financed sickness and old-age insurance. See J. Wright, *The Politics of Populism: Dissent in Colorado* 226–37 (1974).

48. Id. at 230 (quoting *Pueblo Courier*, Nov. 11, 1898).

Preeminent among Colorado trade unionists were the state's miners, and it was the miners' and smelters' struggle for shorter hours that Kelley had in mind in comparing Colorado's experience with that of Illinois. The Populists ensured the election of Governor Davis Waite, a labor sympathizer, in 1893, and in 1895 Democrats and Populists controlled the state Senate and the Republicans had only a one-vote majority in the House.[49] In that context, labor almost passed a broad eight-hour bill covering all mine, mill, and factory workers.[50] Mill and mine owners denounced the bill as unconstitutional, and their allies in the legislature were able to persuade the bill's proponents to agree to ask the state supreme court for an advisory opinion.[51] *In re Eight-Hour Law*[52] declared that the act would be "class legislation" and in violation "of the right of parties to make their own contracts."[53]

Again in 1899 a campaign by the Western Federation of Miners (WFM) and the State Federation of Labor helped produce a viable pro-labor majority in the state legislature. Despite powerful corporate lobbying, the 1899 session passed an eight-hour law for smelters and miners.[54] And again the Colorado Supreme Court declared the hours legislation unconstitutional: "it is beyond the power of the legislature, under the guise of the police power, to prohibit an adult man who desires to work thereat from working more than eight hours a day, on the ground that working longer may . . . injure his own health."[55] For many miners belonging to the WFM, the decision seemed to reflect their political impotence in a state where the courts

49. See id. at 157–58, 186–91.

50. See id. at 235.

51. See id. at 233–34.

52. 21 Colo. 29, 39, P. 328 (1895).

53. *House Journal of the General Assembly of the State of Colorado*, 10th Sess., Mar. 8, 1895, at 711.

54. The bill was modeled after a Utah law that had been sustained by the high court of that state and by the Supreme Court in Holden v. Hardy, 169 U.S. 366 (1898). On *Holden* and the uneven fortunes of hours laws for "hazardous occupations" in the wake of that decision, see infra pp. 50–53.

55. *In re* Morgan, 26 Colo. 415, 427–28, 58 P. 1071, 1076 (1899).

supplied capital with so many trumps.[56] In the summer of 1899, at hearings held in Denver, a WFM organizer told the United States Industrial Commission, "[u]nder the present condition, I would say that the legislature is an unnecessary expense, on account of the courts setting aside anything the legislature may do, providing they see fit."[57]

But the WFM and the State Federation remained ready to do battle within the polity. They "got out the vote"[58] for a succession of procedural and substantive constitutional amendments over several elections in order to clear a path for the hours law.[59] By then the Colorado Fuel and Iron Company and the "Smelter Trust" had formed. The Trust's enormous sway over the state legislature stalled the eight-hour laws for several more years despite authorization from constitutional amendments.[60] The hours laws that finally emerged were reduced to dead letters for another decade by legislative amendments and judicial construction.

In the face of these numbing frustrations with the legal and political process, Colorado's smelters and miners turned to "[d]irect and militant action." The bitter strikes of 1903 and 1904 emerged out of the failures of these reform efforts.[61] The president of the WFM, Charles Moyer, stormed:

> [I]t has been preached to the men that legislation was the only proper means to secure relief. They were led to believe that they could win at the ballot box, and they believe that they did win, but the legislature threw them down . . . After waiting four years, patiently enduring

56. According to a mine owner's spy, one member of the Cloud City local of the WFM bitterly remarked: "If the eight hour law don't suit the s——s of b———s it suits us and they will have to give us eight hours whether they want to or not . . ." Another member, according to the spy, said: "if I could have my way . . . I would kill them all and see if that would be considered unconstitutional." J. Wright, supra Chap. 2, note 47, at 234 (quoting from Report of the Thiel Detective Agency, July 1, 5, and 17, 1899).

57. 12 *Industrial Commission Report on Capital and Labor*, supra Chap. 2, note 41, at 354 (1901) (testimony of Mr. John C. Sullivan, miner, Victor, Colorado).

58. J. Wright, supra Chap. 2, note 47, at 234.

59. See id. at 234–35; Lonsdale, "The Fight for an Eight-Hour Day," 43 *Colo. Mag.* 339, 346–47 (1966).

60. See J. Wright, supra Chap. 2. note 47, at 235–36.

61. See id. at 236.

the hardships and injustices of a twelve-hour system, is it surprising that at last they have arisen in their power to assert their rights?[62]

The miners' uprising "to assert their rights" was transformed by the mine operators into open warfare. With the help of the state's governor and militia, the operators succeeded in crushing the WFM in the Colorado mine fields.[63]

The last battle unfolded in the state supreme court. During the mining-camp strikes, the militia, headed by mining-corporation officials and supported by the governor, had detained strikers and union leaders for many weeks in bullpens, disregarding hundreds of habeas corpus petitions.[64] In 1905 the Colorado Supreme Court, which in nullifying the hours laws had precipitated the long, violent conflict, upheld the wholesale suspension of habeas corpus.[65]

The same year marked the founding of the Industrial Workers of the World (IWW), the distinctly American syndicalist union movement, which vaunted direct action and defiantly proclaimed its exasperation with and scorn for the political process. The WFM membership voted by referendum to affiliate with the IWW. Eighty percent of the membership, most of them probably staunch Populists a decade earlier, voted in favor of affiliation, and they made up a substantial portion of the Wobblies' total constituency in the IWW's first years. Furthermore, WFM leaders Big Bill Haywood and Charles Moyer were prominent among the founders of the IWW.[66] "The men now realize that they will never get relief by legislation, and that they must get it through their own action," Moyer proclaimed.[67] In a similar vein, Haywood declared that American democracy was a sham because the nation's courts and political parties

62. Commission of Labor, *A Report on Labor Disturbances in the State of Colorado, from 1880–1904, Inclusive*, S. Doc. No. 122, 58th Cong., 3d Sess. 138–39 (1905) [hereinafter *Colorado Labor Disturbances*].

63. See M. Dubofsky, *We Shall Be All* 36 (1969).

64. See *Colorado Labor Disturbances*, supra Chap. 2, note 62, at 138–39.

65. See Ex parte Moyer, 35 Colo. 154, 169, 91 P. 738, 740 (1905), aff'd sub. nom. Moyer v. Peabody, 212 U.S. 78, 84–85 (1909).

66. See M. Dubofsky, supra Chap. 2, note 63, at 76–83, 116–18.

67. J. Wright, supra Chap. 2, note 47, at 236.

were in the capitalists' grip. "Direct action" was the answer.[68] Thus did Gompers's more cautious and conservative anti-statism find a radical anti-statist counterpoint. Both were inspired by the obdurate state of American courts and parties.

Pressed toward a Minimalist Politics

Of course, not every state was like Colorado or even Illinois. The limits of the police power varied somewhat from jurisdiction to jurisdiction, and in many cases state legislatures did not push against these limits hard enough to prompt employers' challenges. There were lordly judges, but there were also timorous legislators. State party leaders dealt harshly with legislators who introduced bills opposed by their party's major financial backers. In 1905, for example, the chairman of the New York State Assembly Committee on Labor and Industries told the New York Federation of Labor's lobbyist "that although he wanted to report a nine-hour bill for women the last time he had let the bill out of committee, he had been 'called down good and hard and told not to permit that bill to go out again.' "[69] Nor was it uncommon for labor lobbyists to find their bills replaced by meaningless substitute measures before being reported out by legislative committees.[70]

Nonetheless, by the turn of the century, sixteen states did have some form of legislation limiting the hours of labor for women.[71]

68. See J. Conlin, *Big Bill Haywood and the Radical Union Movement* 117 (1969); M. Dubofsky, supra Chap. 2, note 63, at 158–59.

69. Asher, "Failure and Fulfillment: Agitation for Employers' Liability Legislation and the Origins of Workmen's Compensation in New York State, 1876–1910," 24 *Lab. Hist.* 198, 212 (1983) (quoting Workingmen's Federation of the State of New York, *Report of the Legislative Committee, Proceedings*, 1905). See generally E. Beckner, supra Chap. 2, note 34 (discussing the passage of a ten-hour law for women in Illinois); I. Yellowitz, *Labor and the Progressive Movement in New York State, 1897–1916* (1965) (discussing the efforts of different political parties in New York to further or impede the progress of labor legislation); Massay, "Legislators, Lobbyists, and Loopholes: Coal Mining Legislation in West Virginia, 1875–1901," 32 *W. Va. Hist.* 135 (1971) (discussing legislation regulating coal mines).

70. See Asher, supra Chap. 2, note 69, at 213.

71. See Brandeis, "Women's Hour Legislation," supra Chap. 2, note 41, at 457, 466n43, 469.

None of these laws was as stringent as the one championed by Kelley and struck down in *Ritchie*. Most were hobbled by want of state enforcement, and many, including New York's, which was in the vanguard of labor legislation, were limited to women under twenty-one.[72] All were ten- or twelve-hour laws.[73] Of these hours laws, three prompted constitutional challenges, and all were upheld.[74]

By contrast, no high court in the Gilded Age proved willing to uphold broad hours laws that embraced all adult male workers. Ohio and Nebraska passed such legislation, but both laws were struck down.[75] Slightly narrower laws, limited to mining and manufacturing, like the 1895 Colorado bill, fared no better.[76]

As far as adult male workers were concerned, only hours laws limited to particular "hazardous occupations" or to callings where workers were deemed to be especially vulnerable to overreaching by employers had decent odds of surviving judicial scrutiny. The narrower Colorado eight-hour law of 1899 that covered only smelters and miners was identical to an 1894 Utah statute. The Utah law had been upheld by that state's supreme court as well as the United States Supreme Court in *Holden v. Hardy*.[77] After *Holden* a few state judiciaries seemed ready to ease restraints on hours laws for broader

72. See id. at 467.

73. The Wisconsin and Illinois acts provided for eight-hour days, but the latter was held unconstitutional in *Ritchie v. People* and the former applied only to employers who "compelled" women to work beyond the legal limit. See Brandeis, "Women's Hour Legislation," supra Chap. 2, note 41, at 457 and n2. The following states had laws limiting women's hours in the period 1880–1900 (no enforcement provisions): Connecticut (1887) (no enforcement provisions), Illinois (1893) (struck down in *Ritchie*), Louisiana (1886), Maine (1887), Massachusetts (1874 and 1900), Michigan (1885), (repealed 1893), Nebraska (1899), New Hampshire (1887), New Jersey (1892), North Dakota (1863) (no enforcement provisions), Oklahoma (1890), Pennsylvania (1897), Rhode Island (1885), South Dakota (1863) (no enforcement provisions), Virginia (1890), Wisconsin (1867) (no enforcement provisions). See id. at 399, 457, 466 n43, 469.

74. See Commonwealth v. Hamilton Mfg. Co., 120 Mass. 383 (1876); People v. Charles Schweinler Press, 214 N.Y. 395, 108 N.E. 639, *appeal dismissed*, 242 U.S. 618 (1915); Commonwealth v. Beatty, 15 Pa. Super. 5, 8 Pa. D. 712 (1900).

75. See Wheeling Bridge & Terminal Ry. v. Gilmore, 8 Ohio C. C. 658 (1894); Low v. Rees Printing Co., 41 Neb. 127, 59 N.W. 362 (1894).

76. See, e.g., *In re* Eight-Hour Law, 21 Colo. 29, 39, P. 328 (1895).

77. 169 U.S. 366 (1898).

categories of male workers. Progressive lawyers had begun to use experts' medical and social science evidence successfully to undercut judges' upper-class "common sense" about the bounds of occupational hazards. By 1900, however, support within the labor movement for hours laws other than for women and children had shrunk,[78] and judicial nullification had already had an enduring impact on labor's politics and visions of reform.[79]

78. See infra p. 53.

79. Nonetheless, Progressive-era (1900–1914) cases upholding hours laws for women and "hazardous" male occupations were and still are frequently cited as evidence that the judiciary had only the slightest stymieing effect on the progress of labor reform. See, e.g., M. Keller, *Affairs of State* 369–70 (1977); Warren, "The Progressiveness of the United States Supreme Court," 13 *Colum. L. Rev.* 294, 295–97 (1913) (claiming that the Supreme Court "has been steady and consistent in upholding all State legislation of a progressive type"); see also Urofsky, "State Courts and Protective Legislation During the Progressive Era: A Reevaluation," 72 *J. Am. Hist.* 63, 91 (1985) ("'[T]he doctrine of contract, while exalted by conservatives and set in opposition to the police power, was far from triumphant at the state level, just as it also failed to carry the day in the United States Supreme Court"). But see id. at 90 ("'[S]tate court decisions, however, did go against laws that attempted to support unions").

Another case in point is workmen's compensation laws. Urofsky makes much of the courts' relative toleration toward workmen's compensation laws from 1910 onward. See id. at 85–87. But that is a partial version of the story. It omits the fact that this particular reform was business's and not labor's answer to America's unparalleled rate of industrial injuries and deaths. Business groups like the National Association of Manufacturers sponsored and lobbied for workmen's compensation schemes in the early 1900s. See Lubove, "Workmen's Compensation and the Prerogatives of Voluntarism," 8 *Lab. Hist.* 254, 266–68 (1967). Labor federations, both left and right, hotly opposed them. See Weinstein, "Big Business and the Origins of Workmen's Compensation," 8 *Lab. Hist.* 156, 159–60 (1967). From the 1870s through the early 1900s, organized labor had promoted not workmen's compensation schemes but rather employers' liability laws. These latter bills narrowed or repealed the common law defenses—assumption of risk doctrine, fellow servant, and contributory negligence rules—available to employers against workers' common law tort actions for industrial injuries. Not surprisingly, many of these revisions of the common law during the Gilded Age were defeated or watered down in the legislatures. The courts nullified most of those that passed. See Asher, supra Chap. 2, note 69, at 215. After 1900, however, judges began to incorporate some of the revisions into jury instructions, and employers began to feel their bite. Employers' associations joined middle-class reformers in promoting workmen's compensation schemes as more "rational" and "predictable" alternatives to jury compensation. At the same time, they continued their unstinting opposition to employers' liability laws as "'destructive class legislation.'" Id. at 217 (quoting a letter from Marshall Cushing, Secretary of the National Association of Manufacturers, to an unnamed New York employer). At

Moreover, Colorado was not alone in repudiating the "hazardous occupation" standard, and many state high courts gave the standard a narrow and unpredictable reach.[80] *Lochner v. New York*,[81] decided seven years after *Holden*, is the classic illustration from United States Supreme Court case law.

If the exact borders of the police power regarding hours laws often seemed maddeningly uncertain, the general contours and political implications were clear. Broad, class-based legislative initiatives would not pass constitutional muster. The police power, courts often declared, could be invoked to protect "dependent" and "vulnerable" groups within the labor force, but it could not constitutionally reach the inequalities of fortune and power that arose from the "fact that some men are possessed of industrial property and others are

first, labor stood opposed to workmen's compensation schemes, accurately predicting that workmen's compensation in practice would limit workers' recoveries to impoverishing amounts. See Lubove, supra, at 268–69 (citing a study estimating that compensation equaled no more than "one-fourth of the pecuniary cost of those injuries which the compensation laws profess to cover"). Yet by 1910 labor federations had also grown disillusioned with the prospects for stringent legislative revisions of common law liability rules. Even when legislatures passed such "radical" laws, courts vitiated them. See Clark, "The Legal Liability of Employers for Injuries to Their Employees in the United States," 74 *Bull. Bureau Lab.* 1, 91–120 (1908). Moreover, legislators preferred the workmen's compensation alternative, because it seemed to accomplish the same ends as employers' liability laws, and yet employers endorsed it. See Lubove, supra, at 262; Weinstein, supra, at 160.

Only in this context did labor turn toward supporting workmen's compensation. As was the case with hours laws, courts quashed generations of reform measures and prompted labor to narrow and recast what they sought; then courts haltingly upheld the results. Urofsky and others may be unaware of the details of this story or may think it represents an insignificant judicial intervention in the political process. In either case, they ignore the courts' cumulative effects upon the development of labor's political vision and aspirations.

80. See, e.g., State v. Legendre, 138 La. 154, 70 So. 70 (1915) (invalidating an eight-hour day for firemen); State v. Barba, 132 La. 768, 61 So. 784 (1913) (same); Commonwealth v. Boston and M. R.R., 222 Mass. 206, 110 N.E. 264 (1915) (invalidating a nine-hour day for railroad employees); State v. Miksicek, 225 Mo. 561, 125 S.W. 507 (1910) (invalidating a six-day week for bakeries); Saville v. Corless, 46 Utah 495, 151 P. 51 (1915) (invalidating a six o'clock closing-time restriction for mercantile establishments).

81. 198 U.S. 45 (1905).

not.''[82] This constitutional segmentation of labor into a ''dependent'' class of children, women, and men in certain dangerous or especially vulnerable callings, and an ''independent'' class of ''free adult workers'' who ought not rely on ''state paternalism'' helped fragment not only labor legislation but also workers' group identity.[83] The courts' relative hospitality toward hours laws for women and children encouraged and ratified within labor circles a gender-based division of the working class. The labor movement had once favored ''universal hours laws,'' signifying its class-wide constituency; now it supported hours legislation for those ''dependent'' groups now deemed *outside* the movement, because they could not ''look after themselves'' through collective self-help.[84]

These cases also figured prominently in the crucial 1890s debates in the AFL between the proponents of broad versus minimalist la-

82. Coppage v. Kansas, 236 U.S. 1, 17 (1915); see also Frorer v. People, 141 Ill. 171, 31 N.E. 395 (1892); Godcharles v. Wigeman, 113 Pa. 431, 6 A. 354 (1886). Although the Supreme Court in *Holden* spoke broadly of the growing inequality of bargaining power between industrial worker and employer—see Holden, 169 U.S. at 397 (''The proprietors lay down the rules and the laborers are practically constrained to obey them'')—both the Supreme Court and other federal and state courts continued to reject that inequality as an adequate basis on which to rest legislative ''interference'' in the wage relation.

83. See D. Gordon, R. Edwards, and M. Reich, *Segmented Work, Divided Workers* 119–21 (1982) [hereinafter D. Gordon and R. Edwards]; R. Steinberg, *Wages and Hours: Labor and Relations in Twentieth-Century America* 10–13 (1982); J. Viau, supra Chap. 2, note 1, at 60–74. For works on protective legislation for women, see J. Baer, *The Chains of Protection: The Judicial Response to Women's Labor Legislation* 42–67 (1978), which argues that these cases set a precedent for sex discrimination based on physical differences; A. Kessler-Harris, *Out to Work* 180–205 (1982), which describes women workers' attempts at organizing as well as advocating legislation; Brandeis, ''Women's Hour Legislation,'' supra Chap. 2, note 41, at 457–500, which praises the legislation; and Lehrer, ''Protective Labor Legislation for Women,'' 17 *Rev. Radical Pol. Econ.* 187 (1985), arguing that protective laws helped to undercut workers' organizing. The segmentation of the labor force and labor market is a topic well beyond the scope of this essay, although the political rifts and narrowing of aspirations that do concern us here were certainly reinforced by employers' labor market strategies. See D. Gordon and R. Edwards, supra, at 136–57. Thus, we are dealing with an elaborate set of ''feedback loops'' linking law, employer strategies, and labor politics.

84. See, e.g., J. Baer, supra Chap 2., note 83, at 31; D. Gordon and R. Edwards, supra Chap. 2, note 83, at 204–06; A. Kessler-Harris, supra Chap. 2, note 83, at 180–205; R. Steinberg, supra Chap. 2, note 83, at 78–81.

bor politics. Proponents of voluntarism frequently invoked *Jacobs,
Ritchie, In re Morgan,* and other liberty-of-contract cases in the
closely fought battle over whether the AFL would embrace "independent labor politics" and the eleven-point "political programme"
that had been adopted by England's recently formed Independent
Labour Party. One point of the "programme" was a "legal eight-
hour workday."[85] Speaking to that demand at the 1894 Denver Convention of the AFL, Adolph Strasser of the Cigarmakers, Gompers's
mentor and colleague, declared: "There is one fact that cannot be
overlooked. You cannot pass a general eight hour day without changing the constitution of the United States and the constitution of every
State in the Union . . . I am opposed to wasting our time declaring
for legislation being enacted for a time possibly, after we are dead."[86]

Henry Lloyd, a widely known author and journalist, a champion
of broad labor reform, and a key figure in forging the labor-populist
alliance that founded the People's Party, rose to respond: "We are
told it is unconstitutional. Mr. President, I sometimes wish I had
been born in any other country than in the United States. I am sick
and tired of listening to lawyers and laboring men [like Strasser and
Gompers] declaring everything we ask unconstitutional . . . [I]t is
about time we undertook to change the constitution."[87] And he went
on to describe the depth of support for a legal eight-hour day at the
recent conference in England of the TUC's Labor Representation
League. Unimpressed, Strasser queried: "Is it not a fact that in
England there is no constitutional provision [to stymie an eight-hour
law?]"[88] And he pointed proudly to the craft unions, like the Cigarmakers, that had gained the eight-hour day "by themselves . . .
pass[ing] and enforc[ing] [their own] law without the government."[89]

Invalidated labor laws were powerful evidence of and a metaphor
for the recalcitrance of the American state and the wisdom of voluntarism. Whatever might be true of politics in England or else-

85. *Verbatum Report,* supra Chap. 1, note 60, at 1.
86. Id. at 19–20.
87. Id. at 21 (statement of Henry Lloyd).
88. Id. (statement of Adolph Strasser).
89. Id. at 19.

where, organizing and acting in the private economic realm of the American workplace seemed, increasingly, the only worthwhile avenue for gaining reforms like the eight-hour day.

Over the next decade those who championed a minimalist labor politics prevailed in the shaping of the national (and many state) AFL programs. Of course, such a politics did not mean abandoning all reform by legislation. The voluntarist strategy embraced a significant measure of legislative intervention. Thus, for example, the AFL staunchly supported hours and wages laws for women and children, not only because these groups were deemed "dependent" and in need of state "paternalism," but also to put a floor under wage competition. Such laws were the visible hand of voluntarism. At the same time, by 1910, Gompers and other national AFL leaders were also condemning the very kinds of broad, class-based wage and hours legislation and state-financed social insurance that labor's national organizations in England and elsewhere were demanding and gaining.

Some leaders, like Gompers and Strasser, were more receptive than others to learning the lessons of voluntarism. Their base lay in some of the stronger craft unions and among skilled workers, a constituency for whom minimalist politics could be expected to have greatest pragmatic appeal when broad reforms seemed increasingly elusive.

Skilled workers' unusual bargaining power often enabled them to improve hours and wages and gain workplace reforms that less-skilled workers were unable to gain or defend without legislation. Accordingly, their unions weighed the costs of broad politics (and broad industrial action) more warily than did unions of less-skilled workers.[90] Moreover, Gompers, Strasser, and several other early AFL craft union leaders issued from a specific minority tradition within the American labor movement of the 1870s and 1880s. Rooted in the émigré-Marxism of New York City's English- and North European–born labor leaders, it championed economic action and

90. Sometimes, however, skilled workers proved stalwart champions of broad social reform and organizing the unskilled and unorganized. See J. Green, *The World of the Workers* 68–69 (1980); D. Montgomery, *Workers' Control in America* 67–72 (1979).

the building of workers' own organizations and opposed what it saw as the dominant American labor tradition's "middle class" faith in the efficacy of political reform.[91]

Some important unions in Gilded Age America were predisposed toward voluntarism, but miners were not among them. Their unions cleaved to the tradition that set great store by politics and reform through legislation. Many miners had brought with them from England and Wales a legacy of experience with seeking and reaping the benefits of mine labor legislation.[92] Yet in the late 1890s, even the miners' national leaders reluctantly withdrew some of their earlier faith. Asked by the United States Industrial Commission in 1899 about the operation of mine labor laws during the past several years, United Mine Workers (UMW) president John Mitchell answered that the laws miners had sought most vigorously—"to abolish the truck stores and the screens and such things, and those requiring weekly payments"—"have almost invariably been declared unconstitutional by the supreme courts.[93] Was the problem one of drafting? Was there "no form of law to cover these abuses [truck stores, payment in scrip, and so forth] that would come within the Constitution?"[94] "Our experience," Mitchell replied, "has been that there is not; we have tried different laws . . . and we have tried framing the laws in different ways . . . and it appears that we have always been defeated in the Courts.[95] The situation seemed to demand that miners rely on their "organizations . . . themselves to regulate these abuses."[96] Mitchell conjectured that miners' organizations would have to abandon a broad regulatory program in favor of simply seeking legislation to protect workers' organizations from public and private repression.[97]

91. See S. Kaufman, supra Chap. 1, note 16; N. Salvatore, "Introduction" to S. Gompers, Seventy Years of Life and Labor at xix–xx (N. Salvatore, ed., 1984).

92. See J. Laslett, Labor and the Left 193–94 (1970).

93. 12 Industrial Commission Report on Capital and Labor, supra Chap. 2, note 41, at 48 (1901).

94. Id. at 48–49 (statement of Commissioner North questioning Mitchell).

95. Id. at 49.

96. Id. (statement of Mitchell).

97. See id.

This was the minimalist path toward which many labor leaders' political thinking seemed inclined at that time. The conjuncture of a key moment of collective debate and decisionmaking in labor's political history with the rise of judicial review of labor laws lent unusual significance to these late-nineteenth-century constitutional cases. Together with the entrenchment of the "old political parties," "judicial supremacy" supplied a context in which Gompers and his cohort managed to transform their outlook into the prevailing one. Even those not predisposed to voluntarism recognized the practical and symbolic barriers that the courts had erected to a broad politics; through conscious choices as well as what political scientists would call "decisionless decisions" or the "rule of anticipated reactions," labor's programs and visions of reform gradually narrowed.[98] Thus the courts helped turn minimalist politics from a minority viewpoint of cautious craft unionists into what seemed the surest path to most of the labor movement.[99]

---

98. See J. Gaventa, *Power and Powerlessness* 15 (1980).

99. Judicial review seemed so formidable partly because it was bound up with a broader judicial control over labor legislation and its enforcement. At the turn of the century, most labor laws in most American states remained in the common law mold, requiring enforcement by private civil actions rather than by state officials—at best, they relied on the affected employee or his union to try to prevail on the ordinary state attorneys to prosecute their complaints. See E. Brandeis, "Labor Legislation" in 3 E. Brandeis and D. Lescohier, *History of Labour in the United States*, supra Chap. 2, note 41. Seventeen states did have factory and mine inspectors; there were 114 in all of the United States covering some 513,000 workplaces, and most of these were not full-time inspectors. Many heavily industrialized states had no inspectorate at all. See S. Kingsbury, *Labor Laws and Their Enforcement* 233–35 (1911). And even in the most progressive states, factory and mine inspectors were scarce in comparison to those in England and lacked many of the most important enforcement powers that English inspectors enjoyed. See Forbath, " 'In the Mother Country,' " supra Chap. 1, note 23; G. Price, "Administration of Labor Laws and Factory Inspection in Certain European Countries," *Bulletin of the U.S. Bureau of Labor Statistics*, no. 142, pp. 81–82, February 27, 1914; E. Baker, *Protective Labor Legislation* 281–84 (1924) (on the size, powers, and responsibilities of New York's factory inspectorate); Testimony of Thomas Lappin, 19 December 1900, 14 Ind. Comm. 251 (same); *Annual Reports of the Factory Inspector*, Pennsylvania, 1890–1900; J. Barnard, *Factory Legislation in Pennsylvania: Its History and Administration* (1907); *Annual Reports of the Factory Inspectors of Illinois*, 1894–1900; E. Beckner, *A History of Illinois Labor Legislation*, supra Chap. 2, note 34; W. Brock, *Investigation and Responsibility: Public Responsibility in the U.S., 1865–1900* 148–84 (1984); and on

England, see H. A. Mess, *Factory Legislation and Its Administration: 1891–1924* (1926); A. May and A. Davies, *The Law Relating to Factories and Workshops* (1902).

Thus, courts held sway, and not only could strike down labor laws but also could nullify them by hostile construction or by procedural decisions that tilted against effective enforcement. See, e.g., Cashman v. Chase, 156 Mass. 342, 31 N.E. 4 (1892); Nappa v. Erie Ry., 195 N.Y. 176, 88 N.E. 30 (1909); Finnigan v. N.Y. Contracting Co., 194 N.Y. 244, 87 N.E. 424 (1909) (dismissing a suit for failure to provide adequate notice); Gallagher v. Newman, 190 N.Y. 444, 83 N.E. 480 (1908); Quinlan v. Lackawanna Steel Co., 107 A.D. 176, 94 N.Y.S. 942 (1905), *aff'd*, 191 N.Y. 329, 84 N.E. 73 (1908) (holding that turning on an electric current was not an act of superintendence within the meaning of the Employers Liability Act); see also H. Hurwitz, supra Chap. 2, note 17, at 49–51; infra Chap. 5, notes 85–97 and accompanying text (detailing generation after generation of labor-sponsored statutes—revising common law conspiracy and other doctrines—that were nullified by crabbed judicial construction). Wilson's Commission on Industrial Relations reported: "Many witnesses . . . have asserted with the greatest earnestness that the mass of workers are convinced that laws necessary for their protection . . . cannot be passed except after long and exhausting struggles [and] that such beneficent measures as become laws are largely nullified [through strained constructions] by the courts." *Final Report*, supra Chap. 2, note 33, at 38.

Government by Injunction | 3

Judicial review and administration of labor laws helped prod many labor leaders and unions to abandon broad ambitions for reform in the public political sphere in favor of a more thorough reliance on economic action, strikes, and collective bargaining to ameliorate workers' conditions. Now we turn to the courts' interventions on that plane of economic activity—from judicial impairment of reform by legislation to judicial constraints on reform through collective action.

During the Gilded Age the labor injunction became the principal vehicle of judicial intervention in labor disputes. Indeed, the injunction proved to be "America's distinctive contribution in the application of law to industrial strife."[1] Originating in railway-labor conflicts, the labor injunction found use in major strikes and boycotts in most industries and locales. Where criminal conspiracy trials had been rare, anti-strike decrees became commonplace.

The Origins and Dimensions of Government by Injunction

The substantive law governing the bounds of workers' collective action in America changed little from the beginning of the nineteenth century until the first and second decades of the twentieth. In 1900, strikes to improve wages and working conditions were clearly legal,

---

1. F. Frankfurter and N. Greene, supra Intro., note 9, at 53.

as they had been virtually throughout the century.[2] But boycotting of almost all kinds—both producers' and consumers'—was becoming a tactic that could not legally be urged or carried out. Before the 1890s, courts had barely considered the legal status of many kinds of boycotting activities. By the early twentieth century, common law and antitrust doctrine condemned in needlepoint detail virtually the entire spectrum of peaceful secondary actions aimed at "unfair" (nonunion) goods and materials. Similarly, sympathy strikes and organizing activities fell under an increasingly thorough ban.[3]

2. America began the nineteenth century with a more tolerant legal order than those of England and other European countries. In the United States, in contrast to England and the continent, legal bars to the very existence of trade unions never took root. See A. Fox, *History and Heritage* 83–86 (1985); Witte, "Early American Labor Cases," 35 *Yale L. J.* 825, 825–26 (1926). See generally Jacobs, "Collective Self-Regulation," in *The Making of Labour Law In Europe*, supra Chap. 1, note 62, at 193–241 (historical patterns of legal repression and toleration of unions in European countries); *Labor Relations and the Law* (O. Kahn-Freund, ed., 1965) (collecting essays on law governing trade unionism in European countries). A famous handful of cases in the first quarter of the century seemingly held mere combinations to raise wages criminal. An example is Commonwealth v. Pullis (the Philadelphia Cordwainers Case) decided in the Mayor's Court of Philadelphia in 1806. See 3 *A Documentary History of American Industrial Society* 59 (J. Commons and E. Gilmore, eds., 1910); see also People v. Fisher, 14 Wend. 9 (N.Y. Sup. Ct. 1835); Witte, supra, at 825–28 (documenting early unreported conspiracy cases). These cases are the basis of the view that American labor law's trajectory over the nineteenth century was one from repression toward relative toleration. See, e.g., C. Gregory, *Labor and the Law*, 22–30, 52–82 (2d ed., 1958); D. Leslie, *Cases and Materials on Labor Law* 1–5 (1985); L. Levy, supra Chap. 1, note 44, at 183–206. But in virtually all of these dark-age decisions, the courts relied upon evidence of "coercive" practices that remained outlawed throughout the century. See Witte, supra, at 827 ("[T]he doctrine that a combination to raise wages is illegal . . . withered before it ever took root . . . The defendants in all of [these early-nineteenth-century] cases . . . used means to effect their ends which are generally regarded as unlawful even now"); see also Hovenkamp, "Labor Conspiracies in American Law, 1880–1930," 66 *Tex. L. Rev.* 919, 922 (1988) ("[N]o American case before the 1890s condemned laborers for the simple act of combining in order to increase wages"). Also important, and too often overlooked, were the extremely light sanctions antebellum courts imposed in most instances. See V. Hattam, supra Intro., note 9, at 57–58 ("[N]o American workers were sentenced to jail before the Civil War, and most fines ranged from $1.00 to $10.00" (footnote omitted)); M. Turner, *The Early American Labor Conspiracy Cases* 39–57 (1967); Nelles, supra Intro., note 9, at 542–47 (1931).

3. See, e.g., Bedford Cut Stone Co. v. Journeymen Stone Cutters' Ass'n, 274 U.S. 37 (1927) (holding a refusal by union members to work on stone cut by nonunion cutters

Not the substantive law but its application changed dramatically during the late nineteenth century. Although estimates are incomplete, there seem to have been relatively few criminal conspiracy trials of trade unionists until the 1870s, and sanctions, in general, were surprisingly mild.[4] In the 1870s and 1880s, however, sanctions grew harsher. This new severity emerged within the context of the city-wide boycott and new, more comprehensive strike ambitions on the part of miners and other unions.[5]

In addition to stoking judicial hostility, these developments prompted a swift change in the characteristic form of legal intervention in labor strife. By 1895, conspiracy prosecutions for strike activities had dwindled to a handful each year, while labor injunctions were multiplying. By a conservative reckoning, at least 4,300 injunctions were issued between 1880 and 1930. These amounted to only a small fraction of the total number of strikes for most of those five decades, although by the 1920s the fraction had increased to 25 percent. The proportion of large secondary actions enjoined, however, was substantial throughout this period. In the 1890s, the

illegal under the Sherman Act); Duplex Printing Press Co. v. Deering, 254 U.S. 443 (1921) (holding union machinists' refusal to work on printing presses manufactured by a firm that refused to recognize machinists' union to be an illegal conspiracy under the Sherman Act). See generally Hovenkamp, supra Chap. 3, note 2, at 956–58; infra Chap. 3, note 125 (listing cases and treatises on boycotts, sympathy strikes, and other proscribed goals and activities). Between 1900 and 1930 a few important industrial states' high courts began haltingly to liberalize labor doctrine, legalizing, for example, the closed-shop strike under certain circumstances. See, e.g., National Protective Ass'n of Steam-fitters v. Cumming, 170 N.Y. 315, 63 N.E. 369 (1902). But cf. Anderson and Lind Mfg. Co. v. Carpenters' Dist. Council, 308 Ill. 488, 139 N.E. 887 (1922) (holding that union members cannot interfere with business of a manufacturer operating an open shop); Auburn Draying Co. v. Wardell, 227 N.Y. 1, 6, 124 N.E. 97, 100–01 (1919) (holding that union members may not refuse to handle materials carried by a trucking company with which a teamsters union was in dispute). See generally E. Oakes, *The Law of Organized Labor and Industrial Conflicts* §434 (1927) (noting a general trend toward allowing union members to refuse to work on material produced or transported by non-union labor, as long as the action is not directed against a particular individual). Also in those decades courts began to enforce collective agreements on labor's behalf and to enjoin their violation by employers. See infra pp. 122–24.

4. See M. Turner, supra Chap. 3, note 2, at 39–52; Nelles, supra Intro., note 9, at 542–47; V. Hattam, supra, Intro., note 9, at 52–57.

5. See infra pp. 79–94.

decade that saw the greatest number of sympathy strikes in the country's history, courts enjoined at least 15 percent of recorded sympathy strikes. That percentage rose to 25 percent in the next decade, and by the 1920s 46 percent of all sympathy strikes were greeted by anti-strike decrees. Injunctions figured in virtually every railroad strike; in most strikes in which industrial unionism, "amalgamation," or "federation" was at issue; in most major organizing and recognition strikes, boycotts, closed shop or sympathy strikes or anti-union/open-shop lockouts of significant magnitude; and in a small but still significant and growing portion of ordinary mine-run strikes.[6]

The switch in procedural and remedial form from conspiracy trial to injunction also signified an enormous increase in the pervasiveness of judicial regulation. A vastly greater number of strikers and boycotters—often whole working-class communities—fell under judicial decrees.[7] In the process equity practice and procedure were transformed. Courts cast aside customary limits on the purpose and scope of injunctions to accommodate the injunction's new role as a mode of lawmaking and law enforcement in industrial cities and regions.

Why did judicial involvement in labor strife become so widespread? After all, the nation's courts could have limited the labor injunction to far more extraordinary kinds of strikes and strike activities, and could have wielded the instrument far more cautiously in terms of procedural practices, the generality of persons covered, and the breadth of proscriptive language.[8] Indeed, in so doing they would have preserved a greater continuity with judicial practices

6. See infra Appendix B. A discussion of the methods and sources informing my estimates, as well as more detailed breakdowns of the incidence of injunctions over time and by types of strikes will be found in Appendix B.

7. See infra pp. 104–05.

8. Both kinds of self-restraint were urged by many commentators from the early 1890s onward. See, e.g., Allen, "Injunction and Organized Labor," 28 *Am. L. Rev.* 828, 848–59 (1894); Andrews, "Injunctions against Crimes," 3 *Nw. U. L. Rev.* 219 (1895); Lewis, "A Protest against Administering Criminal Law by Injunction," 33 *Am. L. Reg. and Rev.* (42 *Pa. L. Rev.*) 879 (1894). See generally A. Paul, supra, Intro., note 9, at 142–58 (1960) (summarizing the legal community's reaction to the rise of the labor injunction).

over the half-century since the emergence of trade unionism in the early 1800s.

To explain the exuberant growth of the labor injunction, we must closely examine its historical seedbed. The emergence of the injunction coincided with a sharp increase in the proportion of strikes called and orchestrated by unions. The older, more spontaneous form of strike was a local affair, usually led by informal groups. Now strike calls, demands, and strategies issued not only from local but often from national or regional unions whose organization reached beyond the struck shop or shops.[9] The new era of union-led strikes was also distinguished by tremendous boosts in the numbers of boycotts, sympathy strikes, and control and recognition strikes.[10] The burgeoning of these types of collective action accounts in part for the judicial ire that animated the rise of "government by injunction." Because such strikes and boycotts often involved mobilizing far-flung national organizations or entire working-class communities against a single employer, they rubbed more abrasively against judges' individualism than did an ordinary wage strike. Too often we forget that many of the Gilded Age jurists who forged the era's labor law were thoroughgoing anti-monopolists and quite ambivalent about corporate expansion. To them, workers' "combinations" represented a more violent and menacing version of the same

9. See 1 S. Gompers, *Seventy Years*, supra Intro., note 7, at 244–50; P. Taft, *AFL in the Time of Gompers*, supra Chap. 1, note 2, at 403–11; L. Ulman, *The Rise of the National Trade Union* 425–59 (1955); Montgomery, "Strikes in the 19th Century," 4 *Soc. Sci. Hist.* 81, 89–93 (1980).

10. At no time before or since the decades bracketing the turn of the century did the number of secondary boycotts and sympathy strikes amount to such large proportions of the total number of conflicts. At no time before or since the period from 1880 to 1910 did workers' control issues—work standards and rules, union recognition and authority—bulk so large in the statistics recording strike objectives. See F. Hall, *Sympathetic Strikes and Sympathetic Lockouts* (1898); E. Hiller, *The Strike: A Study in Collective Action* (1928); Amsden and Brier, "Coal Miners on Strike: The Transformation of Strike Demands and the Formation of a National Union," 7 *J. Interdisciplinary Hist.* 583, 585, 591, 604–09 (1977); Montgomery, supra Chap. 3, note 9, at 89–93; Peterson, "Strikes in the United States, 1880–1936," in *United States Bureau of Labor Statistics, Bulletin* no. 651, at 33, 39 (1938).

kind of monopolistic concentrations of economic power that they condemned in corporate "aggrandizements of capital."[11]

In addition to inspiring increased judicial antagonism, the emergence of more carefully coordinated and highly organized unionism inspired more concerted and organized anti-unionism among employers. The success of a string of strikes and boycotts at the turn of the century sprang from the fact that unionists were organized collectively, while businessmen were not. As a result, in the 1900s, dozens of industrial employers' associations, including the National Association of Manufacturers (NAM), were formed. The NAM launched the "Open Shop Drive," as employers' associations embarked on campaigns to defeat sympathy strikes and union label boycotts.[12] At the heart of these campaigns was the creation of law firms and employers' associations' law departments specializing in anti-strike and anti-boycott litigation. The American Anti-Boycott Association (AABA) was the most prominent group of specialized lawyers, and had scores of clients.[13] They fashioned test cases, systematized and publicized new doctrine—and with it, a new anti-union "open shop" public discourse and imagery—and brought scores of federal and state injunction suits.[14]

But employers' authority on the shopfloor was not the only form of authority at issue, nor were trade unionists merely disregarding

11. See Forbath, "Ambiguities of Free Labor," supra Chap. 1, note 8, at 787–90; Hovenkamp, "Labor Conspiracies in American Law," supra Chap, 3, note 2.

12. See generally C. Bonnett, *Employers' Associations in the United States* 367–69 (1922) (describing the structure and purpose of the NAM's open-shop department); D. Brody, *Workers in Industrial America* 24–26 (1980); D. Montgomery, *Fall of the House of Labor*, supra Intro., note 8, at 269–75; B. Ramirez, *When Workers Fight* 93–95 (1978).

13. The American Anti-Boycott Association was founded in 1902 by the Danbury hat manufacturers Charles Merritt and Dietrich Loewe, plaintiffs in Loewe v. Lawlor, 208 U.S. 274 (1908) (the "Danbury Hatters Case") and pioneers of the open-shop movement. Merritt was the father of Walter Merritt, who became the AABA's lead counsel. The AABA was renamed the League for Industrial Rights in 1919. See W. Merritt, *History of the League for Industrial Rights* 4 (1925). Daniel Ernst has written a rich and insightful history of the AABA: D. Ernst, "The Lawyers and the Labor Trust: A History of the American Anti-Boycott Association, 1902–1919" (Ph.D. diss., Princeton University, 1989). See also C. Bonnett, supra Chap. 3, note 12, at 449–74.

14. See C. Bonnett, supra Chap. 3, note 12, at 458–62, 464–65.

legal boundaries. Labor had also erected itself as a rival lawmaker, challenging the courts' and the state's normative authority. As we shall see, labor activists expounded a competing language of rights. They claimed entitlements in jobs and workplaces as well as broad freedoms of action and association and immunities from state coercion. They promulgated rules of workers' control which they dubbed "laws," and sought to enforce them through new weapons and organizations.[15]

Judges shrewdly understood that trade unionists presented a far greater threat to the courts' definition of law and order, insofar as they believed that their unions stood for an alternative, and truer, "legal" order. Judges realized that such "higher law" thinking on labor's part did much to embolden workers to act in defiance of the state.[16] Thus there were two dimensions of meaning in judges' recurrent use of words like "tyranny," "dictatorship," and "usurpation" in characterizing broad strikes and boycotts. Such collective actions were unjustified, irresponsible concentrations of power, but they were also bodies of men presuming to act as self-constituted sovereigns, "attempt[ing]," as the Supreme Court declared in *In re Debs*,[17] to exercise "powers belonging only to Government."[18] Unions and their members, another court complained, fancied themselves "the exponents of some higher law than that . . . administered by courts."[19] Nothing was more common in a Gilded Age or early-twentieth-century trade unionist's formal encounters with the state than to hear an equity judge condemn his union for acting as a "self-appointed tribunal" or "arbiter" seeking to displace the courts' rules of property and contract with its own "laws" and "decrees."[20] Nothing was more familiar than judges' complaints

15. See Forbath, "Ambiguities of Free Labor," supra Chap. 1, note 8, at 800–05.
16. Chapter 5 treats this in some detail.
17. 158 U.S. 564 (1895).
18. Id. at 592.
19. See Otis Steel Co. v. Local 218, Iron Molders' Union, 110 F. 698, 699 (C.C.N.D. Ohio 1901).
20. For one such judicial denunciation recited in court to defendants Samuel Gompers and John Mitchell, see Buck's Stove and Range Co. v. American Fed'n of Labor, 36 Wash. L. Rptr. 822 (D.C. 1908), which denounced "a studied, determined, defiant

that workers were "trampl[ing] upon the law," all the while "assert[ing] imaginary rights."[21] Not mere class bias but rather this special rage at unions as rival lawmakers[22] is crucial to understanding the readiness of Gilded Age courts to embroil themselves in labor strife.

Finally, entwined with the courts' impulse to attack a rival lawmaking authority was the fear that workers' "imaginary" notions of their rights enjoyed substantial sympathy or at least toleration among elected officials in industrial towns and cities. The labor injunction arose out of labor-capital conflict, but equally, as the next three sections all illustrate, it emerged from contests among competing state actors, polities, and normative orders.

The Origins of Government by Injunction in Railway Strikes

The first court orders against strikers were issued during the 1877 railroad strikes. Within a decade federal court decrees had become the prevailing mode of state regulation of railway strikes. These writs issued from federal equity courts holding bankrupt roads in receivership. During the latter half of the nineteenth century the receivership device sheltered a vast number of bankrupt railways.[23]

conflict precipitated in the light of open day, between the decrees of a tribunal ordained by the Government of the Federal Union, and of the tribunals of another federation, grown up in the land." Id. at 842. See also Otis Steel Co. v. Local 218, Iron Molders' Union, 110 F. 698, 699–700 (C.C.N.D. Ohio 1901) (finding that defendant, a "self-constituted body of men" sought to issue its "edicts" against "the complainant [and] the non-union molders," resting its "assumed right thus to dictate to others" on the "unfounded notion . . . that [the molders' union] and its members are the exponents of some higher law than that which may be administered by courts").

21. The Homestead Case, 1 Pa. D. 785, 788 (1892). I return to the contests between courts and local polities in Chapter 4, and to the labor movement's alternative rights discourse in Chapter 5.

22. Cf. Cover, "The Supreme Court, 1982 Term—Foreword: *Nomos* and Narrative," 97 *Harv. L. Rev.* 4, 40–44 (1983) (discussing courts' special hostility toward communities that constitute themselves as rival "non-state based" lawmakers, focusing on religious groups like the Amish and Mormons as well as the civil rights movement, and dubbing this hostility "jurispathic") [hereinafter Cover, "*Nomos* and Narrative"].

23. See Nelles, supra Intro., note 9, at 520. Nelles also details the contrast between American and English judicial practice regarding railroad receiverships. The English

Thus before the era's waves of major railroad labor conflicts began, the federal judiciary had already assumed a role akin to episodic public management of the railways. When the massive strikes of 1877 began, many federal judges with roads under their authority proved receptive to the view that the strikes presented a new necessity for further intervention—for an extension of "our administrative capacities" over roads that were, after all, "public property for the time being."[24]

Because midwestern mayors and governors often sympathized with strikers and failed to quell disruptions of roads that were in receivership, irate federal judges in Indiana, Illinois, and elsewhere took matters into their own hands, ordering their marshals to deputize volunteers or calling out federal troops to put down the 1877 strikes. The underlying writs were addressed to the receivers and the marshals, but in them the judges specifically instructed marshals to apprise the "mob" that obstructing the trains would constitute contempt of court. Some strike leaders were indeed arrested for contempt, and their convictions marked a signal turning point in the history of equity practice. They were the first contempt sanctions exercised against persons neither parties nor named by court orders.[25]

To most contemporary observers this summary punishment of a few strikers was a minor occurrence, and public comment was superficial. One contemporary who perceived a broader significance was Tom Scott, president of the Pennsylvania Railroad:

> It will hardly be contended that the railway companies must become bankrupt in order to make secure the uninterrupted movement of traffic over their lines, or to entitle them to the efficient protection of the

courts resisted undertaking the management of bankrupt railways, while American federal judges gestured toward a similar reluctance but rarely actually declined. See id. at 537–42. More often than not they appointed the existing managers to act as receivers. See id. at 541 and n21.

24. G. Eggert, supra Intro., note 9, at 37 (1967) (quoting telegram from Drummond to Devens, July 23, 1877, and letter, July 25, 1877).

25. See Secor v. Toledo, P. and W. Ry., 21 F. Cas. 968 (C.C.N.D. Ill. 1877) (no. 12,605); King v. Ohio & Miss. Ry., 14 F. Cas. 539 (C.C.D. Ind. 1877) (no. 7,800); Mack, "The Revival of Criminal Equity," 16 *Harv. L. Rev.* 389, 394–95 (1903); Nelles, supra, Intro., note 9, at 524.

United States government . . . The laws which give the Federal courts the summary process of injunction to restrain so comparatively trifling a wrong as an infringement of a patent-right certainly must have been intended or ought to give the United States authority to prevent a wrong-doing which not only destroys a particular road, but also paralyzes the entire commerce of the country and wastes the national wealth.[26]

In the mid-1880s a rash of strikes against Jay Gould's Southwest lines—some of which were in federal receivership—supplied the occasion for an extension of the new equitable domain etched out in the 1877 strike. The Knights of Labor waged these strikes against Gould's lines and won their first major contest. They had succeeded in avoiding conflict with the federal authorities by allowing mail trains (with passenger cars) to move freely through strikebound areas. At the same time, they tied up freight service on Gould's system, yet continued to enjoy public support. State governors sent in militia to preserve the peace but again refused to allow troops to be used to break the strike. A year later Gould provoked more strikes, and, with the courts' help, turned the tide against labor. Circuit judges flatly declared that employees of a receiver who engaged in peaceable but concerted work stoppages that halted operations were in contempt of court. Strike leaders were dealt severe sentences, and most of the strikes were defeated. The Knights blamed the defeats largely on the "legal meshes" into which Gould, like a "fisherman," "gather[ed and took] in" hundreds of strike leaders.[27]

Opportunities to address courts with grievances did not mitigate the harshness of judicial intervention. Shortly after the Jay Gould strike, a number of workers on the Denver and Rio Grande line, in receivership under then Eighth Circuit Judge David Brewer, tested the court's offer to hear their grievances regarding intolerable working conditions. Judge Brewer, in response, delivered a brief homily to the workers on the benevolent law of supply and demand and dismissed their claims as "trivial."[28]

26. Scott, "The Recent Strikes," 125 *N. Am. Rev.* 351, 359 (1877).
27. See R. Allen, *The Great Southwest Strike* 71–91 (1942).
28. See Frank v. Denver & R. G. Ry., 23 F. 757, 758 (C.C.D. Col. 1885). But cf.

Two years later, during the Great Burlington Strike of 1888, the injunction fulfilled its potential as anticipated by Tom Scott. No longer did a railroad company have to ''become bankrupt . . . to entitle it to the efficient protection of the federal . . . courts.''[29] During that strike three federal circuit courts found that the new Interstate Commerce Act[30] endowed the federal judiciary with authority to enjoin railway workers' refusals to handle cars from struck lines, quite apart from whether the latter were in receivership.[31] The railway workers' brotherhoods saw boycotting ''lawfully'' struck roads as an ethical duty; the duty was set out in their constitutions and recognized in many collective agreements with railway employers.[32] But the three federal courts concluded that such boycotts violated the Act's ban on discrimination in interstate traffic on the part of the railroads.[33]

Ames v. Union Pac. Ry., 62 F. 7 (C.C.D. Neb. 1894) (setting aside as inequitable a prior court's grant of receivers' request to abrogate existing contracts between the Union Pacific and various railroad workers' brotherhoods and also to enjoin any strikes protesting the wage cuts).

29. Scott, "The Recent Strikes," supra Chap. 3, note 26, at 359.

30. 24 Stat. 379 (1887) (codified as amended at 49 U.S.C. §1 (1982)).

31. In June 1886, the redoubtable Judge Gresham was the first federal judge to enjoin a strike against a road not in receivership. In granting a temporary order against a minor strike in Chicago, he relied on the Ku Klux Klan Act of 1871, ch. 22, 17 Stat. 13 (1871) (codified as amended at 10 U.S.C. §333; 18 U.S.C. §§371–372, 2834; 28 U.S.C. §§1343, 1861; 42 U.S.C. §§1983, 1985–1986 (1982)), passed by the Reconstruction Congress of 1871, which outlawed conspiracies to injure or oppress citizens in the free exercise of federal statutory or constitutional rights. The railroad's right to engage in interstate commerce, Gresham reasoned, was such a constitutional right. The strike ended before any hearings were held, and no opinion issued. See McMurry, "The Legal Ancestry of the Pullman Strike Injunctions," 14 *Indus. and Lab. Rel. Rev.* 235, 239 (1961).

32. See F. Hall, supra Chap. 3, note 10. An example is Toledo A.A. and N.M. Railway v. Pennsylvania Co., 54 F. 730 (C.C.N.D. Ohio 1893).

33. See, e.g., Chicago, B. and Q.R.R. v. Burlington, C.R. and N.R.R., 34 F. 481 (C.C.S.D. Iowa 1888). This construction of the Act flew in the face of both the House and the Senate's rejection of numerous proposed amendments providing sanctions against strikers who obstructed interstate commerce. See G. Eggert, supra Intro., note 9, at 69–71. The courts also derived their authority to enjoin such discrimination from a provision which, by its terms, only authorized injunctions against violations of orders of the Interstate Commerce Commission. However, some courts followed a broader interpretation of the provision, granting injunctions to prevent violations of the Act, even when no order had been issued by the Commission. See McMurry, supra Chap. 3, note 31, at 240n25.

The old railway brotherhoods were among the most "respectable" of Gilded Age unions, but they were not yet ready to abandon the boycott. The Burlington strikers believed they could have won their fight in 1888 had the boycott continued.[34] The Brotherhood of Locomotive Engineers, for one, preserved the practice. So five years after the Great Burlington Strike, when Grand Chief Peter Arthur authorized a strike on the Toledo, Ann Arbor line, notice of the strike to engineers on connecting lines automatically set a boycott in motion. To avoid strikes on their own roads, the connecting lines' managements, in turn, allowed their engineers to enforce the boycott.[35]

At the behest of the Ann Arbor Road, Judge William Howard Taft of the Circuit Court for Ohio summoned Grand Chief Arthur to his courtroom. Speaking from the bench, Judge Taft assailed the boycotting provision in the Brotherhood's constitution, wishing to:

> make plain . . . to the intelligent and generally law-abiding men who compose the Brotherhood of Locomotive Engineers, as well as to their usually conservative chief officer, what we cannot believe they appreciate, that . . . the existence and enforcement of rule 12, under their organic law, make the whole brotherhood a criminal conspiracy against the laws of their country.[36]

Having chastened the union chief, Judge Taft reaffirmed the extension of federal equity jurisdiction to strikes against lines not in receivership. He also carefully spelled out the distinction between a lawful strike like that waged by the Ann Arbor enginemen and an unlawful boycott like the one waged in their support.[37] That distinction helped justify anti-boycott decrees for decades to come. As a border between enjoinable and unenjoinable collective action, it was more short-lived. The Interstate Commerce Act's bar on "discrimination" in the interchange of freight seemed to reach only

34. See McMurry, supra Chap. 3, note 31, at 243.
35. See id. at 240.
36. Toledo A.A. & N.M. Ry. v. Pennsylvania Co., 54 F. 730, 739 (C.C.N.D. Ohio 1893).
37. See id. at 738 ("Neither law nor morals can give a man a right to labor or withhold his labor for such a purpose").

boycotts of struck roads. But a strike of railway workers against their own employer could obstruct interstate commerce as much as a boycott. Whether the 1887 Act could be made to reach such primary strikes became an academic question, however, as lawyers and judges began to see greater possibilities in the Sherman Antitrust Act of 1890.

The first application of the Sherman Act to industrial strife occurred in a tumultuous New Orleans longshoremen's strike, which tied up the city's interstate and foreign commerce. The U.S. Attorney won an anti-strike decree under the new antitrust law, claiming that the striking unions were "a gigantic . . . combination . . . for the purpose of restraining the commerce among the several states and with foreign countries."[38] Soon after, railroad lawyers won a number of injunctions against primary strikes on the theory that railway workers were illegally restraining trade if they combined and conspired to quit a railroad's service with the "object or intent of crippling the property or its operation."[39]

In this fashion judges constructed what Judge Gresham called the new "administrative capacities" of the federal bench to regulate railway labor relations and conflicts.[40] According to the conventional view of these developments, the courts created their role and repressive policies in the absence of alternatives from other government actors. But this perspective adopts, perhaps too readily, the view of

38. United States v. Workingmen's Amalgamated Council, 54 F. 994, 995 (C.C.E.D. La.), *aff'd*, 57 F. 85 (5th Cir. 1893).

39. Waterhouse v. Comer, 55 F. 149, 154 (C.C.W.D. Ga. 1893); see also Farmers' Loan and Trust Co. v. Northern Pac. R.R., 60 F. 803 (C.C.E.D. Wis. 1894). For accounts of unreported cases, see McMurry, supra Chap. 3, note 31, at 253. This theory implied that any strike on an interstate line was illegal, and to many within as well as without the legal elite, that smacked of industrial bondage. See, e.g., R. Allen, supra Chap. 3, note 27, at 118–121; Lewis, supra Chap. 3, note 8, at 882–86; see also Dunbar, "Government by Injunction," 13 *Law Q. Rev.* 347 (1897) (criticizing excessive use of injunctions against striking workers). Justice Harlan carved out a mediating concept by distinguishing an individual worker's right to quit for higher wages from a group effort that might embarrass or obstruct a road or intimidate new workers from entering its service. See Arthur v. Oakes, 63 F. 310 (7th Cir. 1894). In addition to its readily exploitable ambiguities, this distinction hinged on strikers' means, not their ends; it meant that no railway strike was immune from judicial intervention.

40. See supra p. 67.

the winners—the railroad lawyers and managements, and the courts—that the policies and arsenals of the state governors were simply inadequate, and that the alternative to "government by injunction" was anarchy. In fact, leaving the initiative in the states' hands might have resulted in more, not less, order in railway labor relations, but it would have rested on a different balance of bargaining power and an earlier institutionalization of collective bargaining and arbitration.[41]

The winners' perspective also neglects other national policy and state-building paths glimpsed but not taken, at least partly because the dominant judicial outlook opposed them. Judge Thomas Cooley tried to blaze a different trail when he assumed his post as first head of the Interstate Commerce Commission.[42] Cooley would have encouraged the new federal agency to become an active arbiter in railway labor disputes. Much to his frustration, Judge Cooley's fellow commissioners repeatedly rebuffed his proposals.[43]

Some federal judges offered another alternative. In 1894 the Union Pacific Railroad went into federal receivership; its court-appointed receivers assumed they could reduce wages, change schedules, and dismiss men unilaterally. The receivers filed complaints in the federal courts in the states covered by the line, seeking injunctions to restrain the Union Pacific's workers from striking in response to these company actions. Two federal district judges refused, as did Eighth Circuit Court Judge Henry Caldwell, who presided over the receivership.[44] Instead they directed the recalcitrant line to confer with its workers and provided that the old rules, rates, and schedules, which

41. See G. Eggert, supra Intro., note 9, at 99–102. On this possibility see also the actions taken by a New York state court noted below at Chap. 3, note 46.

42. See Forbath, "Ambiguities of Free Labor," supra Chap. 1, note 8, at 792–94 and 792n87; Jones, "Thomas M. Cooley and 'Laissez-Faire Constitutionalism': A Reconsideration," 53 *J. Am. Hist.* 751, 767–71 (1961); see also S. Skowronek, supra Chap. 1, note 45, at 153–54 ("Before he retired from the Commission in January, 1892, Cooley had articulated the tenets of a new theory of law to fit an alternative mode of regulation in a new American state").

43. See generally G. Eggert, supra Intro., note 9, at 98–103 (describing Judge Cooley's efforts as head of the Interstate Commerce Commission).

44. See id. at 117–135.

the receivers had abrogated, would remain in force until the men agreed otherwise or the receivers proved that they were "in excess of a fair, just, and reasonable compensation."[45] On the eve of the Pullman Strike, then, these courts demonstrated that courts could use their equitable powers to etch out an arbitral, rather than a repressive, role.[46]

By the eve of the Pullman Strike the main elements that composed the federal judicial role in that strike were also in place. Built up over sixteen years of judicial experience, they included: the enjoining of strikes and boycotts on nonreceivership lines; the long experience of collaboration with railroad management and attorneys; the precedents for summoning troops over the heads and against the will of state authorities; the preference for summary proceedings over jury trials; and the transformation of the federal courtroom into "a kind of police court," in Judge Taft's words, when railway workers went on strike.[47] The Pullman Strike was extraordinary for its scale and the corresponding scale of judicial involvement, the executive branch's role, and the Supreme Court's imprimatur. The last was a

45. Ames v. Union Pac. Ry., 62 F. 7, 12 (C.C.D. Neb. 1894).

46. Had more Gilded Age federal courts developed their administrative capacities regarding railway labor disputes in Caldwell's fashion, Congress might have built upon those experiments. There was broad support in Congress for the view that the "best and surest preventive" of strikes, "as paradoxical as it may seem" was not to punish the men for striking but to punish the "superior officers" of the railroad should they "goad[] the men to strike," and to provide for receiverships where railroad *management* failed to avert a strike. House Select Committee, *Labor Troubles in the Anthracite Regions of Pennsylvania,* H.R. Rep. no. 4147, 50th Cong., 2d Sess., at xxx (1889). The congressional committee that put forth this view pointed to a New York railroad strike in which the state judiciary played just such a role. See id. at xxv–xxx. As it was, Congress did not empower the courts to direct railroads to bargain collectively with their employees until the 1926 Railway Labor Act. Even then, the courts were left to infer their enforcement powers. See generally Texas and N.O.R.R. v. Brotherhood of R.R. and Steamship Clerks, 281 U.S. 548, 569 (1930) (holding that congressional "prohibition of interference or coercion in connection with the choice of representatives" creates enforcement power by implication); L. Lecht, *Experience under Railway Labor Legislation* 14–60 (1955).

47. Letter from William H. Taft to Helen H. Taft (July 1894), quoted in 1 H. Pringle, *The Life and Times of William Howard Taft* 135 (1939). I owe to Professor Dianne Avery the suggestion that Pringle's biography contains valuable material on Taft's experiences as an injunction judge.

comprehensive endorsement of the federal judicial role in railway strikes and of the new use of equity in industrial conflicts.

The American Railway Union (ARU) called the Pullman Strike.[48] In 1894 the ARU was a fledgling industrial union, created by Eugene Debs and other former railroad brotherhood leaders to overcome the older brotherhoods' often divisive craft boundaries and their exclusion of the railways' masses of unskilled workers. Correctly fearing a showdown for which the new union was unprepared, Debs urged the ARU membership not to take on the cause of the Pullman Company's desperate workers. Swayed by Pullman's ruthless wage cuts and labor policies and his intransigent refusal to confer with his employees, the ARU membership rejected Debs's counsel and voted a boycott of Pullman cars. An eloquent voice of working-class republicanism, Debs then defended the boycott as the "practical exhibition of sympathy," Christian brotherhood, and republican mutualism.[49] However, in the eyes of virtually all of the nation's legal elite, conservative and reformist alike, Debs represented all that was "lawless" in the labor movement, and the web of sympathetic boycotts of Pullman cars that constituted the "Strike" embodied the movement's most threatening developments.

Judge Taft's letters during the strike capture much of the experience and reactions of conservative jurists. Like many midwestern federal judges in 1894, Judge Taft had ordered a railroad into receivership.[50] "[W]hat has worried me more than anything else," Taft wrote to his wife, "is this railway boycott. I have a force of fifty deputy marshals on one side of the river and of seventy-five on the other. Men are constantly being arrested and brought before me and I am conducting a kind of police court . . . Last night . . . I was the object of fiery denunciations in many meetings."[51]

48. The most thorough and insightful accounts of the Pullman Strike include R. Ginger, *The Bending Cross: A Biography of Eugene Victor Debs* 108–51 (1949), A. Lindsey, *The Pullman Strike* (1942), and N. Salvatore, *Eugene V. Debs* 114–46 (1982).

49. Debs, "Labor Strikes and Their Lessons," reprinted in J. Swinton, *Striking for Life* 324 (1894); see also N. Salvatore, supra Chap. 3, note 48, at 114–46.

50. See Thomas v. Cincinnati, N.O. and T.P. Ry., 62 F. 803, 804–05 (S.D. Ohio 1894).

51. Letter from William H. Taft to Helen H. Taft (July 1894), supra Chap. 3, note 47.

"The situation in Chicago," he observed, "is very alarming and distressing . . . "[52] Governor Altgeld of Illinois disagreed. He had vehemently opposed the marshals and troops ushered in by federal decrees. To him, the "situation" was one of mass demonstrations by strikers and their supporters, but there was neither large-scale destruction of railroad property nor significant violence. For the labor-populist governor, the ARU and the Pullman Boycott were vehicles of reform less daunting and dangerous than the huge corporations that opposed them; for the conservative jurist, they were instruments of anarchy and lawlessness that had to be destroyed. Though Taft was a genial man, his solution was savage: "[U]ntil they have had much bloodletting, it will not be better."[53] In another letter, Taft wrote: "They have killed only six of the mob as yet. This is hardly enough to make an impression."[54]

Federal judges "in nearly every large city west of the Allegheny Mountains" responded to the strike as Taft did; they turned their courtrooms into police courts by issuing roughly one hundred decrees prohibiting the ARU and other unions from threatening, combining, or conspiring to quit in any fashion that would embarrass the railways' operations.[55] They also enjoined refusals to handle the cars of other struck lines. Several of the injunctions, including that against Debs and his ARU, also forebade attempts to induce fellow workers to support the strikes or boycotts. "Injunction writs . . . covered the sides of cars, deputy marshals and Federal soldiers . . . patrolled the yards of railway *termini*, and chancery process [was] executed by bullets and bayonets."[56] The next May in *In re Debs*[57] the United

52. Letter from William H. Taft to Helen H. Taft (1894), quoted in J. Anderson, *William Howard Taft: An Intimate History* 63 (1981). I encountered Anderson's account of Taft's letters to his wife in Dianne Avery's essay, "Images of Violence in Labor Jurisprudence: The Regulation of Picketing and Boycotts, 1894–1921," 37 *Buf. L. Rev.* 1, 21–22 (1989).

53. Letter from William H. Taft to Helen H. Taft (1894), supra Chap. 3, note 52.

54. Id. In the legal scholarship of the period even reformers described Debs as an "irresponsible vagabond" and a "dictator" who "reel[ed] with the intoxication which springs from the possession of almost unlimited power." Book Review, 28 *Am. L. Rev.* 629, 633–34 (1894) (reviewing T. Cogley, *Cogley on Strikes and Boycotts* (1894)).

55. See Allen, supra Chap. 3, note 8, at 847.

56. Id.

57. 158 U.S. 564 (1895).

States Supreme Court unanimously lent its sanction to the new equity device, upholding the blanket injunctions that had issued against the Pullman Strike, and the contempt convictions of Debs and other leaders for violating them.

Justice Brewer in *Debs* credited the decrees with prompting a swift and peaceful acquiescence by strikers, ending what had been an unprecedentedly broad and successful sympathy strike. He concluded that the experience affirmed the broad role the federal courts had staked out for themselves in the policing of strikes.[58] Debs made a similar assessment, insisting that it was "not the army, [nor] any other power, but simply . . . the United States courts[59] that ended the strike. The blanketing of the strike with injunctions and the arrests of scores of leaders for contempt had "demoralized" the strikers.[60]

The broad-based sympathy strikes of the Pullman Boycott crystallized a growing sentiment among railway workers. The strikes were waged to support the hard-pressed employees of the Pullman company, but they also constituted a more general assertion. As the most meticulous recent history of Gilded Age railway strikes observes, the sympathy strike "had taken deep root in the industrial experience of the railroad men."[61] By federating their separate crafts—frequently under the Knights of Labor—and by wielding the sympathetic strike, these railroad workers had begun to assert and win "rights" that craft organizations had failed to gain, even for their narrower constituencies.[62] The workers who rallied to Debs's ARU hoped that thorough organization and the ability to tie up broad

58. See id. at 582–600. Then and now, some commentators have been inclined to dismiss Justice Brewer's assessment of the injunctions' impact as puffery. See, e.g., Mack, supra Chap. 3, note 25, at 401–02.

59. In re Debs, 158 U.S. at 598 (quoting Debs's testimony before the United States Strike Commission).

60. See id.

61. S. Stromquist, *A Generation of Boomers: The Pattern of Railroad Labor Conflict in Nineteenth-Century America* 39 (1987).

62. The successful sympathy strikes that bulk large in the overall railroad strike statistics of the 1880s were over such ambitious control issues as the size of crews and the workers' asserted right to demand the firing of abusive yardmasters and other supervisors. See id. at 34–38.

swaths of the nation's railroad traffic would enable them to extend workers' control further, to a fundamental restructuring of work relations, and even to the "operation of the railroads in the general public interest."[63]

By the early 1890s the formidable legal web the courts had spun around the sympathy strike had already led the old brotherhoods' leaders to use the weapon more cautiously.[64] The leadership condemned efforts like the ARU's to create industrial organizations, and, though tens of thousands of their members participated in the Pullman Boycott, the brotherhoods' leaders denounced it.[65] In the wake of the federal assault on the boycott, the ARU disintegrated. But the breadth of worker support for both the ARU and the boycott encouraged leading railroad managers to reconsider their attitudes toward the old brotherhoods. The brotherhoods "could be enlisted to police a new era of industrial peace in return for a guarantee of their survival."[66]

The participation of the railroad's less-skilled workers had helped fuel the dynamic power of the Knights of Labor and the ARU. The rise of these industrial organizations did much to gain the new and undreamed-of security that the brotherhoods now enjoyed. But the masses of less-skilled workers were left out of the bargain between the brotherhoods and the managers,[67] and the *Debs* decision and "government by injunction" led to the scrapping of the only major weapon by which broader organizations of railroad men had been able to assert the rights of the skilled and unskilled alike.[68]

63. Id. at 46. Eugene Debs told the United States Strike Commission investigating the Pullman boycott that he believed "that if the people owned and operated the railroads in the interest of the people instead of for private gain and profit, that the service would be greatly improved, the condition of the men infinitely better, and another strike would never come." Id. at 39, quoting Debs (footnote omitted).

64. See id. at 39.

65. See id. at 54–98. They threatened boycott supporters with expulsion. Indeed, one brotherhood, the Brotherhood of Railroad Trainmen, purportedly expelled nearly 20,000 men after the strike. See id. at 263–64.

66. Id. at 263.

67. See id. at 262–65. "Shopmen, switchmen, and track laborers enjoyed little more security than they had ever had." Id. at 266.

68. See id. at 265.

Despite Debs's urging, Gompers and the AFL leadership had declined to extend beyond the railways the sympathy strike in support of the ARU.[69] Likewise, the "intelligent and generally law-abiding" railroad brotherhoods chose the Pullman Boycott as the occasion on which to honor Judge Taft's stern suggestion and abandon the boycotting tradition.

Thus, the Pullman Boycott would mark a sorely divisive moment—persuading Debs and many of his kin in the labor movement that independent labor politics and public control over the railways and other industries were indispensable to building broad, inclusive unions, and confirming Gompers and his cohorts in the view that broad, class-based strategies and industrial ambitions were too costly and self-defeating.[70] Such approaches invited brutal repression—now resoundingly endorsed and encouraged by the Supreme Court.

Some students of industrial relations contend that legal repression did not significantly influence the demise of the sympathy strike. They suggest that the tactic was more a protest than a real economic weapon, and argue that it merely impeded the development of "mature" contractual relations.[71]

This criticism falls somewhat wide of the mark. To be sure, such strikes were protests affirming broad commonalities.[72] But many types of Gilded Age and early-twentieth-century sympathetic actions also provided a substantial measure of bargaining strength.[73] Nor were they inherently incompatible with a collective bargaining re-

69. See J. Swinton, *Striking For Life*, supra Chap. 1, note 7, at 306–14.

70. See infra pp. 94–97.

71. See, e.g., E. Hiller, *The Strike: A Study in Collective Action* 62 (1928); L. Reynolds, *Labor Economics and Labor Relations* 645 (1974) (discussing the controversy over secondary boycotts).

72. This is why they recurred after losing their place in labor's official arsenal, and also why their demise must be seen as having profoundly affected the culture as well as the clout of the labor movement.

73. See, e.g., D. Bensman, *The Practice of Solidarity: American Hat Finishers in the Nineteenth Century* 111–50, 202 (1985) (noting sympathy strikes in the hatting industry); D. Montgomery, *Fall of the House of Labor*, supra Intro., note 8, at 269 (noting the use of sympathy strikes by the Chicago Federation of Labor); S. Stromquist, supra Chap. 3, note 61, at 34–40.

gime.[74] In contrast to the experience of the American labor movement, in the late nineteenth and early twentieth centuries in France and England, legislatures lifted legal bans on secondary boycotts and sympathy strikes.[75] The result was not to frustrate the development of collective bargaining but rather to hasten employers' acceptance of it.[76] The AFL tried to bring about just such catalytic reactions in the United States. Legislatures were sometimes willing, but for over three decades the judiciary was not.[77]

The Rise and Repression of City-Wide Boycotts

Shortly after the Great Railroad Strike of 1877, employers began to seek equitable intervention against strikes in other industries. However, "government by injunction" did not find ready footholds in these new contexts. Several factors had made federal courts' interventions in railway strikes unique. First, until the late 1880s judicial interventions occurred only against strikers and boycotters of lines

74. See W. Haber, *Industrial Relations in the Building Industry* 330 (1930) (describing how the sympathy strike was used to protect weaker unions and thereby strengthen their bargaining position). Union constitutions as well as collective agreements with employers in several trades in the 1880s and 1890s included provisions setting metes and bounds for such boycotts. See R. Christie, supra Chap. 1, note 16. Particularly in the construction and carpentry trades, it was common practice in highly organized cities and regions around the turn of the century for collective agreements to provide that only union-made goods would be used on the projects under contract. See, e.g., 2 *Industrial Relations: Final Report and Testimony Submitted to Congress by the Commission on Industrial Relations*, S. Doc. no. 415, 64th Cong., 1st Sess. 1618 (1916) [hereinafter *Industrial Relations*]; R. Christie, supra Chap. 1, note 16, at 162 (noting that work considered "non-union" was excluded from markets); L. Wolman, *The Boycott in American Trade Unions* 50–51 (1916); "Unions May Boycott," 17 *Am. Federationist* 228 (1910) (citing such provisions in Oklahoma building trades and other unions' constitutions and contracts).

75. See M. Perrot, supra Chap. 1, note 23, at 243–307; E. Shorter and C. Tilly, supra Chap. 1, note 62, at 21–25 (1974); Brun, "The Law of Strikes and Lock-Outs in France," in *Labour Relations and the Law*, supra Chap. 3, note 2, at 191–200; Wedderburn, "The Law and Industrial Conflict in Great Britain," in id. at 127–53.

76. See G. Friedman, "The State and the Making of a Working Class: The United States and France" 20 (paper prepared for Social Science History Conference, St. Louis, Mo., Oct. 1986). Friedman also argues persuasively that legalization of large-scale strikes in France bolstered the fortunes of broad, inclusive unionism in that country. See id.

77. See infra Chap. 5.

in federal equitable receivership.[78] Thus, the federal judges were already involved with the roads' management and inclined to view them as "public property for the time being."[79] Second, even as the railway labor injunction spread beyond lines in receivership, the far-flung and quasi-public character of the industry as well as its centrality to interstate commerce and the mails continued to differentiate railroad strikes and their regulation.

For almost a decade, until the late 1880s, the validity of non-railway labor injunctions remained uncertain. Two doctrinal obstacles stood in the way of such expansion. First, in some early Gilded Age cases, courts refused to grant injunctions because the suits, alleging that "ordinary crimes" like assaults and trespass, properly belonged in criminal court.[80] As one state court explained, the mere fact "[t]hat the [criminal] law against this offense is not enforced and observed is no ground for the interposition of a court of equity."[81] Similarly, a federal judge in Colorado stoically declined to expand his equity powers into the domain of state criminal law: "[T]he Constitution of the United States has committed the maintenance of peace and good order to the . . . state governments. If the state government has fallen into the hands of socialists . . . or . . . imbeciles . . . we do not thereby acquire the right to assume control . . ."[82]

In other cases, equity judges declined to issue anti-strike decrees on the grounds that, while the strike activities might interfere with

78. See supra pp. 66–69.

79. G. Eggert, supra Intro., note 9, at 37 (quoting telegram from Drummond to Devens, July 23, 1877; and letter, July 25, 1877).

80. See, e.g., Carleton v. Rugg, 149 Mass. 550, 22 N.E. 55 (1889); see also Hurvitz, "American Labor Law and the Doctrine of Entrepreneurial Property Rights: Boycotts, Courts, and Juridical Reorientation of 1886–1895," 8 *Indus. Rel. L. J.* 307, 313–16 (1986). This ground for denying labor injunctions did not vanish. A handful of state judges, particularly in the South, continued to invoke it in the early twentieth century—prompted perhaps more by a traditional conservative jurisprudence than by sympathy for organized labor. See, e.g., 13 *Machinists' Monthly J.* 499 (1901) (reporting a Kentucky equity court's denial of an injunction against a strike on the ground that plaintiff belonged in criminal court).

81. State v. Patterson, 14 Tex. Civ. App. 465, 470, 37 S.W. 478, 480 (1896).

82. See "Against Injunction," 2 *Am. Federationist* 163 (1895) (quoting United States Circuit Court Judge Hallet of Colorado denying mining company's application for injunction against union miners' interference with strike breakers).

the plaintiffs' work or business, they did not threaten any property right.[83] Since the early nineteenth century, equity jurisprudence had required that injunctions issue only to protect property rights.[84] Although political economists had long held that property was "all that which has exchangeable value," Gilded Age equity doctrine still tended to view property as dominion over things.[85] Thus in an 1881 New York case, despite a machine manufacturer's argument that an iron molders' union striking for a closed shop was interfering with strikebreakers and inducing them to abandon his plant, the appellate court held that these actions, routinely enjoinable by the turn of the century, "did not constitute an invasion of any clear right of property."[86] It would require the proliferation of citywide boycotts to

83. See, e.g., Mayer v. Journeymen Stonecutters' Ass'n, 47 N.J. Eq. 519, 530 (1890) ("[I]n the whole history of this long-continued struggle [between unions and employers], there is but one reported . . . case where a court of equity has [intervened] . . . , and then only to prevent a continuing trespass upon the lands of the complainant").

84. The locus classicus is Gee v. Pritchard, 2 Swanst. 402, 36 Eng. Rep. 670 (1818). For the rule's American lineage see 1 J. High, *A Treatise on the Law of Injunctions* §20b, at 34 (4th ed., 1905). See also Vandevelde, "The New Property of the Nineteenth Century: The Development of the Modern Concept of Property," 29 *Buf. L. Rev.* 325 (1980) (describing the evolution of the notion of property from the Revolutionary period to 1925).

85. Equity courts had long deemed as "things," and therefore protected by injunction, a few intangible rights, most notably those inhering in state-granted franchises, see, e.g., Croton Turnpike Road v. Ryder, 1 Johns Ch. 611 (N.Y. 1815); see also 1 J. High, supra Chap. 3, note 84, §897, at 854; H. McClintock, *Handbook on the Principles of Equity* §150, at 399–402 (2d ed., 1948), and some by the 1890s had begun to protect by decree a business's "goodwill," trademarks, and trade secrets, treating them as property rights of a "pecuniary nature." 2 J. High, supra, §1080, at 835. Still, equity courts generally distinguished "property rights" from "personal and civil rights" deeming the latter to be outside the fold of equity's power to grant injunctions. See generally T. C. Spelling and J. Lewis, *A Treatise on the Law Governing Injunctions* 9–10 and 9n25 (1926).

86. Johnston Harvester Co. v. Meinhardt, 31 N.Y. Sup. Ct. 489, 489 (1881), *aff'g* 9 Abb. N. Cas. 393 (N.Y. 1880). In opinions granting anti-strike decrees in the early 1890s, courts still found it necessary to acknowledge that the cases involved no "direct trespass upon realty" nor other threatened injuries to real or physical property, and to explain why that did not decide the outcome in the union's favor. See Coeur D'Alene Consolidated and Mining Co. v. Miners' Union of Wardner, 51 F. 260, 263 (C.C. Idaho 1892) (noting that although the miners' strike activities only "indirectly" affected the employer's possession and enjoyment of his property, if "[c]arried to their logical conclusion, the owner of property would lose its control and management").

spur judges to surmount these obstacles and extend industrial "government by injunction" beyond the railways.

Proliferate they did. Just as judges began to condemn boycotts of struck cars on the railways, boycotts of "unfair" goods and shops began to flourish in the cities. In 1885 the business journal *Bradstreet's* conducted a national survey of such boycotts. Taking stock of their "prodigious [growth] within two years past," the journal counted 196 such incidents across the country since 1883.[87] The 75 percent success rate was daunting,[88] and the numbers of boycotts continued to multiply over the next few years. In 1886 the Illinois Bureau of Labor Statistics recorded 50 boycotts in that state alone: the outcome was ascertained in 31 of those cases, 14 of which were entirely successful and 26 of which were partly so.[89] In New York, of the 59 boycotts in 1885, the state's Bureau of Statistics of Labor recorded a success rate of 81 percent.[90]

The boycott's aims and the solidarities it established beyond individual workplaces distinguished this weapon from the typical strike. In boycotts, as opposed to strikes, "control" issues—enforcing unions' work rules and standards—predominated over wage demands.[91] In addition, the 1880s boycott was almost always a rich illustration of what treatise writers would soon be calling a "compound" or "secondary" boycott.[92] If a city labor federation, for example, called a boycott against a brewer who persistently hired

87. "Boycotting," 12 *Bradstreet's* 394 (1885). The breakdown by industry reflected the fact that boycotts flourished against employers who produced goods that workers bought as consumers: foodstuffs, soap, newspapers, cigars, hats, clothing, carpets and nails, bicycles, streetcar transportation, and so on.

88. See id. A "successful" boycott was one that drove the boycotted employer to concede the wages or working conditions demanded by his employees when they first went on strike. Generally, labor councils and federations only approved and publicized a boycott when striking workers made a showing that (1) their demands were "reasonable" by industry standards; (2) efforts at conciliation had failed; and (3) a boycott was essential to their victory. See H. Laidler, *Boycotts and the Labor Struggle* 90–97 (1913).

89. See H. Laidler, supra Chap. 3, note 88, at 77–78.

90. See id. at 82–86.

91. See id. at 56–60, 93–95.

92. See, e.g., E. Oakes, supra Chap. 3, note 3, §§427–437, at 655–90; F. Sayre, *A Selection of Cases and Other Authorities on Labor Law* 403–53 (1922).

"unfair" men or spurned union work rules, then it would do more than proclaim his beer "unfair." Representatives would visit saloons and call on them to cease serving his beer or face boycotts and picket lines themselves.[93] Similarly, a boycott against a printer meant notifying all the printer's customers—"hotels, boarding-houses, public schools, railroads and steamships"—that all who continued to patronize the printer would be put on the city labor weekly's "black list."[94] An "unfair" newspaper found its advertising columns filled with blank space as advertisers chose to "leave their space entirely blank, and pay the few cents their contracts called for, [rather] than to jeopardize thousands of dollars of trade that fair labor would be 'compelled to withhold so long as such advertisements appeared.' "[95]

These boycotts provoked courts' anxiety and rage, in part because they mobilized whole working-class populations—broad networks of workers (and their families) not linked to individual workplaces or particular unions. "Their action," as one court remarked, "in the language of the times, was purely sympathetic."[96] They rested on the notion of a moral circulation of goods and money ("keep the money of fair men moving only among fair men,"[97] read a typical circular), a world of exchange relations under the rules and norms of working-class organizations like New York's Central Labor As-

93. See People v. Wilzig, 4 N.Y. Crim. Rptr. 403 (1886).

94. See Crump v. Commonwealth, 84 Va. 927, 945 (1888). The Gilded Age saw the invention of modern advertising. See generally S. Ewen, *Captains of Consciousness* (1976). In its newspapers as well as boycott circulars, placards, and banners, the era's labor movement devised a kind of counter-advertising extolling "fair" commodities, see *J. Knights Lab.*, Sept. 10, 1891, at 4, col. 5 ("Ask your dealers for the clothing made by the solidarity co-operative"), and condemning "unfair" ones, see Crump, 84 Va. at 945 (quoting boycott circular urging "Away With The Goods of this Tyrannical Firm").

95. Barr v. Essex Trades Council, 53 N.J. Eq. 101, 108, 30 A. 881, 883 (1894) (quoting a labor union resolution). New Jersey's high Court of Chancery found that the "various trades unions affiliated in the trades council as is claimed by them, represent a purchasing power amounting to over $400,000 in each and every week." Id. The trades council "put on foot" this power to intimidate many of the paper's dealers, purchasers, and advertisers to cease buying and advertising therein.

96. Id. at 115, 30 A. at 886.

97. Id. at 107, 30 A. at 883.

sembly or the Essex Trades Council,[98] rather than under the norms of the marketplace and the rules of the courts.

Gilded Age trade unionists described their unions' work rules and standards as "laws" or "legislation."[99] Courts found "class legislation" constitutionally intolerable when it emanated from state legislatures. Small wonder that they would assail efforts to enforce such "legislation" when the "laws" and their enforcement both sprang from rival, nongovernmental centers of authority like unions, labor assemblies, and trade councils. Boycotts were proto-political challenges to official authority, as well as to employers. They were waged with a rhetoric not merely of "fair wages" but of "redeeming the republic" from the grasp of "money power judges."[100] Judges saw in the boycott an assault not only on marketplace freedom but on the courts and the state. As a result one New York trial judge dubbed boycotting an odious, "socialistic crime."[101] Another judge declared that "if [boycotts] can be perpetrated with impunity, by combinations of irresponsible cabals or cliques, there will be the end of government."[102] In this mood, courts resolved doctrinal dilemmas, loosened inherited restraints, and extended the labor injunction beyond the railways.

In an effort to shore up the doctrinal obstacles to anti-boycott decrees, boycotters' attorneys would argue that insofar as the plaintiffs sought to enjoin more than peaceful communication they were seeking to enjoin garden-variety crimes.[103] True, equity often en-

98. See Essex Trades Council, 53 N.J. Eq. 101, 30 A. 881 (1894); People v. Wilzig, 4 N.Y. Crim. Rptr. 403 (1886).

99. See Forbath, "Ambiguities of Free Labor," supra Chap. 1, note 8, at 787–90.

100. See Scobey, "Boycotting the Politics Factory: Labor Radicalism and the New York City Mayoral Election of 1884," 28–30 *Radical Hist. Rev.* 280 (1984). The same labor-republican rhetoric—as well as the trope of "boycotting the politics factory"—attended the election campaigns that hundreds of cities' central labor assemblies also orchestrated in these same years. See id. at 287–95. The city-wide labor assemblies and their boycotts were likened in the press and before grand juries to the Paris Commune—to insurrectionary workers' governments. Id.

101. *Wilzig*, 4 N.Y. Crim. Rptr. at 425.

102. Crump v. Commonwealth, 84 Va. 927, 946 (1888).

103. Invoking the principle that equity would not enjoin a crime, they ignored equity's willingness to assert its power to protect property from irreparable injury, even if such

joined people from using their property in a way that amounted to a nuisance, even though the use was also a crime.[104] But that practice lay worlds apart from enjoining thousands of union members and "whomsoever" would aid or abet them from committing any of an indefinite catalogue of criminal offenses such as assault, battery, or trespass. In boycotts, as in railway strike cases, courts candidly justified this innovation on instrumental grounds. Criminal prosecutions, they said, were inadequate to control or deter such "vast conspiracies as these."[105]

Equity judges also had to contend with the unions' argument that boycotts worked no injury to employers' "property." To answer it the courts changed equity's very definition of that term. In place of the inherited view limiting property rights primarily to tangible objects,[106] they adopted the definition that held property to be anything that had "pecuniary" or "exchangeable value" including a man's business or labor. Because boycotts and strikes injured employers' profit-making activities, and therefore their "pecuniary interests," they trenched on employers' "property."

Judges found support for this view of property in a number of contexts. For centuries, the common law had recognized the property interest of "masters" in the labor of their "servants." As late as the 1820s, the common law, in order to guarantee this property right, continued to allow specific performance in certain categories of master-servant relationships: "laborers" and "journeymen" as well as "apprentices."[107] Economic change and anti-slavery ideals brought about the demise of specific performance of service con-

injury stemmed from a crime. But until the Gilded Age that power had been extremely sparingly exercised, and the maxim against enjoining crimes or trenching on trial by jury was frequently invoked by equity judges themselves. See 1 J. High, supra Chap. 3, note 84, §20, at 29–35; Mack, supra Chap. 3, note 25, at 392.

104. Mack, supra Chap. 3, note 25, at 392; see also "Developments in the Law— Injunctions," 78 *Harv. L. Rev.* 994, 1013–19 (1965).

105. T. Cogley, *The Law of Strikes, Lockouts, and Labor Organizations* 342–46 (1894); see also Arthur v. Oakes, 63 F. 310, 327–29 (7th Cir. 1894); Thomas v. Cincinnati, N.O. and T.P. Ry., 62 F. 803 (C.C.S.D. Ohio 1894).

106. See supra p. 81.

107. See R. Steinfeld, *The Disappearance of Indentured Servitude and the Invention of Free Labor in the United States* (forthcoming, Univ. of North Carolina Press, 1991).

tracts. Even then, however, the view that an employer could have a "property" interest in his workers' toil continued to inform the old common law tort action for enticing away another's servants.[108] In the 1870s, courts extended the enticement action to cases involving organized labor.[109] Treating unions' "interferences" with employers' labor supplies as invasions of property rights may have been hard to reconcile with the liberal individualist zeitgeist.[110] However, the goodwill cases in equity, the enticement action at common law, as well as the centuries-old habit of treating servants' labor as masters' property, meant that there were many familiar mental grooves into which the new notions of property could comfortably fit.[111]

But even more often than to these equity and common law precedents, judges turned to recent constitutional cases for the proposition that a "poor man's labor" as well as his employer's "business or

108. See id. See also Orren, "Organized Labor and the Invention of Modern Liberalism in the United States," 2 *Studies in Am. Pol. Dev.* 317, 329–31 (1987). In the latter half of the eighteenth century, courts gradually rearticulated the enticement action in contractual terms: the master's property right was now said to rest in the contract and its fulfillment rather than in the services of the laborer as such. See Note, "Tortious Interference with Contractual Relations in the Nineteenth Century: The Transformation of Property, Contract, and Tort," 93 *Harv. L. Rev.* 1510, 1522–23 (1980) (authored by Nockleby).

109. In Walker v. Cronin, 107 Mass. 555 (1871), defendant, a shoemaker and fledgling union organizer, persuaded a number of plaintiff's employees "to leave and abandon" plaintiff's employment. The court held that plaintiff could collect damages for the injury to his business. "Every one has a right to enjoy the fruits and advantages of his own enterprise, industry, skill and credit," the court declared. Id. at 564. The specific right infringed by the defendant organizer was plaintiff's property right "derived from the [at will] contract[s]" between him and his striking workers. Id. at 567; see also Note, supra Chap. 3, note 108, at 1522–23.

110. One equity judge, rejecting an 1880 employer's petition for an anti-strike decree based on the enticement right of action, declared: "[T]he origin of this kind of actions was at a time of the substantial enslavement of domestic servants, and at the outset it proceeded upon the theory that such servants had not freedom of action which is conceded to that class at the present day . . . [T]he person enticed is a free agent to come and go as he will, responsible only, like other persons, for the violation of his contract or his duty." Johnston Harvester Co. v. Meinhardt, 9 Abb. N. Cas. 393, 400 (1880), *aff'd*, 31 N.Y. Sup. Ct. 489 (1881).

111. I differ somewhat, then, with those who treat the "propertyization" of labor relations in the late nineteenth century as a dramatic shift in legal thought. See Hurvitz, supra Chap. 3, note 80; Vandevelde, supra Chap. 3, note 84.

enterprise" was "property."[112] By the latter half of the 1880s a handful of state high courts, commencing with the New York Court of Appeals in *Jacobs*,[113] had begun to declare than an entrepreneur's or worker's right to pursue his calling or business was a constitutional property right. The analogy seemed clear and compelling: just as much recent labor legislation had sought without justification to exploit "the force of mere numbers" to "dictate" to employers how they might "use their property" or conduct their businesses, so too did the new boycotts.[114] Believing that the right to pursue one's calling was a natural right that the common law had protected ever since it broke free from "feudal fetters," many Gilded Age jurists did not find it anomalous to borrow precedent from public law in determining a private law right. The new constitutional right seemed to them merely a constitutional recognition of long-standing—and inviolable—common law protections.[115] In both contexts, the same

112. Above all, they cited the Slaughter-House Cases, 83 U.S. (16 Wall.) 36, 116 (Bradley, J., dissenting), which noted that "a calling, when chosen, is a man's property and right"; id. at 110 (Field, J. dissenting); and *In re* Jacobs, 98 N.Y. 98 (1885). The anti-boycott injunctions relying on these two substantive due process cases include Barr v. United Essex Trades Council, 53 N.J. Eq. 101, 30 A. 881 (1894); and Brace Bros. v. Evans, 5 Pa. C. 163 (1888). Similarly, in Pierce v. Stablemen's Union, 156 Cal. 70, 103 P. 324 (1909), the California Supreme Court cited to *Ex parte* Jentzsch, 112 Cal. 468, 4 P. 803 (1896), for the proposition that "constitutional liberty means . . . among other rights . . . the right freely to labor and to own the fruits of [one's] toil." *Pierce*, 156 Cal. at 78, 103 P. at 328. The classic liberal marketplace definition of "property" as anything with "exchangeable value" including the "poor man's labor" and his employer's "firm" found its first constitutional expression in Field's and Bradley's *Slaughter-House* dissents, but one can find common law dicta in the same vein in earlier employment contract cases.

113. For a discussion of *Jacobs*, see supra pp. 39–42.

114. See *Essex Trades Council*, 53 N.J. Eq. 101, 30 A. 881; cases cited infra Chap. 3, note 119, concerning unions' presumption to regulate industry; see also Taft, "The Right of Private Property," 3 *Mich. L. J.* 215, 227–28 (1894); D. Brewer, *Report of the New York Bar Association Proceedings* 37–47 (1893).

115. See, e.g., *Essex Trades Council*, 53 N.J. Eq. 101, 30 A. 881; *Slaughter-House*, 83 U.S. (16 Wall.) 36, 93 (Field, J., dissenting); id. at 111 (Bradley, J., dissenting). The notion that a unitary right was involved and had determinate implications across broad public and private doctrinal domains also reflected the habits of mind of a distinctive era in the history of legal thought. See Kennedy, "Toward an Historical Understanding of Legal Consciousness: The Case of Classical Legal Thought in America, 1850–1940," 3 *Res. L. and Soc.* 3 (1980).

new "movement of coercion" justified court-imposed boundaries beyond which such interferences with "the rights of property" by force of numbers became illegal.

Whereas the constitutional cases were rather general and terse in their new definition of property, injunction suits led to a more elaborate redefinition—a kind of refeudalization—of work and employment relations.[116] Where a mid-nineteenth-century employer had been merely at liberty to do business with such customers or suppliers as he chose, he was now found to have a property right in these business relations defensible by injunction against boycotters' pressures. Where he had been merely free to run his shop, and use his machinery, as he willed, he now was found to have a property right to do so that was protected from interference created by a boycott or strike pressing for adherence to union work rules and standards. Where previously he had been merely free to hire whomever he liked, now he had a property interest in his employment relations and in the "natural flow" of labor to his shop or factory.[117]

Because this vision of property allowed virtually any strike to be cast as an interference with an employer's property rights, judges reasserted a set of limiting principles that marked off a realm of

116. Gilded Age trade unionists did not need legal historians to remind them of the old law of master and servant and its recognition of property rights in labor. That history was part of their common culture, and they accused the Gilded Age judges of refeudalizing the law of industrial relations with the labor injunction, just as the judges accused them of refeudalizing it with hours legislation. For labor's accusations, see infra Chap. 5, notes 30–42 and accompanying text; for the courts', see Forbath, "Ambiguities of Free Labor," supra Chap. 1, note 8, at 800. For a provocative argument that American labor law remained "feudal" until the New Deal, see K. Orren, *Belated Feudalism: Law and Liberal Development in the United States* (forthcoming).

117. See, e.g., Oxley Stave Co. v. Coopers' Int'l Union, 72 F. 695 (C.C.D. Kan. 1896); Casey v. Cincinnati Typographical Union No. 3, 45 F. 135 (C.C.S.D. Ohio 1891); Jersey City Printing Co. v. Cassidy, 63 N.J. Eq. 759, 53 A. 230 (1902); Matthews v. Shankland, 56 N.Y.S. 123 (1898); Brace Bros. v. Evans, 5 Pa. C. 163, 166–67 (1888). These developments are well chronicled in Hurvitz, supra Chap. 3, note 80, at 338–44.

Without judicial protection of these "property rights," one anti-boycott decision declared, the country's industrial and transportation systems would "become dependent on the paternalism of the national government, and the factory and the workshop subject to the uncertain chances of cooperative systems." *Essex Trades Council*, 53 N.J. Eq. at 113–14, 30 A. at 885.

legitimate strikes. Judge Taft again took the lead, first on a state and then on a federal bench.[118] Relying on criminal conspiracy doctrine, he suggested that one could identify enjoinable strikes by dint of their objects or motives. The general rule was that strikes seeking no immediate gain for the strikers—defined in narrow terms which, until the early 1900s, did not transcend wages or working conditions—were deemed to be prompted by malice. Within this conceptual framework, many control and work-rule strikes, strikes for union recognition or for closed shops, and all sympathy strikes and producer or consumer boycotts could be categorized as illegal.[119] As

118. See Moores v. Bricklayers' Union, 10 Ohio Dec. Reprint 665 (1889); Casey v. Cincinnati Typographical Union, 45 F. 135 (C.C.S.D. Ohio 1891). For detailed analyses of these two cases and Taft's role in forging new doctrine, see Hurvitz, supra Chap. 3, note 80, at 328–32, 337–39.

119. For cases on union work rules and standards, see Benito Rovira Co. v. Yampolsky, 187 N.Y.S. 894 (1921), which held illegal a strike to enforce union work standards and work rules; Hopkins v. Oxley Stave Co., 83 F. 912 (8th Cir. 1897) (same); Folsom Engraving Co. v. McNeil, 235 Mass. 269, 126 N.E. 479 (1920) (same); W. P. Davis Mach. Co. v. Robinson, 41 Misc. 329, 84 N.Y.S. 837 (N.Y. Sup. Ct. 1903) (same); and Jaeckel v. Kaufman, 187 N.Y.S. 889 (1920) (same). But cf. National Fireproofing Co. v. Mason Builders' Ass'n, 169 F. 259 (2d Cir. 1909) (holding legal a strike to enforce union work standards); Pickett v. Walsh, 192 Mass. 583, 78 N.E. 753 (1906) (same).

For cases condemning strikes for union recognition, see Michaels v. Hillman, 112 Misc. 395, 183 N.Y.S. 195 (1920), which held a strike for union recognition illegal; Tunstall v. Stearns Coal Co., 192 F. 808 (6th Cir. 1911) (same); Reynolds v. Davis, 198 Mass. 294, 84 N.E. 457 (1908) (same); and In re Higgins, 27 F. 443 (C.C.N.D. Tex. 1886) (same).

For cases condemning strikes to force employer to adopt a union, see Folsom v. Lewis, 208 Mass. 336, 94 N.E. 316 (1911), which held a strike for closed shop illegal, and Erdman v. Mitchell, 207 Pa. 79, 756 A. 327 (1903) (same). But cf. National Protective Ass'n of Steamfitters v. Cumming, 170 N.Y. 315, 63 N.E. 369 (1902) (holding a strike to force discharge of nonunion workers legal).

For cases condemning boycotts of "unfair" materials or shops, see Gompers v. Buck's Stove and Range Co., 221 U.S. 418 (1911), which held that workers may not strike or threaten to oppose working for companies producing "unfair" goods; Aikens v. Wisconsin, 195 U.S. 194 (1904) which held as unlawful under a state statute a combination of newspaper managers demanding advertisers pay their papers the same rate as the "injured" party newspaper; Burnham v. Dowd, 217 Mass. 351, 104 N.E. 841 (1914), which enjoined the Bricklayers and Plasterers Union from keeping the plaintiff's business on the "unfair list" of the union; and Auburn Draying Co. v. Wardwell, 227 N.Y. 1, 124 N.E. 97 (1919), which enjoined a boycott by butchers, bakers, plumbers, and others of an "unfair" draying firm. But cf. Bossert v. Dhuy, 221 N.Y. 342, 117 N.E. 582

with the sympathy strike, the demise of the citywide boycott was brought on by its legal repression. In 1886, in New York City alone more than one hundred trade unionists were sentenced to state penitentiary terms in conspiracy and injunction suits. Over the new two years boycotts became less aggressive and scored fewer victories. Trade unions, the state's Commissioner of Labor observed, were no longer resorting to "the boycott . . . as frequently . . . as in former years."[120] It had lost much of its potency "as a war measure." Judicial decisions had "thrown impediments" in the boycotters' path.[121] By the late 1880s the number of reported citywide boycotts everywhere had dwindled substantially, and after 1890 virtually all the state bureaus of labor statistics stopped reporting them.[122] The diminishing numbers can partially be explained by union and assembly reluctance to report on outlawed activities for state publication. There seems little doubt, however, that the particular form of boycotting that flourished in the mid-1880s, rich with political and cultural significance, with its emphasis on active community mobilization, largely died away under a judicial ban.

By the 1890s another, less street-centered and less "disorderly,"

(1917), which held that carpenters may refuse to work on "unfair" wood trim where work conditions surrounding manufacture of the "unfair" material directly affect members of the same union.

For cases condemning unions urging consumer boycotts, see *Gompers*, 221 U.S. 418 (1911), which held union urging of consumer boycott illegal; Loewe v. Lawlor, 208 U.S. 274 (1908), discussed below at p. 000; Brace Bros. v. Evans, 5 Pa. C. 163 (1888). But cf. Robison v. Hotel and Restaurant Employees Local No. 782, 35 Idaho 418, 207 P. 132 (1922) (holding that workers may urge the public to participate in a boycott with a legal purpose); Rosenberg v. Retail Clerks' Ass'n Local 428, 27 Cal. App. 769, 177 P. 864 (1918) (same). See generally E. Oakes, supra Chap. 3, note 3, §§262–305, at 376–402, §§406–472, at 598–740 (discussing the legality of various types of strikes and boycotts); F. Sayre, supra Chap. 3, note 92, at 147–389 (collecting cases on the legality of methods used by labor unions, as well as of goals sought by collective action); id. at 394–467 (collecting cases regarding the legality of boycotts); Hurvitz, supra Chap. 3, note 80 (discussing the development of Gilded Age anti-boycott and anti-strike doctrine).

120. See *1887 Annual Report of New York State Bureau of Statistics of Labor* 521.

121. Id. By 1892 the number of boycotts reported to the Commissioner had fallen to less than half of those reported in 1890. Compare *1890 Annual Report of New York State Bureau of Statistics of Labor*, vol. 2, at 1170, with *1892 Annual Report of New York State Bureau of Statistics of Labor*, vol. 2, at 230.

122. See H. Laidler, supra Chap. 3, note 88, at 71.

form of boycotting had emerged. This more far-flung boycott relied on publicizing "unfair" products through labor newspapers and journals and organizers dispatched to speak at other cities' labor assemblies. The new weapon proved well-suited to swaying the growing number of employers producing for regional or national, rather than local, markets.[123] From the late 1880s through the early 1900s, the Knights of Labor and AFL journals carried "We Don't Patronize" lists and "Boycott Departments" announcing boycotted goods.[124] Both organizations created centralized "Boycott Committees" to ensure that unions across the country received notice of boycotts launched in different locales. One finds journals and newspaper articles and "departments" expertly tracing the paths of "unfair" goods into distant markets.[125] The 1890s and early 1900s were punctuated by a series of vigorous national boycott campaigns, waged by the Hatters, Ironmolders, and several other national craft unions. Most were highly successful, winning strategic concessions from large, obdurate manufacturers and generating broad-based coalitions among once-parochial workers and unions.[126]

123. See id. at 60–63; D. Bensman, supra Chap. 3, note 73, at 215–17; L. Wolman, supra Chap. 3, note 74, at 96–98.

124. See, e.g., "To the Order Wherever Found, Greetings," *J. Knights of Lab.*, Sept. 10, 1891, at 3, col. 2 (presenting a circular directing Knights to "leave the boots and shoes made by Messrs. Thomas and Co. severely alone" and reproducing the brand marks used by the firms); "St. Louis Cigars," *J. Knights of Lab.*, Dec. 9, 1897, at 3, col. 4; "St. Louis Theatre Boycotted," *J. Knights of Lab.*, Jan. 28, 1897, at 3, col. 2; "Boycott Worthley's Shoes," *J. Knights of Lab.*, Feb. 9, 1893, at 4, col. 1.

125. See, e.g., "Dodging the Boycott," *J. Knights of Lab.*, Oct. 1, 1891, at 4, col. 4 (detailing "aliases" under which "unfair" Massachusetts shoe manufacturers were selling shoes in the South and Southwest). On boycotting departments see L. Wolman, supra Chap. 3, note 74, at 28–29. As the numbers of boycotted goods on its national "We Don't Patronize" list began to mushroom, the AFL undertook to rationalize and discipline the calling of boycotts, and by all accounts these procedures helped enhance their effectiveness. See H. Laidler, supra Chap. 3, note 88, at 109–15; P. Taft, *AFL in the Time of Gompers*, supra Chap. 1, note 2, at 264–66; L. Wolman, supra Chap. 3, note 74, at 113–15. Union locals created consumers' leagues and committees to dissuade members from buying nonunion bicycles, cigars, shoes, and so forth. These leagues claimed credit for driving "unfair goods" out of town and bringing union-made goods into local stores. See D. Bensman, supra Chap. 3, note 73, at 196–98.

126. See generally L. Wolman, supra Chap. 3, note 74, at 101–28 (describing labor's ability to foment far-flung boycotts and their use in obtaining employer concessions); see

Successes like these prompted the creation of the American Anti-Boycott Association. The Association was founded by two nonunion hat manufacturers in Danbury, Connecticut, Dietrich Loewe and Charles Merritt, in the summer of 1902 when Loewe refused to recognize the hatters' union. All but ten of Loewe's men had struck in support of the union. After several months he assembled a new "scab" crew and resumed production. These circumstances prompted a boycott, and the AFL placed Loewe's firm on its "We Don't Patronize" list. The hatters took aim at Loewe's distribution network. Wherever his hats were sold, one of the United Hatters' six full-time agents or a rank-and-file activist appeared. In Richmond, Virginia, for example, two out-of-town hatters spent "several weeks" persuading the local trade and labor council to put a retailer on their unfair list.[127]

The boycott hurt Loewe, as he expected it would, and he turned to the courts, commencing a suit that would eventuate in the Supreme Court's Danbury Hatters opinions. In 1908, *Loewe v. Lawlor*,[128] the Supreme Court's first Hatters opinion, confirmed what a majority of lower federal courts had held: that the Sherman Act applied to combinations of workers.[129] It then held that the hatters' urging consumers "through the common newspapers and union prints" to boycott goods that had crossed state lines was illegal both under the Act and at common law, as was boycotting retailers who handled

also D. Bensman, supra Chap. 3, note 73, at 192–98 (discussing the success of the hatters' union in making workers conscious of their interdependence); 7 *Industrial Commission Report on Capital and Labor*, supra Chap. 2, note 41, at 189 (presenting testimony of Garment Workers' Union secretary reporting the success of the union label in garnering outside support for the union).

127. The hatters' efforts reached as far as the West Coast. In San Francisco, the "labor council passed a resolution . . . in response to an appeal by the local hatters' union: ' . . . all friends of organized labor, and those desiring the patronage of organized workers, will not buy goods from Triest and Co. . . . ' " D. Bensman, supra Chap. 3, note 73, at 203 (quoting D. Robinson, *Spotlight on a Union* 86 (1948)).

128. 208 U.S. 274 (1908).

129. See id. at 292. Earlier federal court rulings on the application of the Sherman Act to strikes and boycotts included United States v. Debs, 64 F. 724 (C.C.N.D. Ill. 1894), and United States v. Workingmen's Amalgamated Council, 54 F. 994 (C.C.E.D. La.), *aff'd*, 57 F. 85 (5th Cir. 1893). For a federal court rejecting the Act's application to labor, see United States v. Patterson, 55 F. 605 (C.C.D. Mass. 1893).

the hats.[130] In its second Danbury Hatters opinion seven years later, the Court upheld the federal trial court's ruling that enabled Loewe to collect treble damages from some 248 Connecticut members of the hatters union.[131]

By reaching out for mutual help beyond the narrow horizons of hat finishing, first through amalgamating with related crafts, then by joining the Knights and the AFL, the hatters forged bonds that enabled them to preserve their workplace strength against increasingly recalcitrant employers. Their boycotts forced all but a handful of firms to grant union recognition. "Only the Supreme Court, with . . . *Loewe v. Lawlor*, was able to overcome the hatters' new strategy."[132]

The closest contemporary student of union label boycotts like the hatters' wrote that "plans for conducting [boycott] campaigns [were] discussed with a naive disregard of the law; resolutions to boycott were endorsed in journals and convention proceedings with a degree of publicity that actually courted legal interference."[133] The record demands a more complex assessment. Few union leaders actually disregarded the law regarding boycotting. Although they defied the law, most of them seem to have followed its development with surprising care, reporting on cases to their constituents, and criticizing judicial opinions in painstaking detail—all to affirm their unions' respect for law and to show why defiance of this branch of the law was justified.[134]

130. *Loewe*, 208 U.S. at 308.

131. See Lawlor v. Loewe, 235 U.S. 522, 536–37 (1915); D. Bensman, supra Chap. 3, note 73, at 203–08. Counsel for plaintiffs was Walter Merritt, manufacturer-plaintiff and AABA-founder Charles Merritt's son. The Danbury Hatters case launched Walter on his career as the first nationally prominent anti-union lawyer. Merritt had gleaned these 248 defendants by combing the real estate and bank records of Danbury, Norwalk, and Bethel to determine which of the union's 2000 Connecticut members had homes or bank accounts. He then attached those assets. See id. at 202–03.

132. D. Bensman, supra Chap. 3, note 73, at 217.

133. L. Wolman, supra Chap. 3, note 74, at 130.

134. See, e.g., 14 *Machinists' Monthly J.* 251, 252 (1902) (reporting a Missouri Supreme Court opinion upholding the right to publicize a boycott); "Van Cleave Seeks Injunction against A.F.L.," 14 *Am. Federationist* 783, 784 (1907) (criticizing plaintiff's allegations in the *Buck's Stove* boycott case); "Supreme Court Decision in the Hatters'

However, open defiance of anti-boycott decrees largely ceased after the Supreme Court's decisions in *Loewe v. Lawlor* and *Buck's Stove*.[135] Gompers and other leaders continued for a time their principled disobedience of injunctive bans on publicizing boycotts in speech and print.[136] But "unfair" lists gradually disappeared from union journals, and boycotting lost its prominent place in the labor movement's arsenal and common culture.[137]

We have seen the courts' part in purging broad sympathy strikes and boycotts from labor's arsenal. We should conclude this section by noting how judicial suppression of these weapons figured in labor's broader strategic deliberations. By the mid-1890s, both federal and state high courts had made plain that the law was implacably opposed to broad unionism and the kinds of aggressive, industry-, community-, and class-based tactics it often entailed. Railway boycotts in the 1880s and early 1890s gave rise to the revealing phrase "Gatling-gun injunctions,"[138] and gave the lie to Hamilton's famous characterization of the judiciary as the branch that wields no sword.[139] The fate of the Pullman Boycott seemed to confirm that broad, inclusive strikes would run up against violent state opposition, and that state force would arrive with high legal sanction.

Case—Affects All Organized Labor. A Symposium Giving Opinion and Comment by Men of Affairs," 15 *Am. Federationist* 161 (1908) (presenting detailed comments and critiques by twenty-one trade union leaders—scrutinizing and assailing common law doctrine and judicial interpretations of the Sherman Act, comparing English and American law); "Unions May Boycott," 17 *Am. Federationist* 228 (1918) (reporting trial court decision in Oklahoma). In the process they began to refine and teach an alternative common law and constitutionalism that we will take up in Chapter 5.

135. Gompers v. Buck's Stove and Range Co., 221 U.S. 418 (1911), was a contempt case against Gompers and other national AFL officials for publicizing a boycott against an "unfair" iron-molding firm in defiance of a District of Columbia trial court injunction. The trial court sentenced Gompers to one year in prison, two other AFL leaders to nine and six months. See Buck's Stove and Range Co. v. A.F.&L., 36 Wash. L. Rptr. 822 (D.C. 1908). The Court rejected the defendants' first amendment pleas, 221 U.S. at 436–37, but dismissed the contempt proceedings. See id. at 452.

136. See infra pp. 143–45.

137. See H. Laidler, supra Chap. 3, note 88, at 64, 118–19; L. Wolman, supra Chap. 3, note 74, at 134–35.

138. See, e.g., J. Swinton, supra Chap. 1, note 7, at 252, 458.

139. See *The Federalist* no. 78 (A. Hamilton).

For these reasons most labor leaders argued for moderation. Peter Agnew, a New Orleans delegate to the 1894 Denver Convention, reminded his fellow trade unionists of the fate of a broadly backed strike against the Texas & Pacific Railway. "Judge Pardee, who had appointed the receivers, granted them a writ, and it told the U.S. Marshals to come cavalry and infantry and crush the strike, and they did."[140] "A few years later," Agnew continued,

> came the general sympathy strike called by the Workingmen's Amalgamated Society to support the longshoremen. Colored and white workers struck, teamsters, printers, hearse drivers and carriage drivers, musicians and carpenters and streetcar workers. The whole city was tied up. Then Judge Billings decided the strike was against the Interstate Commerce Law and we were summoned to his courtroom and he told us that the strike was outlaw and we would all go to jail and have the U.S. Army here again besides if we didn't call it off.[141]

The New Orleans delegate's recollections prompted another delegate, Samuel Johnston, a railway shop craftsman, to complain:

> Didn't the A.R.U. [Pullman] strike teach us anything? We clamored for an interstate commerce law. Yes and we got it. Got it shot into us at Chicago and in New Orleans and prodded into us in California with bayonets . . . Judge Woods decided that interfering with the passage of streetcars was a violation of the interstate commerce law. And yet we howl for more.[142]

Johnston's complaint captured the mingled lessons that many union leaders and activists were drawing. Broad unionism and broad reform politics alike assumed a minimally tolerant and accessible state. But the American state had begun to seem intractably enemy territory. Even when labor won, it lost. Not only were labor- and populist-inspired reforms struck down or nullified by interpretation; they were turned violently against labor. Experiences with Gilded Age injunctions grounded, as most federal decrees were, on the Interstate Commerce and Sherman Acts gave rise to a voluntarist

140. *Verbatum Report*, supra Chap. 1, note 60, at 30.
141. Id. at 30–31.
142. Id. at 31.

parable. Trade unionists spoke and wrote about how they had agitated for legislation against the trusts and monopolies only to have the Sherman Act invoked most successfully not against trusts but against strikes and boycotts. Like the Interstate Commerce Act, the Sherman Act "simply resulted in the arrest and imprisonment of union men"; it supplied a "modern warrant for calling workers' efforts to protect their common interests actions . . . in restraint of trade."[143] Laws intended to protect the nation's "toilers" proved "instead the incubators of our modern injunction and trial without jury."[144]

Even the proponents of protective legislation like hours laws were stymied by this injunction-inspired parable about the treacherous court-dominated state. One close observer of AFL politics remarked: "Year after year the Federation . . . has gone on record as vehemently opposed to the eight-hour day by legislative enactment and in favor of direct action as the exclusive means of securing the shorter work day."[145] Each year, the progressive "minority led by the Socialist delegates" strove to reverse the "traditional policy of the Federation"[146] And each year, they encountered Gompers's objection. "Legislative enactment, he has always contended, means the subjection of organized labor to the courts. And subjection to the courts, he has consistently held, means subjection to tyranny. Upon this contention he has repeatedly staked his leadership in the American Federation of Labor . . . "[147]

In the shadow of so many broken big strikes and bootless broad initiatives, many thought it wise to conserve and build upon what "worked"—minimalist politics, craft unionism, high dues, and restrained but well-calculated strike policies.[148] Of course, not every-

143. S. Gompers, *Labor and Common Welfare* 45 (1919) (excerpt from Annual Report of AFL Convention, Detroit, Mich., Dec. 11, 1899).

144. Id.; see also Valesh, supra Chap. 2, note 46, *Verbatum Report*, supra Chap. 1, note 60, at 48–49, 52–54.

145. "The Predicament of Organized Labor," *New Republic*, Dec. 2, 1916, at 114.

146. Id.

147. Id.

148. See C. Tomlins, supra Intro., note 9, at 60–61; see also H. Laidler, supra Chap. 3, note 88, at 131–33 (noting the increasing conservatism in the AFL's use of the boycott weapon); L. Ulman, supra Chap. 3, note 9, at 425 (describing a national union strike

one in the labor movement drew the same lessons from the state of courts and parties. A substantial minority of AFL trade unionists remained attached to the vision of a broad, inclusive movement. They were more inclined toward Debs's thinking than Gompers's.[149] But these were the lessons drawn by most of the leaders of the powerful craft unions that were the AFL's dominant bloc.

policy restraining locals from striking too often); Foner, supra Chap. 1, note 42, at 68 (commenting on a union movement uninterested in posing a political challenge to capital).

149. While the Pullman injunction and the 1890s courts helped persuade Gompers to embrace a minimalist politics and a cautious, narrower unionism, they converted Debs to socialism. See N. Salvatore, supra Chap. 3, note 48, at 136–37, 149–51.

4 | Semi-Outlawry

Adopting a more disciplined and restrained strike policy after the turn of the century did not free AFL unions from the courts. The unions continued to rely on tactics that the courts condemned: boycotts, refusals to haul or work on unfair goods, control strikes, closed shop strikes, organizing strikes, and picketing. The huge growth of AFL membership in the early 1900s, from about 375,000 in 1899 to about 1,700,000 in 1904,[1] sprang from union victories that rested on increasingly well-coordinated use of these weapons. As I showed in Chapter 3, such developments bred new employers' associations, new anti-union litigators, open-shop drives, and expanding numbers of injunction suits, which in turn halted AFL expansion.[2] A similar pattern repeated itself in the 1910s and 1920s. Wartime government policy from 1917 to 1919 opened the door to unions in places and industries hitherto closed.[3] By the mid 1920s, however, open-shop drives, supported by unprecedented numbers of anti-strike decrees,[4]

1. See S. Perlman, *History of Trade Unionism in the United States*, supra Chap. 1, note 5, at 163.

2. See 4 S. Perlman and P. Taft, *History of Labour in the United States*, supra Chap. 1, note 1, at 523–24 (comparing the roles of economic downswings with open-shop drives and hostile state action in accounting for trends in AFL union membership, and attributing substantially greater weight to the latter for the period from 1900 through the 1920s).

3. See R. Hoxie, *Trade Unionism in the United States* 413–22 (2d ed., 1924).

4. At least 1000 anti-strike decrees issued in the 1900s and again the 1910s, and at least 2,800 in the 1920s. Injunctions issued against 3–5% of all recorded strikes in the first two decades; 25% of all recorded strikes were enjoined during the 1920s. See infra Appendix B.

had robbed the Federation of over 25 percent of its total 1919 membership and half of its wartime gains.[5]

But how significant were the courts in this process that sapped labor's strength? Labor historians tend to discount the influence of judges' words and deeds on the unfolding of ground-level events like strikes. "Much more important than injunctions and the famous court precedents," writes Montgomery, "was the behavior of local police."[6] "Law and society" scholars agree; far more important than judicial doctrine in the "real world" are the purely discretionary decisions of local officials and lowly administrators.[7] Is this realist perspective apt in this case, and, insofar as it is, how explain trade unionists' endless preoccupation with judge-made law during the years from 1900 through the early 1930s? We need to scrutinize more closely how injunctions, judge-made law, and court-minted rhetoric actually figured in workers' experiences.

The Usurpation of Local Polities

The clash of federal courts with state governors was only the most spectacular example of the contests injunction judges waged with elected state officials.[8] As one labor journalist remarked, the injunction did "away with local grand juries, local petit juries, local officers [and elected officials] of all kinds."[9] Together with the swiftness of ex parte orders, the "doing away" with juries was one of the chief attractions of equity over criminal law from the employer's perspective. As early as 1879, the industry journal *Iron Age*

5. See 4 S. Perlman and P. Taft, supra Chap. 1, note 1, at 524; P. Taft, *AFL in the Time of Gompers*, supra Chap. 1, note 2, at 233.

6. D. Montgomery, *Fall of the House of Labor*, supra Intro., note 8, at 271.

7. See Friedman, "American Legal History: Past and Present," 34 *J. Legal Educ.* 563, 570–71 (1984); Macaulay, "Law and the Behavioral Sciences: Is There Any There There?" 6 *Law and Pol'y* 149, 166–67 (1984); Moore, "Law and Social Change: The Semi-Autonomous Social Field as an Appropriate Subject of Study," 7 *Law and Soc'y Rev.* 719 (1973).

8. State judges were often *more* prone to issue injunctions than were federal judges, even though they were subject to direct elections. For conjectures as to why this might have been so, see supra pp. 33–34.

9. *National Labor Standard*, Aug. 15, 1901, at 1, col. 3.

noted that iron manufacturers prosecuting conspiracy cases often found themselves stymied by local juries. Pointing to the activities of federal equity courts during the 1877 railroad strike, the journal proposed injunction proceedings as an alternative to "useless jury verdicts."[10]

A classic instance of the vexations of relying upon juries to condemn broad strike tactics occurred in the aftermath of a tumultuous teamsters' strike in Chicago in 1905.[11] The teamsters' action began as a sympathy strike in support of the city's garment workers, but it swiftly became a battle waged by the employers, several of the city's large department stores, to break the teamsters' power. The strike produced strong-arm tactics on both sides. It ended inconclusively with the teamsters and their Labor Council weakened but hardly quelled. When the employers successfully demanded a criminal conspiracy prosecution against the strike's leadership, the jury surprised the prosecution and the press by returning a verdict of not guilty.[12] To celebrate their vindication, the teamsters paraded through Chicago's streets: their wagons were swathed with banners declaring, "The Sympathetic Strike Is Legal."[13]

Another Chicago garment industry strike, two decades later in 1924, dramatically confirmed the persistence of sharp differences between judges' and juries' reckonings of the legality (or legitimacy) of labor protest. During the dress and shirtwaist strike of 1924, law courts with juries tried roughly nine hundred strikers for statutory offenses such as intimidation and assault of strikebreakers. Two convictions resulted. Equity judges tried 258 cases, most of which involved peaceful picketing or persuasion that violated the terms of injunctions against inducing "breach of contract" by strikebreakers.

10. *Iron Age*, June 5, 1879, at 14, col. 2.

11. See H. Meyers, "The Policing of Labor Disputes in Chicago," 635–37 (Ph.D. dissertation, University of Chicago, 1929).

12. The foreman explained the jury's rationale: "Violence . . . and corruption . . . were testified to, [but] even if all the testimony were true, [they] are no evidence of a conspiracy . . . as alleged in the indictment. A sympathetic strike is not a conspiracy." *Chicago Tribune*, June 12, 1905, at 4, col. 1; see H. Meyers, supra Chap. 4, note 11, at 637.

13. See H. Meyers, supra Chap. 4, note 11, at 657.

Of the 258 contempt cases, 255 resulted in convictions; 208 of the convictions were for peaceful picketing. The equity courts meted out more than 50 jail sentences ranging from three weeks to six months.[14]

However, injunction proceedings circumvented more than just local juries. In the first instance, an injunction suit could be used to override the judgments of local authorities, whom courts as well as employers constantly accused of siding with strikers.[15] Sentencing strikers for contempt of a decree against picketing, a federal judge in Iowa voiced an utterly typical reproach: "there would not have been the slightest occasion for bringing this case, had there been any . . . honesty of purpose by the local authorities . . . Intimidation [and] force . . . were all winked at, because . . . certain peace officers [believed] that they would be kindly remembered on future election days . . . "[16] Again and again, federal judges echoed the old Federalist dismay about local polities and their faction-driven disregard for the lawful rights of property. Local officials were "lawless," "blameworthy," "irresponsible," and sometimes "subversive" in their derelictions of duty.[17] Often the seeming derelictions

14. See id. at 978–79, 984.

15. See, e.g., Schenectady Ry. v. Mayor, 121 Misc. 4, 5, 199 N.Y.S. 827, 828 (N.Y. Sup. Ct. 1923) (deeming mayor's actions in connection with a streetcar workers' strike "subversive of law, of property rights, and of orderly government"). A Pennsylvania Supreme Court judge, appointed especially to preside over the conspiracy prosecutions that emerged out of the Homestead ironworkers' strike, complained from the bench that the strikers were encouraged in their "erroneous view[s] of the law" by those whom he characterized as "demagogues, who pander to the mob, and . . . politicians who hunger for votes." The Homestead Case, 1 Pa. D. 785, 788 (1892).

16. Atchison, T. and S. F. Ry. v. Gee, 139 F. 582, 584 (C.C.S.D. Iowa 1905).

17. For reported examples, see American Steel and Wire Co. v. Davis, 261 F. 800, 802–03 (N.D. Ohio 1919); Niles-Bement-Pond Co. v. Iron Molders Local 68, 246 F. 851, 858–60 (S.D. Ohio 1917), *rev'd on jurisdictional grounds*, 258 F. 408 (6th Cir. 1918), *aff'd*, 254 U.S. 77 (1920); Employers' Teaming Co. v. Teamsters' Joint Council, 141 F. 679, 688–89 (C.C.N.D. Ill. 1905), *rev'd*, 163 F. 16 (7th Cir. 1908); Otis Steel Co. v. Local 218, Ironmolders Union, 110 F. 698 (C.C.D.N. Ohio 1901); United States v. Sweeney, 95 F. 434, 441–42 (C.C.W.D. Ark. 1899); Consol. Steel and Wire Co. v. Murray, 80 F. 811, 815 (C.C.N.D. Ohio 1897); see also 14 *Machinists' Monthly J.* 255 (1902) (reporting federal judge's condemnation of Indianapolis mayor's toleration of labor protest during machinists' strike).

actually sprang from local officials' fulfillment of their duties of office—but according to norms that differed from those of the courts. Local officials in towns with strong union traditions often held a different view of legitimate strike goals as well as a different view of allowable picketing and protest activities.[18] Since the courts regarded many kinds of strikes, and most boycotts, as illegal by dint of their objectives, they had little trouble barring virtually any form of communicative activity connected with them.[19]

Local officials certainly did not always favor strikers,[20] but when they did, they often clashed with the state and federal judiciary. Indeed, local officials' indignation at judicial intervention was frequently no less voluble than that of trade unionists. In 1901, for

18. In towns with strong union loyalties, local officials often condoned harsh verbal intimidation of strikebreakers. In such towns, even a blackened eye, a broken nose, or a stray brick heaved at a strikebreaker usually did not seem grounds for complying with employers' demands to suppress all picketing, particularly during contests over a union's very survival. More serious violence against strikebreakers rarely went unpunished, no matter how numerous the labor vote. See, e.g., *Anti-Injunction Bill: Complete Hearings before the Committee on the Judiciary of the House of Representatives on the Bill (H.R. 89) Entitled "A Bill to Limit the Meaning of the Word 'Conspiracy' and the Use of 'Restraining Orders and Injunctions' in Certain Cases,"* 58th Cong., 1st Sess. 440–41 (1904) (statement of James E. MacCloskey, Jr., of Pittsburgh, Pa., counsel for the Harbison-Walker Refractory Company) (describing, in testimony of counsel for company seeking to drive union from plant, local constable's and county sheriff's refusal to prevent the fired "union men from . . . clamoring at our gates . . . stoning our workmen, and following them in mobs"); "One Dead and Many Injured in Riots," *Chicago Inter-Ocean*, Apr. 30, 1905, at 3 (reporting police suppression of violent assaults on strikebreakers in strongly unionized Chicago); see also Mullins Body Corp. v. I.A.M., Quaker City Local No. 568, 3 *Law and Lab.* 149 (N.D. Ohio 1921).

19. See supra Chap. 3, note 119.

20. Probably, local officials were more often responsive to employers' than to trade unionists' views of legitimate strike activities. Compare F. Couvares, supra Chap. 1, note 6, at 29–30 (1984) (arguing that in many smaller industrial cities and towns and some larger ones where workers were a substantial portion of the electorate, elected officials were tolerantly neutral or even occasionally pro-union in strike situations), H. Gutman, supra Chap. 1, note 3, at 236–37, 254–58, and D. Walkowitz, *Worker City, Company Town* 214–15 (1978), with G. Adams, *Age of Industrial Violence, 1910–1915* 176–203 (1966), R. Goldstein, *Political Repression in Modern America from 1870 to the Present* 45–55, 561–63 (1978), and Montgomery, " 'Liberty and Union': Workers and Government in America, 1900–1940," in *Essays from the Lowell Conference on Industrial History, 1980 and 1981* 145–57 (O. Ford, P. Marion, and R. Weible, eds., 1981).

example, a large printing company owned by one Conkey moved to Hammond City, Illinois, to avoid Chicago's powerful typographers' and pressmen's unions. In the face of Conkey's vow to maintain an open shop, several Chicago locals set about organizing the new plant.[21] Conkey secured a broad order against all picketing and persuasion by the unions, but organizers and union members continued to picket on the city park ground beside Conkey's plant. The local city council supported the unions.[22] One alderman visited the pickets on the day of a city council meeting. Enraged, he reported to the council that one of Conkey's private police had ordered him off the city park grounds for violating the injunction. The mayor told the Park Committee chairman, "[I]f any of [Conkey's] bogus officers . . . get on that patch of green have them arrested."[23] But, according to the typographers' journal, the "thugs" were not arrested. Indeed, the Hammond City police began to enforce the provision of the court order enjoining strikers and organizers from meeting trains from Chicago to try to persuade strikebreakers hired by Conkey to return home.[24]

Every injunction represented a new, particularized set of legal commands for strikers that supervened the policies and discretion of local officials. It is surprising, in fact, how many injunctions also directly addressed these officials. A justice of the peace in Pennsylvania, for example, was enjoined by a federal court from issuing warrants against strikebreakers carrying concealed weapons, while one in West Virginia was enjoined from hearing criminal charges against private police. Two city councilmen in Duluth were jailed for contempt for publicizing a boycott. So too were a mayor in New Jersey and another in New York. The mayor and chief of police of

21. They vowed to seek recognition "from the youngest, smallest girl in the binderies to the sturdy pressmen." *Chicago Tribune*, Aug. 28, 1901, at 5, col. 4.

22. So too did a number of local businessmen who sent a delegation to visit Conkey urging him to settle with the unions. *Chicago Tribune*, Aug. 30, 1901, at 3, col. 4. On small merchants' and businessmen's frequent ties with the labor movement, see F. Couvares, supra Chap. 1, note 6, at 29–30, and H. Gutman, supra Chap. 1, note 3, at 254–58.

23. *Chicago Tribune*, Aug. 28, 1901, at 5, col. 4.

24. See "The Chicago Strike," 26 *Typographical J.* 625 (1905).

Cleveland were enjoined from enforcing a city ordinance prohibiting the employment of private police as out-of-state strikebreakers during the steel strikes of 1919.[25]

The omnibus injunctions against the railway strikes of the 1880s and 1890s supplied the model for courts to enact "criminal codes" for entire working-class communities. It was not uncommon for such decrees to address ten thousand workers and "whomsoever" would aid and abet them. The model spread swiftly to other industries. For example, in 1896, all the trade unionists of Kansas City were addressed in an anti-boycott order; in 1905, California's scores of thousands of union women and men found themselves similarly addressed; and that same year, all the printers in Chicago and thirty other cities fell under blanket anti-strike decrees.[26] A federal injunction addressed all the nation's bituminous coal miners in 1919, and the omnibus injunction continued to flourish in the 1920s. During a streetcar strike in Indianapolis, the city's entire working class, "having knowledge of the existence of this order," were enjoined from aiding the strikers; while in West Virginia and southwestern Pennsylvania, whole mining counties came under permanent injunctions.[27] Beginning in the late 1890s, the "plastering" of work-

25. 2 Law and Lab. 26 (1920); 13 Am. Federationist 13 (1906); 8 Machinists' Monthly J. 211 (1896). See American Steel and Wire v. Davis, 261 F. 800 (N.D. Ohio 1919); see also Schenectady Ry. Co. v. Whitmyer, 121 Misc. 4, 6, 199 N.Y.S. 827, 828–29 (N.Y. Sup. Ct. 1923) (enjoining mayor of Schenectady to protect strikebreakers rather than directing plaintiff to cease operating its streetcars during strike). During a machinists' strike in Quaker City, the mayor had out-of-state strikebreakers arrested and brought to his office where he roughly "told them to go back where they came from," and urged strikers to "kick them out of town." A federal court enjoined the practice. Mullins Body Corp. v. I.A.M., Quaker City Local No. 568, 3 Law and Lab. 149 (N.D. Ohio 1921).

26. See "A War Whoop," 8 Machinists' Monthly J. 211 (1896); Loewe v. California State Fed'n of Labor, 139 F. 71 (C.C.N.D. Cal. 1905) (issuing anti-boycott decree running against all members of constituent unions of state Federation of Labor and all persons associating with them); A. R. Barnes and Co. v. Chicago Typographical Union No. 16, 232 Ill. 402, 83 N.E. 932 (1908); H. Meyers, supra Chap. 4, note 11, at 490.

27. See H. Blankenhorn, The Strike for Union 46, 91–94, 132–35, 214 (1923) (describing strikes and injunctions in Virginia, West Virginia, and southwestern Pennsylvania); F. Sayre, Cases on Labor Law 757 (1922) (printing unreported case, United States v. Frank J. Haves (C.C.D. Ind. 1919)); Advance, June 2, 1922, at 5, col. 3; "The Misuse of Injunction," United Mine Workers' J., Sept. 4, 1902, at 5, col. 3 (discussing injunctions against West Virginia miners).

places and workers' neighborhoods with copies of injunctions—"on telegraph poles and freight cars [and buildings, on scabbing teamsters' wagons] . . . reading it to [groups of] strikers and others" and "publishing it in newspapers"[28]—became both a new mode of serving the courts' writs and a symbol of the courts' presence as lawmakers and regulators of industrial conflict.

In a variety of contexts, courts usurped from local elected officials bits of power over labor's public sphere and the permissible limits of protest. A single injunction's language often ranged from the broadest and vaguest proscriptions to the most minute catalogue of strike tactics and customs and even particular songs, catcalls, and jeers. Injunctions forebade everything from "interfering with plaintiff's business"[29] or with plaintiff's employees by "violence, intimidation, persuasion or otherwise," to shouting "scab," marching with cowbells and tin cans, publishing unfair lists in local newspapers, holding meetings, or urging boardinghouse owners and shopkeepers to refuse service to strikebreakers. Like substantive due process cases striking down reform legislation, but in a narrower and harsher fashion, decisions like these revealed employers' legal resources for trumping workers' political influence.

Courts and the Uses of Police, Guards and Troops

In the early twentieth century, state coercion and violence against strikers was substantially greater in the United States than in other industrial nations. Elsewhere, by the early 1900s, strikes, secondary actions, and labor protest were no longer in a legal twilight. Strikers were no longer semi-outlaws, and police and troops arrested, injured,

28. See *Report of a Hearing before the Committee on the Judiciary of House of Representatives*, S. Doc. no. 58, 56th Cong., 2d Sess. 2 (1900) (statement of Clarence Darrow).

29. The unpublished memoranda of the Commission on Industrial Relations include a list of 100 "blanket injunctions" containing provisions forbidding "interfering with plaintiff's business in any manner whatsoever" or like language. See F. Frankfurter and N. Greene, supra Intro., note 9, at 50n9 (citing E. Witte, *Report on the Use of Labor Injunctions*, app. B (1915) (unpublished memorandum)).

and killed significantly fewer of them than in the United States.[30] How then did the republic's courts and judge-made law figure in strikers' encounters with police and other local officials? How did they affect the uses of private guards and state and federal troops?

Generally, where a particular sheriff, mayor, or other local official tolerated picketing, injunctions could prod him to toughen his policies. In February 1917, for example, when the ladies' garment workers of Chicago struck to institute the protocol system that prevailed in New York, the "irreconcilables" among the manufacturers secured several blanket decrees against strikers even approaching their shops. These decrees brought a sharp turnabout in the policy of relative toleration that had prevailed for the strike's first few days.[31] The federal judge who heard the irreconcilables' ex parte petitions for temporary restraining orders was determined to exert his authority swiftly against the large "illegal" strike. He chided

30. The statistics for the United States are rough but grim. In the 1890s, roughly 2 workers were killed and 140 injured for every 100,000 strikers. In the same decade in France, for every 100,000 strikers roughly 3 (or 137 fewer) were injured; only 70 French strikers were *arrested* per 100,000. For the United States, national arrest rates are simply impossible to compile. In Illinois, the arrest rate for the latter half of the 1890s was at least 700 per 100,000 strikers, or ten times that of France; in New York for that decade it was at least 400. Between 1902 and 1904 (the three years between 1880 and 1920 for which we have the most detailed and reliable figures), at least 198 people were killed and 1,966 were injured; for every 100,000 strikers, one worker was killed and 1,009 were injured. See G. Groat, *Organized Labor* 189 (1916); G. Friedman, supra Chap. 3, note 76; see generally United States Commissioner of Labor, *Report on Strikes and Lockouts*, H.R. Doc. no. 882, 59th Cong., 2d Sess. (1906) [hereinafter *Report on Strikes*] (reporting results of investigation of strikes and lockouts, 1901–1905, with summaries from 1881 to 1905). For a comparative analysis of strikes and unions, see G. Friedman, supra Chap. 3, note 76, which compares the government strike policies of France and the United States and their impact on the two nations' labor movements; and Taft and Ross, "American Labor Violence," in *Violence in America* 281–395, 380 (H. Graham and T. Gurr, eds., 1969), which notes that "[t]he United States has experienced more frequent and bloody labor violence than any other industrial nation . . ."

The repressive character of state policy engendered more violence in the United States. Further, more was, and still is, at stake in strikes in the United States than elsewhere. Abroad, labor's share of the social product depended and today still depends far more than here on legislation and bargaining between nationwide organizations and representatives. See D. Hibbs, *The Political Economy of Industrial Democracies* 78–79 (1987); Bok, supra Intro., note 1, 1417–19, 1436–39; Rogers, supra Intro., note 1.

31. See *Chicago Daily Tribune*, Feb. 18, 1917, at 10, col. 3.

city and police officials. Instructed to enforce the court's orders scrupulously, police arrested 1,000 pickets in the first two weeks of the strike. Five strike leaders were quickly sentenced to prison terms of one to two and one-half months for speaking at rallies or advising or participating in the picketing. The newspaper of the Amalgamated Clothing Workers (ACW), the *Advance*, blamed the "injunction judge" for defeating the strike; a Chicago sociologist concluded that the strikers' victory had been doubtful in any case, but that the injunctions and the sentencing of the local leaders had "settled all doubt and demoralized the strikers."[32]

Garment workers' organizers reported similar experiences in other campaigns. In Buffalo, for example, during the ACW's 1923 organizing drive, employers secured temporary restraining orders and the police began "wholesale arrests for violation of the injunctions, and interpret[ed] and enforc[ed] these injunctions . . . in a way to interfere with picketing of shops which are not protected with injunctions.[33]

Where city or town administrations were ill-disposed toward strikers, injunctions were hardly necessary to stiffen police policy toward picketing or publicizing strikes.[34] Nonetheless, employers sometimes got them, and strikers complained that the injunctions were invoked by employers, police, and the press to justify measures like arming strikebreakers or jailing pickets.[35]

Only in the mining counties of Pennsylvania and West Virginia and in railroad and railroad shopmen's strikes did consistently large numbers of strikers serve significant jail time for violating decrees.[36]

32. See *Advance*, Mar. 30, 1917, at 1, col. 2; *Advance*, Mar. 9, 1917, at 7, col. 1.
33. *Advance*, June 29, 1923, at 1, col. 6; see also *Advance*, Aug. 4, 1922, at 1, col. 3 (reporting enforcement by Baltimore police of injunction against picketing).
34. Often, as in the 1922 general strike in Philadelphia's garment industry, police barred picketing before a rash of injunctions issued doing the same. See *Advance*, Sept. 8, 1922, at 1, col. 4.
35. See, e.g., 14 *Machinists' Monthly J.* 28, 29–30 (1902).
36. See H. Blankenhorn, supra Chap. 4, note 27, at 133 (stating that during a typical miners' strike in Pennsylvania "hundreds of local leaders" were in prison "for many months" serving sentences for violating anti-strike decrees); see also Letter from W. H. Taft to H. H. Taft, supra Chap. 3, note 47 (describing "men . . . constantly being arrested and brought before" Judge Taft as he "policed" the enforcement of one anti-strike decree

From the 1890s through the 1920s, the largest number of jail sentences for contempt arising from an injunction in a single Chicago strike appears to have been 53 sentences meted out during the 1924 dress and shirtwaist industry strike.[37] In the years from 1904 to 1932, New York State equity judges jailed a total of 51 people for violating court orders.[38]

But if jail terms for violating court orders were relatively rare, arrests were not. Figures of 1,000–2,000 arrests in a three-to-four-week strike were not uncommon for large strikes; figures of 100–200 arrests were not unusual in smaller ones.[39] Occasionally, the repeated arrests of peaceable strikers, flatly barred from all communication with strikebreakers, would win the sympathy of city newspapers, merchants, professional elites, and politicians. These might exert pressure on an otherwise intransigent employer to confer and compromise with the union.[40]

For organized workers, the picket line was a means of persuasion

issued during the Pullman Strike). See generally *Report of the United States Coal Commission, Civil Liberties in the Coal Fields*, S. Doc. no. 195, 68th Cong., 2d Sess. 161 (1925) [hereinafter *Civil Liberties in the Coal Fields*]; A. Lindsey, *The Pullman Strike* 164–171 (1967) (describing masses of arrests and sentences based on anti-boycott decrees).

37. See H. Meyers, supra Chap. 4, note 11, at 971.

38. See C. Swayzee, *Contempt of Court in Labor Injunction Cases* 46–47 (1935). Nonetheless, prison sentences remained a far more frequent outcome of contempt proceedings against strikers than of criminal trials or police court proceedings. The 1924 Chicago garment industry strike, noted above, gave rise to 900 criminal trials resulting in two convictions and one jail sentence, see H. Meyers, supra Chap. 4, note 11, at 957, compared to 258 contempt proceedings netting 255 convictions and, as noted, 53 jail sentences, see id. at 971. The contrast is more remarkable when one considers that the offenses tried in the criminal courts typically involved assaults and batteries or threatened violence; those tried in equity did not. See id. at 957, 971; see also id. at 959 (stating that in 1924 garment industry strike employers "foresaw the futility of the [criminal process] . . . and turned to the injunctions as a more effective method" of securing penal sanction against strikers).

39. Such figures were also common in strikes unattended by injunctions. Court-sanctioned arrests on this scale happened often enough to put the "law" squarely on the side of such strike-policing policies. For every picket line declared illegal by an injunction, there were countless other picket lines condemned by lesser officials relying on the "law" as injunction judges had fashioned it. See infra pp. 125–26.

40. See, e.g., H. Meyers, supra Chap. 4, note 11, at 485 (describing such support for the 1905 Printers' Strike in Chicago).

and, at the same time, a form of protest against injustice and betrayal. In their attitude toward strikebreakers, pickets were often ambivalent: sometimes they tried to persuade, exhort, cajole, or shame; at other times they tried to menace and intimidate.[41] The courts, however, recognized no such distinctions. They deemed picketing inherently intimidating and typically permitted no more than one or two persons at each workplace entrance to serve notice of a strike's existence: as Chief Justice Taft wrote, these persons acted as "missionaries."[42]

In light of this strict judicial response, what might have been, and elsewhere was,[43] the scene of peaceful, if vociferous, protest became the scene of arrests and more or less violent frays. Such scenes encouraged employers, officials, and the press to portray the striking union as lawless and irresponsible.[44] These images, in turn, fueled harsher prohibitions and sanctions, greater employer intransigence, longer strikes, and mounting anger, violence, and demoralization

41. About picketing in coal miners' strikes, Heber Blankenhorn wrote:

"A dilemma early confronts mine strikers: 'How shall the scabs be treated? Treat 'em pretty, persuade 'em? Or cut 'em dead, drive 'em out?' . . . [A] year after the strike began, union meetings in Somerset were still at times debating violently that question . . .

"The picket line is the heart of a strike, in a mine camp where only the highroad is not company-owned . . . The only chance the striker has to see or count or speak to the strikebreakers is the fleeting moment . . . when the strikebreakers cross the road on their way to and from the mine mouth. There is time for only a manner and a phrase . . .

"The theory of picketting [*sic*] truthfully reflects this dual attitude of union men to strikebreakers; besides being persuasion, picketting is also protest. It is meant to advertise first the existence of a strike, then the plight and the endurance of the strikers, their families and their union. To enforce the protest, women and children frequently take to the picket line, with symbols of ridicule or shame; offering the strikebreakers bread crumbs and pennies 'if you're so hard up you gotta work in a scab mine' . . . Shouting 'scab' having been ruled illegal, pickets would innocently scratch themselves in the sight of strikebreakers or their children called 'cuckoo' in cheery bird-lover tones." H. Blankenhorn, supra Chap. 4, note 27, at 130–32.

42. See American Steel Foundries v. Tri-City Central Trades Council, 257 U.S. 184, 207 (1921).

43. On the relative toleration toward labor protest on the part of state officials in France and England, see G. Friedman, supra Chap. 3, note 76; A. Fox, supra Chap. 1, note 62.

44. See, e.g., "Labor and Equal Rights," 7 *Am. Federationist* 164 (1900) (noting that the "capitalistic press" depicts strikers as outlaws); "Writ in Kellogg War," *Chicago Daily News*, July 20, 1903, at 1, col. 1. See generally E. Witte, supra Intro., note 9, at 121.

among strikers. City elites would rarely intervene on behalf of unions embroiled in showdowns like these.

To avoid such consequences, striking unions frequently submitted to court-ordered bans on picketing. How important picketing was to the success of a particular strike and how wounding its repression depended on several considerations: the level of organization of a particular industry in a particular locale, the skill of the labor force, and the availability and social identity of strikebreakers. The anti-union printing employers' association, the Chicago Typothetae, obtained injunctions against a 1905 printers' strike that barred all picketing and all other communication with either customers or strikebreakers—and also prohibited offering strikebreakers free transportation out of Chicago, free union membership, or money. The typographers' union by and large obeyed. They ceased picketing and stopped orchestrating boycotts or wooing strikebreakers. But neither these inhibitions nor the threatened jailing of several union officials undermined the highly skilled and thoroughly organized printers' strike. Moreover, a blanket decree against such patently sober and responsible, "conservative" trade unionists outraged liberal opinion at the same time that it stiffened the union's resolve. One by one, the majority of the Typothetae's Chicago members signed union contracts and the city's printing trade remained predominantly "closed shop," notwithstanding the illegality of closed-shop strikes.[45]

A socialist union in a less skilled and more sprawling trade, the ACW in New York, boasted a similar immunity from defeat by injunction. In 1921, more than three hundred employers refused to renew an industry-wide agreement that established joint arbitration of contract disputes. Their refusal provoked a strike, and the strike was met by several blanket injunctions barring all picketing. After several hundred arrests during the first month of the strike, the ACW decided to obey the decrees and rely solely on community and neighborhood committees, cooperative kitchens and cultural activities, work-sharing in "settled" shops, rallies, and meetings to discipline their ranks and sustain morale. The strategy worked.

45. See H. Meyers, supra Chap. 4, note 11, at 476–98.

The bosses cannot "make coats by injunction," an ACW official reminded a meeting of shop chairmen during the fifth month of the strike:

> These manufacturers, these Broadway millionaires . . . are shoving in a bundle here and a bundle there . . . but if they have become good sneaks who steal around in the night to place their orders in settled shops we have become good detectives and we have succeeded in stopping much of the work. As long as no one will go inside shops to do scab work, the injunctions can't harm us.[46]

Elsewhere, however, the ACW could not rely upon the same depth of organization or upon the strong labor and socialist culture of New York's Jewish immigrant workers. Elsewhere, it did not enjoy the same support among liberal professionals and reform politicians. The *Advance* repeatedly declared that injunction cases "threatened the life of all labor organizations." They were "gattling [sic] gun[s] on paper . . . trained on our organization."[47] The ACW filed appeal after appeal seeking to legitimate industry-wide strikes and to deprive open-shop employers of the power to use court-sanctioned public and private force against strikers.[48]

In fact, injunctions were intimately associated with employers' use of private guards as strike police. In major strikes in many industries, employers saw private police as far more reliable enforcers of the inevitable anti-strike decrees than sheriffs or municipal police. Strikers have left us numerous accounts of having been assaulted by company-hired "sluggers"[49] with copies of injunctions in their hands.[50]

46. *Advance*, Apr. 15, 1921, at 1, col. 1. The official, Abe Shiplacoff of the New York Joint Board, reported that the situation was generally favorable. Five hundred shops had settled with the ACW, and had agreed to resume collective-bargaining relations and joint arbitration of grievances and disputes. He closed his talk with an admonition that rested on familiar religious imagery: "[Y]ou can wash your hands of all kinds of dirt, but the stain of your doing scab work you can never wash off." Id.

47. "At the Hustings," *Advance*, Nov. 1, 1918, at 4, col. 1.

48. See infra pp. 118–25.

49. See Letter from A. Wharton, IAM organizer from St. Louis, Mo., reprinted in 24 *Machinists' Monthly J.* 153, 153–54 (1912) (reporting company guards' injunction-sanctioned violence).

50. See H. Blankenhorn, supra Chap. 4, note 27, at 74–75 (noting "the 'serving'

Even Reverend Frederic Seidenburg, the chairman of a Chicago Church Federation commission investigating the 1924 ladies' garment workers' strike in that city, experienced such a run-in:

> I stopped in front of one of the [manufacturing shop] buildings on the doorway of which was a copy of the injunction issued by Judge Sullivan against the Garment Workers' Union. I started to read the bill when a big husky fellow brushed up against me.
>
> In an offensive manner he pulled from one of his pockets a copy of the injunction and handed it to me saying, "If it will do you any good, here is a copy." He did not wear a uniform, so I asked him where his badge was and if he was empowered to make arrests. "Just so long as I am physically able, I can make arrests," he replied in a bullying manner. "Well," I replied, "I am somewhat physically able myself, so according to that I can make arrests too."
>
> In polite language this fellow was what you call a slugger.[51]

In mining towns the companies would print the court's writ by the thousands, and their private guards would "serve" the papers on the miners in their houses, "sometimes pleasantly, 'Sorry boys but I guess that fixes you,' sometimes unpleasantly 'Now you sons of bitches, you can walk to the mine and back home and that's all.' "[52]

In some cases, courts not only issued the writs that the company guards carried and posted but also deputized the guards. In the Harriman Line Strike of 1913, for example, the federal courts made deputy marshals of hundreds of strikebreakers and guards on the payroll of the Illinois Central. As a result, a union lawyer explained to Wilson's Commission on Industrial Relations, "the men . . . think that the Government is conferring rights that belong to it and delegating them to [labor's] opponent in the controversy and is the cause of much discontent among the men."[53]

wholesale of printed injunction papers, especially of injunctions of a six-year old dead and gone strike").

51. *New Majority*, Mar. 22, 1924, at 1, col. 1–2.

52. H. Blankenhorn, supra Chap. 4, note 27, at 30.

53. 10 *Industrial Relations*, supra Chap. 3, note 74, at 9934 (testimony of Mr. Frank Comerford, Attorney for Illinois Central System Federation). Examples of courts' de-

Outside the context of mine and railway strikes, however, courts rarely deputized private police, strikebreakers, or "sluggers"; instead, they left this task to the sheriff or police chief. This was the case in several of the large strikes in Chicago during this era.[54] In all of them, the "sluggers' " presence found a kind of legitimacy in the fact that they were enforcing courts' orders.[55] The "sluggers" were an unsavory lot, but the strikers, after all, were deemed outlaws and dangerous conspirators.[56] Police chiefs and sheriffs frequently made a private profit contracting out their public authority. They

putizing guards and strikebreakers are many. See, e.g., A. Lindsey, supra Chap. 3, note 48, at 165 ("United States marshals were granted unrestricted freedom to recruit men, and many thousands of deputies were thus sworn in as temporary law-enforcing agents"); E. Witte, supra Intro., note 9, at 116 (noting that in about a dozen cases courts have taken steps to police their injunctions); Dail-Overland Co. v. Willys-Overland, 263 F. 171, 180 (N.D. Ohio 1919) (appointing the head of company-paid private police force as court's "chief special officer to take charge of and enforce the opening and operation of said plant"), *aff'd sub nom.* Quinlivan v. Dail-Overland 274 F. 56 (6th Cir. 1921); N.Y. Trust Co. v. Amalgamated Ass'n of Street and Elec. Ry. Employees, 11 Law and Lab. 176, 176 (E.D. La. 1929) (directing appointment of deputy marshals to enforce decree); Clarkson Coal Mining Co. v. United Mine Workers, 9 Law and Lab. 290, 291 (S.D. Ohio 1927) (directing marshal "to see that this injunction is enforced . . . [and] to call to his assistance such persons, either as Deputy Marshals or otherwise . . . as he may deem necessary"); "Federal Court Intervenes," *N.Y. Times*, July 7, 1897, at 1, col. 3 ("Judge [W. H.] Taft gave an order to the United States Marshal to consult with the receivers and send to Jefferson County . . . a sufficient number of [marshals and deputies]").

54. For example, the Kellogg Company Strike of 1903, the Teamsters 1905 strike, the men's clothing industry strike in 1910, the ITU strike of 1912, and the 1917 and 1921 men's clothing industry strikes all involved such deputization. See H. Meyers, supra Chap. 4, note 11.

55. See id.

56. See, e.g., "Tells of Dark Plot," *Chicago Daily News*, July 31, 1903, at 1, col. 1 (describing pickets as "part of a deep conspiracy"); "Writ in Kellogg War," *Chicago Daily News*, July 20, 1903, at 3, col. 1 (noting that labor leaders and rank and file "anarchists of to-day have given up their old belief of explosion and in bomb throwing.").

Injunctions may have "plastered" large strikes somewhat less frequently outside Chicago. In Chicago, one of the city's machinists observed: "A strike isn't looked upon as a real strike . . . until there is an injunction against it." "Injunction against Caldwell Strikers," 16 *Machinists' Monthly J.* 42 (1904). But the mass deputizing of private guards occurred everywhere. The researchers of the 1912–1915 Commission on Industrial Relations found it in many of the era's best-known strikes. See *Final Report*, supra Chap. 2, note 33, at 73–80.

charged employers a flat fee per day for each deputy they recruited, outfitted, and provided with room and board.[57]

However, the record also yields stories of contrary sheriffs who refused to deputize company-hired guards and instead deputized strikers to police their own ranks and to keep company guards in line. These bold choices led to heated and violent jurisdictional conflicts between pro-union sheriffs and anti-union courts. The struck coal or iron company would petition the court that the sheriff's striker-deputies were violating the court's injunction. The court would deputize the company's guards, who, in turn, would arrest the sheriff's deputies—in the act of, say, accompanying a union parade—for aiding and abetting the violation of the injunction. In other cases, the company would cite the sheriff's deputies for contempt for having arrested a number of the court's company-hired deputies for brandishing guns at strikers.[58]

When the "property rights" of mine and iron-mill operators were insecure in the hands of local lawmen, the operators and owners turned to more detached state authorities. If injunctions overrode the judgment of local officials, the Pennsylvania state militia—dubbed the "Cossacks" by the state's Slovakian immigrant miners and mill hands—literally rode over the striking miner-citizens and their local sheriffs.[59] One organizer leading a struggle to unionize a Bethlehem, Pennsylvania, steel plant reported on the Cossacks' intervention:

57. Late-nineteenth- and early-twentieth-century Pennsylvania law reports contain suits by sheriffs on unpaid bills for such services. See, e.g., Clark v. Cook, 197 Pa. 643, 47 A. 851 (1901) (upholding a sheriff's right to demand compensation for such contracted services); McCandless v. Allegheny Bessemer Steel Co., 152 Pa. 139, 25 A. 579 (1893) (same).

58. See *Report on the Miners' Strike in Bituminous Coal Field in Westmoreland County, Pennsylvania in 1910–1911*, H. R. Misc. Doc. no. 97, 62d Cong., 2d Sess. 123–28 (1912). One such sheriff, John Shields, refused to jail several of his striker-deputies after they had been arrested and convicted by a justice of the peace for trespassing on company property in pursuit of company-hired deputies who had shot at strikers. The operators launched a criminal action against Sheriff Shields; he was indicted by a grand jury for malfeasance in office, and eventually sentenced to thirteen months in the state penitentiary. While Shields served his sentence, the voters of Westmoreland County elected him a county commissioner. See id.

59. See W. Foster, *The Great Steel Strike and Its Lessons* 120–33 (1920); J. Guyer, *Pennsylvania's Cossacks* (1924); B. Smith, *The State Police* 54–65 (1925).

"We all know what the injunction means during strikes, but this means injunction on horseback, riding into homes, clubbing and arresting people without the least provocation."[60]

Mother Jones probably participated in more miners' strikes between the 1890s and 1910s than any other UMW organizer. She testified to Wilson's Commission on Industrial Relations about injunction judges' critical role in harrying organizers and unleashing state violence upon striking miners.[61] When she was summoned before such judges for speaking to strikers, Mother Jones's "soft voice" and "silver hair" sometimes moved them to spare her the harsh sentences meted out to fellow organizers, and simply to "thunder" at her to leave the state. Instead, she would return to the coal fields.[62]

The United States Supreme Court first entered these distant battles in the coal fields with *Hitchman Coal & Coke Co. v. Mitchell*.[63] *Hitchman* sustained the familiar federal judicial practice by which UMW organizing was enjoined as an infringement of the operators' "property interest" in the nonunion status of their miners.[64] The protected interest arose from the "yellow-dog contracts" that nonunion or union-weary operators required miners to sign as a condition of employment.[65] One could not work in a West Virginia mine or

60. "Report of Vice-President Keppler," 22 *Machinists' Monthly J.* 344, 345 (1910).

61. See 11 *Industrial Relations*, supra Chap. 3, note 74, at 10619–45 (1916) (testimony of Mother Jones).

62. See "A Great Interest Is Being Manifested in Trial of 'Mother' Jones," *United Mine Workers' J.*, July 3, 1902, at 2, col. 1; "Judicial Iniquity," *United Mine Worker's J.*, July 31, 1902, at 4, col. 3.

63. 245 U.S. 229 (1917).

64. See id. at 260–61. This practice was, however, not universal. See Diamond Block Coal Co. v. United Mine Workers, 188 Ky. 477, 222 S.W. 1079 (1920) (dissolving a state court injunction restraining organizing on the basis of operators' right against interference with yellow-dog contracts). For reformers' criticism of the yellow-dog contract, see Ernst, "The Yellow-Dog Contract and Liberal Reform, 1917–1932" 30 *Lab. Hist.* 251 (1989).

65. Such contracts were not new. In the 1870s and 1880s they were called "iron clad" contracts, and they were among the grievances Gilded Age labor sought to remedy by legislation. See E. Beckner, supra Chap. 2, note 34, at 16–17. From the 1880s until the passage of the Norris-LaGuardia Act in 1932, virtually every anti-iron-clad or anti-yellow-dog law that was passed was struck down. See infra Appendix A, Part I(A); infra

in the nonunion mines of southwestern Pennsylvania without signing such a contract. When UMW organizers sought to enlist the restive southern miners, federal and state courts would enjoin all organizing efforts as infringements on the operators' right in the nonunion status of their employees. The redoubtable old equity lawyer Justice Pitney saw in the organizers' efforts to enlist the contract-bound miners a new incarnation of an ancient wrong, enticing away a rival's servants; in his view, "any court of equity would grant an injunction to restrain this as unfair competition."[66] By upholding the equity device in this context, *Hitchman* helped legitimate the savagery with which the mine operators policed their company towns. In *Hitchman*'s wake, scores of yellow-dog injunctions against the UMW blanketed West Virginia's coal counties and blocked all attempts to organize the state's miners.[67]

The role of *Hitchman* in local proceedings and policing in mining towns is captured in an account of the organizing strikes of 1922 in the nonunion mines of Somerset county in southwestern Pennsylvania, written for the Bureau of Industrial Research and submitted to the U.S. Coal Commission. This passage describes the first of several court proceedings during the ten-month strike, this one in the "lofty court room of Common Pleas of Somerset County":

> The barons of Somerset, sitting in a row within the rail, and the miners crowding all available seats, heard the injunction argued . . .
>
> The Consolidation case is called first, as a test; the injunctions for Berwind-White, the Hillman Coal and Coke Co., the Quemahoning and a dozen others are of one stripe.

Appendix C, §A. Until the early 1900s, the contracts were enforced by employers' unaided power to intimidate. Then, mine operators' attorneys and others discovered their expedience in injunction litigation. Used most pervasively in the nonunion coal fields, yellow-dog contracts were also used to support injunctions in the shoe- and garment-making industries. See Ernst, supra Chap. 4, note 64.

66. 245 U.S. at 259.

67. See generally W. Lane, *Civil War in West Virginia* 68 (1921); E. Witte, supra Intro., note 9, at 224. The writs barred union organizers from holding meetings, publishing information about the UMW, distributing food to miners striking for union recognition, and paying court costs for appealing evictions from company-owned houses. See, e.g., International Org., UMW v. Red Jacket Consol. Coal and Coke Co., 18 F.2d 839 (4th Cir. 1927); Gasaway v. Borderland Coal Corp., 278 F. 56 (7th Cir. 1921).

The operators' lawyer quickly divulges their case. "We intend to prove that this is a conspiracy. If outsiders get our miners to quit work *even by persuasion*, they are committing an illegal act. Especially when accompanied by meetings.

"What is the purpose of these defendants? To unionize the miners and injure our business. We have a legal right to conduct our business as we see fit, the right to run non-union mines.

"These acts of organization,—strike cards, meetings,—are unlawful acts."

The judge requests him to cite his authorities.

Counsel begins reading, "245 U.S. p. 229 Hitchman vs. Mitchell." As he reads on into the notorious magna charta of the open-shop in America, the judge asks whose opinion that is.

"Justice Holmes—no Pitney's, 1917. It proves that the union activities are illegal."

The judge tells him to read on; he wants full light on this case. At last counsel concludes and demands: "What standing have they in court when the Supreme Court of the United States says *it is unlawful* to go in and organize a non-union mine?"[68]

Relying on Hitchman and on "iron-clad" anti-union contracts both oral and written, the county court granted the injunctions. The account continues:

> [T]he fundamental legal position of the operators, the basis of their acts for a year was the United States Supreme Court decision in the Hitchman case. "Our position is exactly the same as that of the West Virginia non-union companies;" and what they wanted was injunctions like the West Virginia injunctions . . . to enforce the outlawry decreed by the Supreme Court.[69]

The UMW's court-fashioned outlawry lent a thin but hard coat of legality to the activities of Cossacks, Baldwin-Felts guards, and other public and private troops in the coal fields. Where state government forces were not so formidable or so readily available, or private armies not so readily tolerated, federal troops sometimes intervened. Between 1886 and 1930, the U.S. Army came close to

---

68. H. Blankenhorn, supra Chap. 4, note 27, at 35–36 (emphasis in original).
69. Id. at 92.

being a national police force;[70] as one professional officer described it, "[t]he army is now a gendarmery."[71] Although appeal by a state governor remained the traditional ground for federal troop intervention, the federal labor injunction became an increasingly common alternative[72] that enabled employers to circumvent governors who did not share their estimate of "disorder." In all, federal or state troops were employed in more than five hundred disputes between 1877 and 1903, or nearly once in every sixty strikes.[73]

Labor's Resort to Injunctions

Although the dominant theme of organized labor's encounters with the legal order between World War I and the New Deal was one of intolerance, occasional judicial solicitude provided a faint counter-theme. The 1920s not only witnessed the greatest number of anti-strike injunctions (roughly 2,100); they also saw a handful of injunctions issued on labor's behalf to enjoin employers from breaching collective agreements, to forbid a lockout, to protect pickets from violence by company guards, or to protect union members from discharge or blacklisting. These pro-labor decrees numbered no more than twenty-five. The vast majority of trade unionists probably remained unaware of them. Probably most of those who knew about them saw the experience as a sideshow, a happy distraction from the main drama of judicial repression. But this sideshow turned out to be a dress rehearsal for the new legal order, for New Deal labor law and policy.[74]

---

70. See Taft and Ross, supra Chap. 4, note 30, at 281–95 (discussing the role troops played in suppressing strikes, boycotts, and picketing).

71. See Hacker, "The United States Army as a National Police Force: The Federal Policing of Labor Disputes, 1877–1898," 33 *Military Aff.* 255, 260 (1969) (citation omitted).

72. See id. at 258.

73. See F. Wilson, *Federal Aid in Domestic Disturbance: 1787–1903*, at 260 and n.a. (1903).

74. See Fraser, "Dress Rehearsal for the New Deal: Shop-Floor Insurgents, Political Elites, and Industrial Democracy in the Amalgamated Clothing Workers" in *Working-Class America* 212 (M. Frisch and D. Walkowitz, eds., 1983).

It is fitting that Franklin Roosevelt's principal counselor on labor matters—and organized labor's chief representative in the New Deal administration—was Sidney Hillman. No union leader differed more sharply from Gompers and the AFL leadership in his faith in the positive uses of politics, law, and state power. Throughout the 1920s, Hillman was the socialist president of the left-wing industrial union, the Amalgamated Clothing Workers (ACW).[75] Like the International Ladies' Garment Workers' Union (ILGWU), also a socialist union organized along industrial rather than craft lines, the ACW was excluded from the AFL. These two unions spearheaded labor's resort to the injunction.

During the 1910s and 1920s, the ACW and ILGWU also went further than any other of the nation's unions in forging the kind of collective bargaining arrangements that would come to characterize "modern" labor-management relations under the 1935 National Labor Relations (Wagner) Act.[76] A vivid picture of the garment workers' "dress rehearsal" of New Deal labor policies emerges serendipitously from a legal defense mounted by the ACW in a 1920 injunction suit in Rochester, New York. Plaintiff was an "open shop" clothing manufacturer who claimed that in picketing his shop the union was prompted by no legitimate motive but rather simply sought to destroy plaintiff's business because he had fired his union workers and decided to operate on an open-shop basis.[77] The union's counsel was Felix Frankfurter. Setting out to prove that the union was "actuated by a legitimate motive of bettering the economic conditions of its members and of the trade," Frankfurter presented an ambitious Brandeisian case.[78] By conveying the history of the

75. See id. at 212.

76. 49 Stat. 449 (1935) (codified as amended at 29 U.S.C. §§151–169 (1982)).

77. See Michaels v. Hillman, 112 Misc. 395, 183 N.Y.S. 195 (1920); Coolidge, "Michael Stern and Co. vs. The Amalgamated," 110 *Nation* 759 (1920). Further, plaintiff alleged that the ACW aimed not at improving the wages and working conditions of its members but at overthrowing "private ownership." At issue for the union, then, was the legitimacy of its organizing strikes, and of its campaigns to create city-wide collective bargaining regimes in the nation's garment centers. See Chenery, "War and Peace at Rochester," *The Survey*, May 1, 1920, at 185.

78. See Chenery, supra Chap. 4, note 77, at 185. Through the "logic of social fact" and by presenting "economic exhibits" of the benefits of collective bargaining, the union's

garment industry over the previous decades, he sought to show that, until the advent of industrial unions like the ACW and the ILGWU, cutthroat competition among the trade's thousands of tiny shops had fostered economic insecurity for employers and employees alike. Both small employers and labor managers from large-scale garment manufacturers testified that the ACW had brought "law and order" to a once-chaotic industry. With the enthusiasm of converts, they described the industry-wide agreements instituted by the union: the grievance conciliation and arbitration machinery, the contract adjustment boards, the no-strike pledges, and the policing against "guerrilla warfare," the standardization of wages, and the improvements in productivity.[79]

In some places, like New York, the ACW began these sophisticated arrangements before World War I, through patient organizing, alliances with a small group of powerful retailers and far-sighted employers, and massive general strikes.[80] In others, like Rochester, union organizers were unsuccessful until the war. Then, they proceeded under the auspices of the federal War Department. Reform-minded personnel from the War Department's Board of Control of Labor Standards worked out an agreement between the ACW and most of the men's clothing manufacturers of Rochester. At the federal officials' urgings, a Labor Adjustment Board was created. Under its aegis, the business agents of Rochester's garment trades union and employers' labor managers grew so accustomed to compromise

---

defense set out to refute the archaic assumptions underlying injunctions like this one. See Soule, "The Case against the Injunction," 110 *Nation* 576 (1920).

79. See Chenery, supra Chap. 4, note 77; Soule, supra Chap. 4, note 78, at 576. These features of the Amalgamated (and ILGWU) contractual regimes made them working models of what labor law academics of the 1950s and 1960s would come to call "mature collective bargaining." See Stone, "The Post-War Paradigm in American Labor Law," 90 *Yale L. J.* 1509, 1511 (1981).

In the spring of 1920, however, the Rochester trial judge was unimpressed with this testimony and with Frankfurter's carefully prepared case. Rather than determining the nature or legality of the Amalgamated's objectives, the judge focused solely on whether the picketing had been characterized by intimidation or violence. He concluded that it had and made permanent his injunction. See Michaels v. Hillman, supra Chap. 4, note 77.

80. See Fraser, supra Chap. 4, note 74, at 221–22.

that workers would tell their business agents that they sounded like the boss, and the manufacturers complained to their labor managers, "You talk like the union."[81]

The structure and culture of the nation's garment industry made many employers uniquely open to unionization. The union brought a measure of stability. Many found that the new system, which workers embraced with much nudging and policing by the union, brought greater efficiency than the "type of Prussian discipline" that was imposed from above by the foreman and the boss.[82] Even these forces within this unique industry were not sufficient to sustain a durable, institutionalized scheme of collective bargaining without help from outside. The same intense competitiveness and dwarfish scale of production that made some turn to unionization for stability encouraged others to undercut it. Even extraordinary wartime demand for uniforms, lucrative government contracts, and a tight labor market would not have been enough to consolidate collective bargaining in garment districts like Rochester's. "[I]t was the visible hand of the government that proved decisive."[83]

When the war ended, the government's hand was withdrawn. Business leaders, from machine-making to railways to mining to garments, successfully pressed for rapid dismantling of the government's wartime industrial administrations, which had encouraged wage standardization and recognition of unions. Unions fought bitterly to maintain wartime gains.[84] Hundreds of employers, like the one who brought the Rochester suit, refused to renew contracts, and renewed instead the open-shop campaign.

81. Chenery, supra Chap. 4, note 77, at 185. Hillman and Frankfurter were well acquainted with the wartime federal government's role in encouraging this new spirit. Hillman had collaborated closely with federal personnel throughout the country. Just before the war ended, Frankfurter was appointed chair of a new War Labor Policies Board, and he, in turn, appointed Hillman to an advisory board for making recommendations on modernizing the New York clothing industry. See Fraser, supra Chap. 4, note 74, at 220.

82. See Fraser, supra Chap. 4, note 74, at 217 (quoting Meyer Jacobstein, labor manager for a large Rochester firm).

83. Id. at 219.

84. See V. Conner, *The National War Labor Board* 158–86 (1983); D. Montgomery, *Fall of the House of Labor*, supra Intro., note 8, at 392–400.

Most AFL leaders agreed with Gompers: it was not merely quixotic but dangerous to turn to the courts to fill the regulatory void created by Washington's withdrawal.[85] Gompers simply wanted the courts to leave labor alone—to abide by the injunction-curbing provisions of the Clayton Act.[86] But Hillman and his socialist and progressive counterparts in other unions were keen to keep alive the possibility of invoking law and public power on labor's behalf. A New York City judge proved receptive.

In late 1921, most of the members of an association of New York ladies' garment manufacturers had had enough of a key aspect of the garment industries' new unionized labor system. They wanted to abandon the week-work system and return to piecework. Knowing that such a revision would be unacceptable to the ILGWU, the Cloak, Suit and Skirt Manufacturers Protective Association broke with its practice of the previous several years and failed to confer with the union. Instead, the association simply adopted a resolution, "that . . . each and every member will operate his factory on the piece-work system."[87] As the association's resolution went into effect, the union declared that it violated the contract between the association and the union and called a strike. The employers' association gained a preliminary injunction against picketing.[88] A few weeks later the ILGWU's president, Benjamin Schlesinger, represented by Morris Hillquit, the International's counsel and vice-president of the Socialist Party, won a preliminary injunction enjoining the employers from conspiring to violate the collective agreement by abrogating its terms respecting weekly wages.[89] Read-

85. See, e.g., Witte, "Labor's Resort to Injunctions," 39 *Yale L. J.* 374 (1930) (noting that enthusiasm for resort to the courts was found chiefly in the left wing of the labor movement, and quoting AFL Executive Committee report to the 1922 annual convention of the Federation to condemn the use of injunctions by labor as a "snare and a delusion"); see also Gompers, "What about Injunctions? Shall We Fight Them, Use Them, or Violate Them?," 15 *Lab. Age* 15, 15–18 (1926).

86. See infra pp. 154–58.

87. Schlesinger v. Quinto, 117 Misc. 735, 744, 192 N.Y.S. 564, 568, *aff'd*, 201 A.D. 487, 194 N.Y.S. 401 (1922).

88. See *Quinto*, 117 Misc, at 745, 192 N.Y.S. at 568–69.

89. See id. at 748–49, 192 N.Y.S. at 570–71. For the union's contemporaneous account of these events, see "International Obtains Temporary Injunctions against Pro-

ing his opinion from the bench, the Manhattan trial judge recited some of the history that the Rochester judge had deemed irrelevant. The workers, he observed: "regarded [the week-work system] as a great stride forward in their struggle to raise their standard of life . . . Besides the constant disputes that arose as to what the employee should receive for a particular garment, the workers contend that the piecework system was an incentive to work with an intensity injurious to their health . . . "[90]

Turning to the question of whether the manufacturers' resolution constituted a breach of the parties' collective agreement, the judge concluded that it did. Even more important, he decided that the plaintiffs were entitled to equitable relief. The novelty of the application, declared the court, lay only "in the respect that for the first time an employees' organization is seeking to restrain their employers' organization from violating a contractual obligation."[91] But, the court ruled, "the door of a court of equity is open to employer and employee alike."[92] Some "nisi prius adjudications rendered in [labor] disputes" had, in the court's judgment, "reflected a somewhat imperfect understanding of the trials and hardships experienced by the workers in their just struggle for better living conditions."[93] This decree, the opinion implied, began to correct that flawed understanding.

In support of its opinion the court relied chiefly on "the well-known case of *Hitchman Coal & Coke Co. v. Mitchell.*"[94] *Hitchman*, as the court read it, stood for the proposition that a combination to procure a concerted breach of contract by the members of an organization like a union—or an employers' association—is an unlawful conspiracy, and all acts in furtherance of it are enjoinable.[95]

tective Association," *Justice*, Dec. 2, 1921, at 1, col. 1; and Hillquit, "Injunctions against Employers," *Justice*, Dec. 9, 1921, at 7, col. 1.

90. *Quinto,* 117 Misc. at 737, 192 N.Y.S. at 565.

91. Id. at 744, 192 N.Y.S. at 569.

92. Id.

93. Id. at 745, 192 N.Y.S. at 569.

94. Id. at 746, 192 N.Y.S. at 570. For a discussion of Hitchman, 245 U.S. 229 (1917), see supra pp. 115–17.

95. See *Quinto,* 117 Misc. at 746–47, 192 N.Y.S. at 569.

After quoting from the *Hitchman* injunction, the court dictated its own order: defendant officers of the employers' association were enjoined from "supporting, aiding or assisting [its] members . . . in any effort to abrogate the existing contract as to the week-work system or increase the labor hours in their establishments . . . [and, inter alia, from] continuing any act in furtherance of the conspiracy above set forth by means of speech, writing, meeting, or any other method."[96]

The opinion's author was Judge, later Senator, Robert Wagner, chief sponsor of the Wagner or National Labor Relations Act, the centerpiece of New Deal labor legislation and the basis of the modern law of collective bargaining and industrial relations. Upheld on appeal, [97] *Quinto* became the leading precedent relied on by unions in the forty-odd cases they brought seeking to enjoin breaches of trade agreements as well as other employer actions, such as discharges of union members, blacklisting, interference with meetings, and beatings by company guards.[98] In Detroit, a few months after *Quinto*, a trial judge denied a cigar manufacturer's petition for an anti-picketing decree against locked-out union cigarmakers protesting the manufacturer's new open-shop policies. Instead, the judge granted the union a decree directing the manufacturer to abide by the union contract he had breached.[99] Shortly after *Quinto*, a New York court upheld the validity of a counterclaim brought by the ACW seeking equitable relief against an employer's blacklisting and discriminating against union members as well as the employer's

96. *Quinto*, 117 Misc. at 749, 192 N.Y.S. at 571.

97. 201 A.D. 487, 194 N.Y.S. 401 (1922).

98. The most comprehensive inventory of injunctions sought by labor was compiled by Witte, "Labor's Resort to Injunctions," supra Chap. 4, note 85. That article includes an appendix listing all such cases located by Witte, reported and unreported, both pre- and post-*Quinto*. See id. at 380–87. *Quinto*, Witte agrees, was a turning point. See id. at 375. Before it, virtually none succeeded. After *Quinto*, in the decade preceding the New Deal, Witte's list reveals that some 15 decrees (of the 42 sought) were granted on unions' behalf. Of these, 4 were later dissolved. See id. app. at 380–87.

99. See "Refuse Injunction to Open-Shop Boss," *New Majority*, May 14, 1921, at 5, col. 3.

interference with peaceful picketing.[100] The most careful contemporary chronicler of the labor injunction, Edwin Witte, was able to locate more than a dozen such suits by labor that succeeded during the decade preceding Norris-LaGuardia and the Wagner Acts.[101]

The number of injunctions granted employers dwarfs this handful gained by unions. Still, the progressive reformers did manage to demonstrate the kinds of protections that could be written into law. Some circles cheered these accomplishments,[102] but Gompers and the councils of the AFL excoriated those labor leaders and lawyers who resorted to the injunction. They feared that pro-labor decisions like *Quinto* might lend new legitimacy to courts' curbs on labor at the very moment when "government by injunction" was coming under renewed scrutiny and attack by lawmakers.[103]

If Gompers and the AFL leaders seemed overwrought about issues of legitimacy, they had reasons. The most devastating effects of judge-made labor law were indirect. They flowed from the way that law shaped or "disfigured," in Gompers's words, the very language with which not only judges but "newspapers . . . [and] the common people" talked about the labor movement.[104] Court-drawn images

100. See *Advance*, Aug. 11, 1922, at 1, col. 4. The trial court held that the union had stated a cause of action against the plaintiff, Rogers Peet, for plaintiff's malicious arrests and violent interferences with lawful picketing, and for plaintiff's efforts to refuse employment to striking union members. See id. at 2, col. 1.

101. See Witte, "Labor's Resort to Injunctions," supra Chap. 4, note 85, at 380–87. Four of these decrees were granted under the 1926 Railway Labor Act, which served as the chief statutory precedent and model for the Wagner Act. See I. Bernstein, supra Intro., note 9., at 215–20 (1960).

102. In spite of its rarity, labor's resort to injunctions was widely noted in legal and labor journals as well as in the progressive press. See, e.g., Mason, "Labor Turns to the Injunction," 231 *N. Am. Rev.* 246 (1931). Legal reformers like Witte and progressive journals like *The Nation* and *The New Republic* applauded *Quinto. Law and Labor*, the journal of the American Anti-Boycott Association, applauded, too. *Law and Labor* pointed to the garment workers' resort to injunctions as evidence that labor, which had always spurned the courts, was finally realizing the "usefulness and wisdom of the law in the maintenance of industrial freedom." "Employers' Association Enjoined from Combining to Breach Union Contract," 4 *Law and Lab.* 35, 40 (1922).

103. See infra pp. 159–63.

104. Speech of Samuel Gompers, Labor Lyceum, Brooklyn, N.Y., Apr. 19, 1908, reproduced in AFL Records, Samuel Gompers Era, 1886–1924, microfilm reel no. 110 at 9; see also "Judge Kohlsaat's Injunction," 37 *Iron Molders' J.* 686 (1901) (arguing

and prohibitions enabled hostile employers and public officials to treat ordinary protest and mutual aid as the deeds of outlaws.[105] An injunction against picketing could vanquish a strike, but for every picket line enjoined, many more were broken up without court decrees by local officials who invoked the illegality of picketing, boycotts, organizing, and closed-shop strikes. The courts had woven a powerful web of associations between strikers' use of economic "coercion" and their use of brute physical force, between popular images of criminal conspirators and the legal construction of virtually all secondary actions as conspiracies in restraint of trade, and between picketing in any fashion and threats of violence. Thanks to these associations, anti-union employers found a resonant vocabulary in court-minted rights talk,[106] while unions' actions were dubbed "conspiracies" not only by employers and judges but also by journalists drawing on charged legal images of strikers' activities.[107] Often, trade unionists assailed by local police and company "thugs"—but with no injunction in sight—would nonetheless blame the denial of their "freedom of action . . . association . . . [and] expression"[108] on judge-made law.[109]

that court's portrayal of strikers as "thugs" shapes view of ordinary newspaper readers).

105. See, e.g., Conlon, "Strikes," 11 *Machinists' Monthly J.* 195 (1899) (complaining that injunctions "poison the minds of the public against the workmen"); Gompers, "The Essence of Labor's Contention on Injunctions," 15 *Am. Federationist* 611, (1908) ("Injunctions . . . make outlaws of men" who are innocent of any unlawful . . . act").

106. By invoking the rights of the nonunion worker, open-shop employers' associations justified anti-union intransigence. See, e.g., *Hearings on the Anti-Injunction Bill*, 58th Cong., 1st Sess. 179 (1904) (statement of Edwin Freegard, Secretary of the United Typothetae of America) ("[Y]ou must not take away from [the nonunion worker] the right of selling his labor to whom he pleases, for whatever he pleases . . ."); "Position of Rival Factions: Both Sides Make Statements," *Chicago Inter-Ocean*, April 28, 1905, at 1, col. 4.

107. See, e.g., "Labor and Equal Rights," supra Chap. 4, note 44, at 164–65 (noting that the "capitalistic press" depicts unions as outlaws); "Miners Are Indicted as Trust Heads," *United Mine Workers J.*, Dec. 4, 1913, at 1, col. 1 (quoting grand jury report depicting UMW organizers as "a menace to the peace and property and even the lives of citizens"); "Tells of Dark Plot," *Chicago Daily News*, July 31, 1903, at 1, col. 1.

108. "Labor's Bill of Rights," 32 *Machinists' Monthly J.* 43 (1920).

109. "Miner's Convention Is On," *United Mine Workers J.*, Jan. 22, 1914, at 1, col. 1.

The anti-injunction campaigns that are the subject of Chapter 5 sought to end these burdens. The AFL struggled for legislation that would raze the court-constructed barriers to peaceful collective action. At the same time, trade unionists strove to counter the law's "disfigurement" of organized labor in public discourse. Through words and deeds, they created alternative legal narratives and forged an alternative language of labor's "rights."

Strategic imperatives, but not only strategic ones, inspired these words and deeds. AFL leaders and rank-and-file members had strong claims to respectability. Enlightened politicians and employers courted them. The leaders were men of affairs, the builders and managers of major national organizations. During the Wilson era and World War I, as we have seen, they even began to find themselves ushered inside the national administration. The rank and file were skilled workers who saw themselves as proud citizens indispensable to the nation's industrial might. From this perspective, organized labor's semi-outlawry was disturbing for noninstrumental reasons. By legitimizing employers' intransigence and the heavy-handed policing of strikes, this semi-outlawry put the onus of violence and "disorder" upon trade unionists; it meant that even the most respectable trade unionist was always vulnerable to being treated like an outlaw, a "thug," or an anonymous revolutionary. The common experience of being dressed down by an injunction judge—the trial judge in *Buck's Stove* accused Gompers of "insolent . . . defiance"[110]—symbolized, in an intensely personal, galling fashion, the precariousness of trade unionists' respectability.

So, as I turn to this world of organized labor's culture and self-understanding, I should underscore that one cannot understand in purely strategic terms the thousands of editorials, speeches, and protests about judge-made law by trade unionists. Psychological stakes, as well as strategic goals, fueled labor's struggle for a secure legal status.

110. Buck's Stove and Range Co. v. A.F.L., 36 Wash. L. Rptr. 822, 842 (D.C. 1908).

5 | The Language of the Law and the Remaking of Labor's Rights Consciousness

As the AFL emerged from the calamities of the 1890s, it retreated from many of labor's earlier ambitions. Not "positive" regulation or reconstruction of industrial relations, but simply escaping the burdens of semi-outlawry, became the AFL's chief political goal from the late 1890s through the 1920s. It contested judge-made law everywhere: in the courts, but equally in the legislatures and in the public sphere.

"Labor's Whole Gospel Is Liberty of Contract"

The struggle for legitimacy led Gompers and countless others at every level of labor leadership to immerse themselves in common law doctrine, equity jurisprudence, and constitutional law. They had scant faith in litigation as a way to change the borders of legitimate collective action. But the law's social and political authority compelled speaking in the law's terms. Labor, moreover, was drawn to mining the fine radical veins of legal tradition. The result was a subtle but pervasive change in the labor movement's dominant language of protest and consciousness of rights. Legal discourse helped shape new principles and new parameters of argument; it infused new meanings into inherited ideals like "equal rights." Trade unionists also came to defend, and even to understand, specific outlawed union activities using new arguments, analogies, and metaphors inspired by the common law.

In the 1880s and early 1890s, labor leaders generally hewed to a republican outlook that held that being forced to sell one's labor conflicted with a worker's status as a citizen. They condemned the labor market of industrial capitalism as a system of "wage slavery." Citizens of a republic had to be economically "independent" and had to enjoy a rough measure of social and economic equality.[1] Their rights discourse also sprang from a republican understanding of law's chief object: not to secure private "rights" but to ensure over time the social and economic conditions for civic trust and for ordinary producer-citizens' participation in self-government.[2]

Whereas Gilded Age courts held that the Constitution often forbade legislative intervention in labor-capital relations, the Knights of Labor and other Gilded Age labor reformers appealed to legislatures and the public with the argument that the Constitution frequently *required* it. Wrote one eight-hours law advocate:

> The laws do not compel anyone to work a longer time than may be acceptable to him; but when a man is without means to subsist upon, his wants compel him to work, and he must ask for employment as a favor from someone who has the *property* required to carry on some kind of productive work. In plain language, *property is a tyrant and the people are its slaves . . .*[3]

Where once ownership of productive property had been widespread among workingmen, now a single class had "monopolized" the tools of industry. According to Gilded Age trade-union spokesmen, the emergence of industrial capitalism was not a natural outcome of technological progress but, again, the result of one class arraying against another "the powers of the world . . . all the wealth, and even the law itself."[4] Under such circumstances, it was

1. See Forbath, "Ambiguities of Free Labor," supra Chap. 1, note 8, at 801–06.

2. See id. See generally Michelman, "Possession vs. Distribution in the Constitutional Idea of Property," 72 *Iowa L. Rev.* 1319 (1987) (describing the traditional republican conception of law's basic purposes).

3. D. Montgomery, *Beyond Equality*, supra Chap. 1, note 6, at 239 (quoting *Revolution*, Dec. 24, 1868, at 395, which quotes the *Philadelphia Daily News*) (emphasis in original).

4. L. Fink, *Workingmen's Democracy*, supra Chap. 1, note 6, at 4 (quoting the Knights of Labor manifesto). Restoring workers' status as equal participants in the economy and

monstrous for courts to attack hours laws on the ground that "such legislation destroys the great right of freedom of contract."[5] In fact, in an industrial age, the Constitution as understood from labor's republican perspective "obliged" legislators to interfere to protect the sovereign citizen against the "insidious inroads of the usurping power of corporate greed."[6] Preserving a "republican form of government" now demanded "amending the work of the founders" to "engraft republican principles on property and industry."[7]

During the late 1890s, however, AFL leaders abandoned these radical republican claims upon the government. Their protests began to echo the freedom-of-contract rhetoric of liberal constitutional doctrine and late-nineteenth-century common law. Prompted by state- and court-taught lessons, they became disillusioned with the prospects for broad legislative reform and chary of the state's violent hostility to labor radicalism. In contrast to their predecessors in the Knights of Labor or the 1880s AFL, they no longer proposed to use legislation to quell the "tyranny of capital." "Labor," Gompers declared, "does not depend on legislation. It asks . . . no favors from the State. It wants to be let alone and to be allowed to exercise its rights."[8]

By the early 1900s, AFL leaders had embraced a rigid anti-statist liberalism that assailed but also resembled the philosophy of their judicial adversaries. Labor's freedom to pursue "responsible" strikes and boycotts, AFL spokesmen insisted, was secured by the

polity required a "republicanization of industry"; preserving a republican constitution demanded "workers' cooperative ownership of the factories, mines and railroads." Forbath, "Ambiguities of Free Labor," supra Chap. 1, note 8, at 808 and n142 (quoting Powderly, "Address of the Grand Master Workman," in *Proceedings of the Knights of Labor General Assembly* (1881)).

5. McNeill, "Declaration of Principles of the Knights of Labor," in *The Labor Movement: The Problem of To-day*, supra Chap. 2, note 3, at 478; see also L. Fink, *Workingmen's Democracy*, supra Chap. 1, note 6, at 7 (stating that because labor was demoted to "just another factor of production . . . the [labor] contract was not and could not be entered into freely").

6. See Forbath, "Ambiguities of Free Labor," supra Chap. 1, note 8, at 873.

7. McNeill, supra Chap. 5, note 5, at 462.

8. Gompers, "Judicial Vindication of Labor's Claims," 7 *Am. Federationist* 283, 284 (1901).

same legal principles that guaranteed their antagonists entrepreneurial freedom and liberty of contract. "The whole gospel" of the labor movement, Gompers proclaimed, "is summed up in one phrase . . . freedom of contract—organized labor not only accepts, but, insists upon, *equality of rights and of freedom*."[9]

In courts, congressional hearings, and union journals, the AFL used these terms to attack the injunction and to demand anti-injunction legislation. The closest Gilded Age analogue to the early-twentieth-century AFL's anti-injunction campaigns were the labor movement's campaigns from the 1870s to the early 1890s to reform criminal conspiracy law. The "anti-conspiracy law" campaigns, like the anti-injunction campaigns, sought to undo judicial restraints on workers' collective action. But one will search in vain for arguments inspired by common law or liberty of contract in the testimony, speeches, and writings of the Knights of Labor as they pursued "anti-conspiracy" legislation. Just as they excluded lawyers from membership,[10] so they spurned lawyerly rights talk in their protests against the wave of conspiracy prosecutions against boycotters during the 1880s. Instead, the Knights' protests and arguments typically relied on invocations of natural rights and the Declaration of Independence.[11] Another decade of increasing judicial interventions persuaded the AFL that it could not afford to ignore the language of the law.

In contrast to the Knights' protests, the AFL's common-law-inspired attacks on state repression drew in their train not only affirmations of liberty of contract but also acceptance of the naturalness of the capitalist marketplace, the inevitability of marketplace conflict, and the legitimacy of the competitive freedom enjoyed by corporations. When criticizing anti-boycott decrees, for example,

9. Gompers, "Justice Brewer on Strikes and Lawlessness," 8 *Am. Federationist* 121, 122 (1901) (emphasis in original).

10. See L. Fink, *Workingmen's Democracy*, supra Chap. 1, note 6, at 24.

11. For example, in 1886, Knights executive George McNeill had this to say about the courts' recent condemnations of boycotts: "[W]hether the exercise of the boycott is judicious or injudicious, justifiable or unjustifiable in certain instances, the innate right of man to the privilege of exercising his moral power . . . to withhold trade cannot be safely denied." McNeill, supra Chap. 5, note 5, at 489.

AFL spokesmen would insist that had the action taken by the labor organization instead been taken by manufacturers, it "might have been fairly considered a legitimate battle of trade with which a court of equity should not have interfered."[12] However, courts granted "a certain class immunity against the ordinary vicissitudes and hazards of business."[13] Not labor but capital sought special treatment from the state, in the form of judge-made exemptions from "opposing forces it would have to encounter if recognition were given to the principle of equality before the law."[14] When the courts embraced these claims on behalf of employers, the AFL argued, they betrayed their own first principles. The common law principle of competitive freedom ought to mean that capital, like labor, was obliged to seek its objectives (an open shop against a closed one, a speed-up against observing union standards) by testing its market power against labor's, not by claiming from the state special protection. "Equality of rights" demanded no less.

Trade unionists did not resort to this common law, marketplace-rights rhetoric simply for outsiders—to justify themselves to judges, legislators, or middle-class reformers. They heartily embraced the language. Thus, it came to abound in the correspondence sections of union papers. For example, the secretary of a printers' union local in Chicago relied on this form of rights rhetoric in reporting in his union's national paper on his local's 1905 battle against an aggressive open-shop drive. The local was defying a blanket injunction against all "interference" with nonunion employees. Notwithstanding that defiance, he assured the *Typographical Journal*'s readers, "[w]e are doing business strictly within the limits of the Constitution":[15]

> The right to persuasion under the promise of better conditions . . . is the present question facing the nation . . . The employer who offers more money to the employee of his competitor is in our class of lawbreakers . . .

12. *Limiting Federal Injunctions: Hearings on H.R. 23635 before a Subcommittee of the Senate Committee on the Judiciary*, 62d Cong., 2d Sess. 394 (1912) (statement of T. C. Spelling).
13. Id. at 395.
14. Id. at 396.
15. "Letter from George J. Knott," 28 *Typographical J.* 184, 186 (1906).

. . . [A] manufacturer expects to make sales by claiming his product is of better quality and cheaper in price than his competitors'. He must, according to the [employers' association and the courts] . . . , be amenable to the law because he is interfering with a competitor's business.

. . . Rivalry between unions and employers' associations is no more wrong than the same methods employed between business rivals.[16]

Thus, trade unionists uncovered the common law's contradictory commitments to competitive freedom on the one hand and security of property interests and contractual expectations on the other. Labor's arguments enjoyed a handful of judicial endorsements. Among the first was that of Justice Holmes. His famous essay "Privilege, Malice, and Intent,"[17] as well as his dissent in *Vegelahn v. Gunter*,[18] underscored the same contradiction. Holmes acidly pointed out that the common law doctrines that protected employers' businesses from union interference—rules based on security of property and contractual expectations—stood in contradiction to common law principles of competitive freedom.[19] If highlighted in labor cases as they were elsewhere, these contrary principles could readily support denying anti-strike decrees in circumstances where they were routinely granted. Recourse to these principles, therefore, could not decide cases. One had to make a policy judgment, and Justice Holmes, for one, favored extending to labor organizations much the same freedom of action that businesses enjoyed. By 1910, a small group of state and federal judges had joined Holmes in endorsing labor's equal rights in what he called the "struggle for life."[20] Greeted with fanfare

16. "Letter from George J. Knott," 27 *Typographical J.* 563, 565–66 (1905). For additional examples of labor's common-law-inspired laissez-faire rights rhetoric, see Walker, "Injunctions Writs Mock Justice," *Chicago Fed'n News*, May 16, 1925, at 1–2, col. 1, which recounts a speech by the President of the Illinois Federation of Labor; Gompers, "Judicial Vindication of Labor's Claims," supra Chap. 5, note 8; and "Working Girls Jailed by Injunction Judge," *New Majority*, Aug. 9, 1924, at 7, col. 2.

17. 8 *Harv. L. Rev.* 1, 7–9 (1894).

18. 167 Mass. 92, 44 N.E. 1077 (1896).

19. See 167 Mass. at 106–07, 44 N.E. at 1080–81.

20. See, e.g., Allis-Chalmers v. Iron Molders' Union, 150 F. 155 (C.C.E.D. Wis. 1906) (upholding the right to urge fellow union iron molders to boycott work that the strikers' employer has sent out to other foundries); Hopkins v. Oxley Stave Co., 83 F.

in AFL conferences and the labor press,[21] these opinions lent momentum to the new liberal labor outlook. Increasingly addressing labor's grievances in the courts' terms, labor's spokesmen contended for a more thoroughgoing application of the common law principle of competitive freedom.

In some important ways, then, the courts had recast the outlook of labor's national leaders. The burden of the law's antagonism made abolishing the injunction and the courts' strict limitations on collective action the AFL's top political priority.[22] By the same token, "liberty of contract" beckoned as the surest way to legitimate collective action and the trade unionism that rested on it. In this light, it is clear that Gompers's voluntarism has not been fully understood by students of American labor history. The classic studies treat it as a quintessential expression of American labor's "pragmatism" and lack of "class consciousness."[23] More recent accounts explain it as an organizational ideology that protected the AFL unions' undiluted authority over their constituents.[24] Still others explain AFL volun-

---

912, 936–38 (8th Cir. 1897) (Caldwell, J., dissenting); National Protective Ass'n of Steam Fitters v. Cumming, 170 N.Y. 315, 326, 63 N.E. 369, 371 (1902) (upholding the right to strike for closed shop by refusing to work with nonunion members, on the grounds that the union action is akin to "every day acts of the business world" protected by the "principle of competition"). Neither *Cumming* nor *Allis-Chalmers* ever became the majority view on these questions. But maverick opinions continued to appear. See, e.g., Great N. Ry. v. Brosseau, 286 F. 414 (D.C.D.N.D. 1923).

21. See, e.g., "A Just Court Decision," 15 *Am. Federationist* 76 (1908) (commending a Brooklyn appellate division decision reversing a grant of an injunction against a strike to enforce a closed shop agreement); Gompers, "Judge Holdom's Injunction Frenzy," 13 *Am. Federationist* 156, 157 (1906) (quoting the Supreme Court of Indiana upholding the right to peaceful argument and persuasion); Gompers, "Judicial Vindication of Labor's Claims," supra Chap. 5, note 8 (discussing National Protective Ass'n of Steam Fitters v. Cumming, 170 N.Y. 315, 63 N.E. 369 (1902), which upheld closed-shop strikes); Ireland, "The Attitude of Courts toward Organized Labor," 14 *Machinists' Monthly J.* 262 (1902) (detailed accounts of several state court opinions); "Judge Refuses to Block Shirt Workers' Strike," *Advance*, May 28, 1920, at 1, col. 2; "Peaceful Picketing Is Upheld in Omaha Suit against Labor Unions," *Advance*, Nov. 2, 1917, at 8, col. 1.

22. See M. Karson, *American Labor Unions and Politics* 42–73 (1958); W. E. Walling, *American Labor and Democracy* 20 (1926); E. Witte, supra Intro., note 9, at 124.

23. See S. Perlman, *A Theory of the Labor Movement*, supra Intro., note 4.

24. The leading version of this view is Rogin, "Voluntarism: The Political Functions of an Anti-Political Doctrine," 13 *Am. J. Pol. Sci.* 234 (1969).

tarism as a rigid expression of Gompers's antagonism toward his socialist foes within and without the AFL.[25] All these views ignore the extent to which AFL voluntarism and advocacy of a collective lassez-faire policy for labor were a constrained but canny response to the inescapable power of the courts and common law over labor's fortunes. The voluntarism of the AFL in the Gompers era expressed the deep disillusionment with reform by legislation that resulted from labor's experiences with the legal order. Ironically, it also recast the labor movement's inherited "equal rights" ideology in the common law's classical liberal mold.

Labor's Constitution

From the 1890s to the 1920s, labor's spokesmen painstakingly criticized countless judicial opinions. At the same time, they forged an alternative legal language. Like the dominant legal language, it rested on premises that ratified many of industry's asymmetries of power. That was its hegemonic aspect: in adopting legal and constitutional rhetoric, AFL leaders abandoned more radical ways of describing and criticizing the nation's political economy. They entered a discourse in which the legitimacy of corporations' power over economic life was not "dangerously questioned."[26] However, legal and, particularly, constitutional rhetoric also contained recessive radical strains and possibilities.

Labor's laissez-faire legal arguments hinged on analogies between unions' strikes and boycotts against employers and competitive tactics used between business rivals. The analogies were persuasive only insofar as workers' collective action enjoyed the same presumption of legitimacy and social worth that the law accorded the

25. See S. Kaufman, supra Chap. 1, note 16, at 190–213; B. Mandel, *Samuel Gompers* 197–98 (1963). See generally J. Green, supra Chap. 2, note 90, at 77–80 (discussing the growth of the Socialist Party after 1910).

26. See E. Genovese, *Roll, Jordan, Roll* 25–28 (1974); see also W. Adamson, *Hegemony and Revolution: A Study of Antonio Gramsci's Political and Cultural Theory* 140–47, 170–79 (1980); Lears, "The Concept of Cultural Hegemony: Problems and Possibilities," 90 *Am. Hist. Rev.* 567 (1985).

collectivization of capital in business enterprises.[27] Almost nothing in the dominant discourse supported such a presumption.[28] The "right of free labor," as the courts construed workers' liberty of contract, was a relentlessly individualistic doctrine.[29] In what legal terms, then, might trade union spokesmen justify extending the individual worker's marketplace liberty to strikers and the collective activities of organized labor? The answer lay in two other strands of labor jurisprudence. In addition to collectivizing the principles of liberty of contract and competitive freedom, labor also drew on the first and thirteenth amendments.

The language of the antislavery movement and the thirteenth amendment lent special constitutional import to labor's attacks on coercive judicial deeds and doctrines. This language also expressed the view that the dignity and independence of free labor were inscribed in the Constitution. Labor spokesmen attacked the "feudal" or "slavish" tenor of the doctrine that employers had a property right in their contracts with workers or in the expectation that their workers would return each day to toil in the employers' plants.[30] They also attacked the anti-strike decree itself as an indirect way of enslaving strikers, a "judicial reenactment of slavery."[31]

27. On the legitimation of the collectivization of capital in corporations in the late nineteenth and early twentieth centuries, see J. W. Hurst, *The Legitimacy of the Business Corporation in the Law of the United States, 1780–1970*, at 58–73 (1970). See also Horwitz, "*Santa Clara* Revisited: The Development of Corporate Theory," 88 *W. Va. L. Rev.* 173, 179–86 (1985) (tracing the conceptualization of the corporation in the late nineteenth century).

28. See C. Tomlins, supra Intro., note 9, at 60, 61–68; Hovenkamp, supra Chap. 3, note 2, at 925–32.

29. See Forbath, "Ambiguities of Free Labor," supra Chap. 1, note 8, at 773–79.

30. See, e.g., *United Mine Workers' J.*, Sept. 9, 1897, at 4, col. 1. The UMW journal editorial page proclaimed, "The chattels slave was ordered by his master to work . . . The wage slave receives his orders just the same, the only difference being instead of a master the federal judge gives him his orders . . ." Id.; see also Howerth, "The Kingdom of God and Modern Industry," 14 *Am. Federationist* 541, 542–43 (1907). On the medieval origins of these doctrines, which still bore the imprint of precapitalist masters' property in their servants, see R. Steinfeld, supra Chap. 3, note 107, at 216–38.

31. See, e.g., Gompers, "Government by Injunction," 4 *Am. Federationist* 82 (1897); Gompers, "Taft, the Injunction Standard Bearer," 14 *Am. Federationist* 785, 788 (1907) ("It is an indirect assertion of a property right in men . . ."); "To a Federal Judge,"

According to Gompers, the employment relation was "a personal not property relation"; no property rights but merely "personal liberties or privileges" inhered in it.[32] In support, Gompers resorted to constitutional history:

> The civil war was a protest against the sacred rights of property of man in man as enunciated by the Supreme Court of the United States in the Dred-Scott decision. So . . . we find the movement of the workers . . . in formidable protest against a reaction as represented by the dominant power of wealth and as expressed through the judiciary . . .
>
> . . . [The courts] are endeavoring to retake from the masses the rights that have been dearly bought, secured and guaranteed.[33]

The idea that the thirteenth amendment was a "glorious labor amendment" that enshrined not only self-ownership but also labor's dignity and independence animated countless anti-injunction speeches and pamphlets.[34] However, the AFL did not invent this idea. The Reconstruction era congressmen who championed the amendment constantly spoke of it as a charter for Free Labor.[35] The thirteenth amendment, they declared, stood as a repudiation of the doctrine that "capital" may "own Labor" or reduce it to a "mere

13 *United Mine Workers' J.*, Aug. 7, 1902, at 3, col. 3 (poem deriding judges' use of anti-strike decrees to "drive [workers] back to slav'ry days again").

32. Gompers, "Judicial Invasion of Guaranteed Rights," 17 *Am. Federationist* 297, 299 (1910) [hereinafter Gompers, "Judicial Invasion"]. The AFL's arguments anticipated the Realist critique of labor law's transmuting privileges into rights. See, e.g., Cook, "Privileges of Labor Unions in the Struggle for Life," 27 *Yale L. J.* 779, 786–801 (1917) (criticizing the judicial reasoning of early-twentieth-century Supreme Court cases limiting the rights of labor to unionize). T. C. Spelling seems to have first elaborated this Hohfeldian style of criticism of the labor injunction. See T. C. Spelling and J. Lewis, supra Chap. 3, note 85, §§110–126, at 224–82.

33. Gompers, "Judicial Invasion," supra Chap. 5, note 32, at 297–98.

34. See V. Olander, "The Constitution, the Free Man, and the Slave" (radio talk), reprinted in *Ill. State Fed'n Lab. Newsl.*, May 30, 1925, at 5, col. 1–3; see also Furuseth, "No Property Rights in Man: The Essential Principle of Protest against Injunctions in Labor Disputes," 13 *Am. Federationist* 310, 313 (1906) ("[The typical injunction violates the] fundamental principle of American law . . . that there shall be no property rights in man").

35. See Forbath, "Ambiguities of Free Labor," supra Chap. 1, note 8, at 778.

tool.''[36] They vowed that the amendment would forever protect against the degradation or coercion of "free labor" "both black and white.''[37] These associations swiftly flowed into the labor movement's rhetorical resources, but it remained to link the thirteenth amendment with labor's "right to strike."

Victor Olander, president of the powerful Illinois Federation of Labor, forged that link most carefully. The "vital case" for Olander was *Bailey v. Alabama*,[38] which struck down an Alabama statute that provided criminal sanctions for breach of a labor contract paid in advance. "What the State may not do directly [apply its coercive arm to hold laborers to their toil]," the *Bailey* court reasoned, "it may not do indirectly.''[39] The fact that the thirteenth amendment's framers' expressly hoped to avert debt peonage against southern blacks was significant for the court. The court's condemnation of indirect state compulsion was significant for Olander and other labor jurists. "The slave is a slave because he is by law prevented from leaving the service of those for whom he works," Olander explained in a radio address.

> He may not withhold his labor. He is not permitted to consult freely with his associates. And if he joins with others of his kind for the purpose of securing a proper return for his labor, he is guilty of rebellion. When an injunction judge issues a restraining order, obedience to which has the effect of restraining men from exercising their constitutional rights in a manner calculated to improve the[ir] condition[] . . . , he is . . . compelling them to accept the shameful garb of slaves.[40]

A black trade unionist also built upon *Bailey*. "Let us call your attention to the Thirteenth Amendment," his anti-injunction "Mem-

36. See Vandervelde, "The Labor Vision of the Thirteenth Amendment" 138 *U. Pa. L. Rev.* 437 (1989) (detailing Civil War and Reconstruction-era congressmen's understanding of the amendment).

37. Id. A strong case can be made that many of these congressmen saw the amendment as protecting against a broader range of economic coercions than the physical compulsion of slavery. See id.

38. 219 U.S. 219 (1911).

39. Id. at 244.

40. V. Olander, supra Chap. 5, note 34, at 5, col. 1.

orial" began; "[i]t grew out of the suffering of our race." "It is idle," he continued, "to say that because the injunctions do not directly compel men to work that they therefore do not tend to interfere with freedom."[41]

> In [*Bailey v. Alabama*] . . . the Supreme Court of the United States [condemned a labor contract law] the purpose of which was to, by indirect pressure, hold men to their jobs; [the court declared that] "what the state may not do directly, it may not do indirectly." By indirection, in many instances throughout the State of Illinois, men have been forced to return to work through injunctions which have broken their [strikes].[42]

Entwined with the AFL's thirteenth amendment critique of the labor injunction was its invocation of the first amendment. Like the other elements of labor's jurisprudence, this one emerged in fragments, on the run. The deepening involvement of the late-nineteenth-century courts in the repression of strikes spawned a sense of constitutional crisis in the labor movement. The legal order itself, and not merely hostile state officials, seemed to be allying itself with corporate greed. "Constitutional liberty has been bludgeoned to death," declared Eugene Debs in 1897 in support of the UMW's call for a national labor conference to protest government by injunction:

> and labor [has been] bound and gagged for the perpetual exploitation of corporate capital. There is no relief in the courts . . . From the justice of the peace to the justice of the supreme court the injunction has full sway. [C]itizens are forbidden to open their lips and walk on public highways. Sheriffs, marshalls and other petty officers . . . shoot and club workingmen if they are not servile and obedient . . . [43]

41. "Injunction Interferes with Freedom," *Chicago Fed'n News*, June 6, 1925, at 2.
42. Id.
43. "Debs Joins St. Louis Call," *J. Knights Lab.*, Aug. 26, 1897, at 1, col. 5. The same front page of the Knights' journal carried the conference call issued by the UMW's Executive Board. The call declared that the "present great miners' strike . . . is no longer a mere struggle between employe [*sic*] and employer." The judiciary's involvement has transformed the "struggle [into one] between tyrannical courts and the whole people" for the preservation of constitutional rights. Nat'l Exec. Bd., United Mine Workers of America, "A Circular! To Organized Labor, Its Various Divisions, Subdivisions, and to

As far as the labor movement was concerned, the courts' definition of "property rights" swallowed up the first amendment. Injunctions against peaceable persuasion, meetings, publications, parades, and picketing stripped workers of their rights as citizens solely because they were an enterprise's labor supply. Decrees against these activities prompted invocations of the first amendment and its republican roots. When the Pennsylvania Supreme Court, for example, affirmed a lower court decree restraining the officers and members of a machinists union for " 'interfering' with the business and apprentices of a certain employer,''[44] the *American Federationist* queried, "What did the officers of the union do? How did they injure the business of the employer?''[45] The AFL journal recited the plaintiff employer's allegations: the plaintiff exacted from each of his workers an oral promise not to join any union. The defendants were charged with "endeavoring to entice" these workers to breach their "covenants" with plaintiff, and thus posing a threat of ruin to his business.[46] Why was the defendants' conduct unlawful? "No coercion or force was used . . . ''[47] The affidavits relied on by the trial court revealed "no evidence that means other than moral suasion and argument had been employed. Has not a man a right to induce another to violate an agreement ignorantly and foolishly made?''[48] The courts of Pennsylvania had issued and "affirmed an injunction against men whose only 'offense' was the promotion of self-help and legitimate combination among wage-workers!''[49] So doing, courts like Pennsylvania's denied to workers and trade unionists rights "which every other citizen enjoys—to counsel, to communicate . . . Their protest, their uniting peaceably to redress a wrong, have been destroyed.''[50]

All Reform, Social, Educational, and Scientific Bodies, Who Condemn Government by Injunction and the Use of Force to Coerce the People and Deprive Them of Their Rights as American Citizens," *J. Knights Lab.*, Aug. 26, 1897, at 1, col. 1–2.

44. "More Abuse of the Injunction," 8 *Am. Federationist* 216, 217 (1901).

45. Id.

46. See id.

47. Id.

48. Id.

49. Id.

50. "Anti-Injunction Bill," 7 *Am. Federationist* 101 (1900) (reprinting Gompers's testimony to the House Judiciary Committee on a 1900 anti-injunction bill). Other ex-

However slight a feature of the courts' constitutional vision, the first amendment had long stood for the sanctity of the republican notion of public liberty in the political culture of protest and reform. It signified citizenly association, mutual counsel and deliberation, protest and uniting peaceably to redress wrongs.[51] Courts construed the communicative activities associated with union organizing and labor protest as coercive interferences with employers' property rights and with nonunion workers' liberty of contract.[52] This construction made legal repression of labor protest unproblematic. In adopting it, however, the courts spurned that alternate tradition which held these communicative activities to be the very essence of republican freedom. By linking labor protest with this alternative tradition, labor leaders could argue that the courts were violently one-sided—not only in their treatment of labor versus capital but also in their treatment of the Constitution.[53]

Slowly, a growing portion of the nation's political elite would come to share labor's sense of constitutional crisis. By the 1920s, senators and congressmen frequently complained that the courts had defined the rights of property so as to threaten workers' constitutional freedoms and to erode the first and thirteenth amendments.[54]

A Great Popular Defiance

Alternative constitutional interpretations can be left in the margins. Large numbers of people committed to those interpretations in the

amples of labor leaders' and rank-and-file trade unionists' appeals to the first amendment in their protests against labor injunctions are Gompers, "Van Cleave Seeks Injunction against A. F. of L.," 14 *Am. Federationist* 784, 785 (1907); "Letter to the Editor: Resolutions Adopted by Sparks, Nevada, Local," 21 *Machinists' Monthly J.* 553, 554 (1909); and "Judge Wallops Painters," *New Majority*, Apr. 26, 1924, at 5, col. 3.

51. See, e.g., J. Smith, *Freedom's Fetters* 136–43, 428–31 (1956).

52. Even those jurists who led the way in defending workers' right to strike held out no significant legal toleration, let alone constitutional protection, for labor protest activity. See, e.g., American Steel Foundries v. Tri-City Cent. Trades Council, 257 U.S. 184, 204, 206–07 (1921) (Taft, C.J.) (holding that in order to limit "interference" with others at the entrance and exit of petitioner's plant, picketers could station only one representative at each point); Arthur v. Oakes, 63 F. 310, 329 (7th Cir. 1894) (Harlan, J.).

53. For further examples, see infra pp. 160–161.

54. See infra pp. 159–61.

face of state violence and prison terms are harder to ignore. Sometimes, only the latter kind of tenacity can test and undermine the
political elite's commitment to an existing order. From the 1900s
through the 1920s, a widening campaign of massive and articulate
defiance of the courts helped the labor movement win support for
its exiled constitutional claims.[55]

Such defiance proved potent for two reasons. First, defiance provoked repression, and repression disturbed the consciences of lawmakers and reformers in ways that a less visibly coercive regime
could not. Secondly, increasing defiance of increasingly frequent
injunctions made sustained legal and constitutional arguments and
protests an ever more common accompaniment of strikers' arrests.
Such protests demonstrated that workers found the judge-made rules
of the game not merely inconvenient but illegitimate. Lawmakers

55. Mass protests accompanied this campaign. In Denver, for example, to protest an
equity judge's jailing of sixteen miners for one-year sentences, the city's trade unions
mounted a "monster" march on the state capitol building. "We had more than 19,000
people in the parade . . . six bands and more than 200 banners," an organizer reported.
The banners bore such inscriptions as "We do not believe in judge-made laws," "Who's
afraid?," "O justice, what crimes are committed in thy name," "Liberty is in the air,
and insurgency is in the saddle," and "Government by injunction must go." "Report
of Benjamin F. Perry from Denver, Colorado," 23 *Machinists' Monthly J.* 269 (1911).
Mass protest meetings and rallies were also frequent. See, e.g., "Labor Day at Jamestown," 20 *Machinists' Monthly J.* 56 (1908) (reporting Gompers's speech in defiance of
an anti-boycott decree at a Labor Day rally); "Shall Judge-Made Law Prevail?," 19
Machinists' Monthly J. 545, 550 (1907) (describing "mass meetings . . . all over the
country at which organized labor is discussing [the recent injunction] . . . decision");
"Garden Meeting Thunders Anti-Injunction Protest," *Justice*, Sept. 24, 1926, at 1
("Speakers denounce . . . attempt to crush Cloak strike by judge-made law—[union]
President Sigonan . . . [and] Congressman LaGuardia . . . address[ ] 20,000 strikers in
Great Arena—Labor movement pledges uncompromising resistance . . ."); "Mass Meeting to Greet Our 'Prisoners' ," *Justice*, Jan. 20, 1920, at 1 (noting a mass meeting
honoring garment workers released from prison after serving sentences for violation of
injunction). For a provocative discussion of the relation between alternative legal interpretations and readiness to confront state violence, see Cover, "Violence and the Word,"
95 *Yale L. J.* 1601 (1986). Cover also developed the notion of a social movement creating
"exiled constitutional narratives" to describe how the civil rights movement used civil
disobedience. See Cover, "*Nomos* and Narrative," supra Chap. 3, note 22, at 47. The
early-twentieth-century labor movement's anti-injunction battles constitute a major but
neglected chapter in the history of civil disobedience in America.

and reformers laid at the courthouse door a growing part of the blame for the ungovernability of the American industrial order.[56]

The message that defiance of labor injunctions was justified was implicit in the constitutional critiques of Gompers and others, and principled disobedience to injunctions was official AFL policy from the late 1890s until the passage of Norris-LaGuardia and beyond. AFL national leaders first publicly defied an injunction in 1897 when Gompers joined Mother Jones and John Mitchell of the UMW, James Sovereign of the Knights, and Eugene Debs in speaking at scores of enjoined rallies and meetings in support of an enjoined West Virginia miners' strike.[57] The AFL was not alone in its official policy of defiance. Among the principles of the IWW was this: "Strikers are to disobey and treat with contempt all judicial injunctions."[58] Confronted by a commissioner of the federal Commission on Industrial Relations in 1913, IWW leader Bill Haywood responded, "Well I have been plastered up with injunctions until I do not need a suit of clothes, and I have treated them with contempt."[59]

Sober business unionists like Gompers and Mitchell would join picket lines or speak at assemblies in defiance of omnibus anti-strike decrees.[60] "Contempt of court," Gompers proclaimed, was "obe-

---

56. See infra p. 59.

57. See 2 S. Gompers, *Seventy Years*, supra Intro., note 7, at 198–205; "Injunctions Unrespected: As a Factor in Strikes They Must Go," 4 *Am. Federationist* 159 (1897). The same year, Andrew Furuseth urged that defiance of injunctions should be official AFL policy. See R. Harvey, *Samuel Gompers* 65–66 (1936). On Furuseth's role in the anti-injunction movement, see infra pp. 154–56. At the 1908 AFL Convention, Furuseth proposed a duty to go to prison rather than acquiesce to unconstitutional decrees, and the proposal was adopted the following year. See Am. Fed'n Lab., *Report of the Proceedings of the Twenty-Ninth Annual Convention* 311–14 (1909); Am. Fed'n Lab., *Report of the Proceedings of the Twenty-Eighth Annual Convention* 219–22 (1908).

58. 11 *Industrial Relations*, supra Chap. 3, note 74, at 10578 (1916).

59. Id. at 10580. Like the IWW, the AFL's socialists closed ranks with Gompers on this question. After Gompers was sentenced to a year in jail for violating the *Buck's Stove* injunction, the socialists withdrew their candidate for the Federation presidency and declined to challenge Gompers's reelection. See J. Weinstein, *The Decline of Socialism in America, 1912–1925*, at 38 (1967).

60. In 1903 Mitchell wrote: "[W]hen an injunction . . . forbids the doing of a thing which is lawful, I believe that it is the duty of all patriotic and law-abiding citizens to resist . . . It is better that half of the workingmen of the country remain constantly in

dience to law."[61] This philosophy was echoed by local union leaders and rank-and-file strikers. In Chicago in the winter of 1905, for example, the head of the city's Woodworkers' Union counseled a mass meeting of striking printers: "Defy the law. Judge-made law is not good law."[62] A labor leader in Milwaukee told President Wilson's Industrial Commission that he distinguished sharply between the law and what injunction judges said. He always advised strikers, "if you're sure you're right, if you're convinced of judicial invasion of your rights, stand for your rights and take the consequences."[63] Strikers did so, some in high spirits,[64] others dreading the prison cell.[65]

When two streetcar-workers organizers were jailed for speaking in defiance of a federal injunction and the strikers' morale ebbed in

jail than that trial by jury and other inalienable and constitutional rights . . . be . . . nullified." J. Mitchell, *Organized Labor* 336 (1903). In the same vein, a Colorado miner, referring to an enjoined strike in that state, wrote that "they may arrest . . . all the . . . leaders that are in Colorado, but we have hundreds more, and we are bound to win." "Our Strike in Colorado," *United Mine Workers J.*, Dec. 18, 1913, at 1, col. 1; see also "Labor Day at Jamestown, Letter to Editor by Secretary of I.A.M. Local No. 441, Portsmouth, Virginia," 20 *Machinists' Monthly J.* 56, 56–57 (1908) (discussing Gompers's speech at a rally in defiance of an anti-boycott decree, and adding, "We say bravo to Mr. Gompers . . . Mr. Gompers [should] pay no attention [to the decree] so that the worst may happen and workingmen then be aroused as to the seriousness of this injunction curse").

61. *Pamphlets in American History*, Microfiche L69(I) (1969).

62. "Would Curb Judges' Power—Unionists Also Urge Compositors to Ignore Holdom's Injunction," *Chicago Daily News*, Nov. 6, 1905, at 1, col. 3.

63. 11 *Industrial Relations*, supra Chap. 3, note 74, at 10683. Along with "taking the consequences," some took other steps along the path of civil disobedience and nonviolent protest we associate with other, later movements. Women garment workers picketing in defiance of an anti-strike decree started a "hunger strike club," pledging "to refuse food and drink if put in jail for disobeying the court order." See "Girls on Strike Ignore Two Judges," *Chicago Herald*, Feb. 20, 1917, at 5, col. 2.

64. See, e.g., "44 Chicago Dress Strike Pickets Begin Serving Prison Terms," *Justice*, June 18, 1926, at 1–2, cols. 2–3 (reporting that 25 Chicago dressmakers marched to the sheriff's office to "give up in a body," "dressed in bright frocks and with bunches of flowers," vowing "to defy Judge Sullivan's injunction . . . again" when released from jail).

65. See, e.g., "Contempt of Court or Contempt for a Vicious System?" *Ladies' Garment Worker*, June 1912, at 1, 6 ("[F]our of the [striking corset workers in Kalamazoo] broke down nervously as the confinement next to common drunks, insane patients, and other prisoners . . . proved too great a strain").

the face of a judicial warning that they were all knocking on the penitentiary door, John Frey of the Machinists reminded them:

> We are not without our sacred precedents.
> When judicial decisions held that the colored man was a chattel to be bought and sold . . . when he was looked upon as an article of commerce and a commodity, it was the clergymen of this state who organized the underground railway. It was the clergymen and their congregations . . . who defied the decision of the United States Supreme Court and held that every human being was free and that they would do all in their power to avoid and evade the decisions of the highest judicial tribunal.[66]

So, in addition to the worker's constitutional right to "come and go at will," the anti-slavery movement supplied the AFL with precedent for other claims: that official legality could be counterfeit, that it could be opposed by a truer understanding of the law, and that such an understanding could sanction disobedience.

It is hard to imagine that more than a handful of the thousands of workers who violated court decrees from the 1890s onward regarded themselves as the sort of disenfranchised proletariat that takes its outlaw status for granted. Like their national leaders, the rank and file of the anti-injunction movement found in the antinomian constitutionalism bequeathed by the anti-slavery movement a language for expressing the rightness and "Americanness" of defying "unjust law":

> I was brought before the Hon. Judge Wright, of the United States Circuit Court at Danville, Ill. . . . on a charge of contempt of court. When he sentenced me he said that I had committed no crime. "There was nobody hurt, nobody robbed . . . nor nobody insulted. All there was to it was a little talk and very little of that. So I sentence you to 30 days in the Vermillion County jail . . . " I had told a boarding house lady, a neighbor of mine, not to board the I.C. [Illinois Central] strikebreakers. That was the first time in my life that I ever was arrested. And I am not ashamed of that arrest. I did not strike against the [railroad]. I was forced to quit their services or denounce the

66. Frey, "Yellow Dog Contracts and Contempt Charges," *Ill. State Fed'n Lab. Weekly Newsl.*, Aug. 14, 1926, at 1, col. 2.

liberty of my fellow men that our forefathers shed their blood to give
to us. I love the [railroad] . . . But I would rather suffer 10 times
what I have rather than stand up and see the . . . railroad managers
pick the stars off Old Glory . . . [67]

That is how a midwestern railway shopman explained his violation
of a federal injunction during the 1913–1915 strike against Harriman
lines. Injunctions also blanketed an 1897 strike in western Pennsylvania's bituminous coal fields.[68] The decrees forbade the striking
miners to assemble or march "in proximity" of the mines, but the
strikers defied the orders.[69] At the height of the strike, some one
thousand strikers, Polish, Italian, and Hungarian immigrants,
marched with an American flag at their head, toward the mines of
Hazleton, hoping to call out their fellow miners there.[70] Along the
"dusty highway," the marchers were stopped by a courier with
news that the Hazleton police force awaited them. According to one
contemporary report, the miners hesitated, and their Italian leader
paused to consider the issue.

> The leader thought. He slowly raised his head and with a voice steady
> as the earth on which he stood, exclaimed: "I gotta the right! I am a
> American citizen. I have my papers. They cannot stoppa us. For-
> ward!" He pulled his naturalization papers from his pocket and
> wave[d] [them] aloft.
> The army revived. Enough! They were protected . . . [71]

They marched triumphantly through the city and closed down a mine
on the other side.[72] In New York, a Polish garment worker wrote
in Yiddish in *Justice*, the ILGWU's paper, "The union protects us
workers against capitalism and the Constitution protects the

67. 10 *Industrial Relations*, supra Chap. 3, note 74, at 9932–33.
68. See Kuritz, "The Labor Injunction in Pennsylvania, 1891–1931," 29 *Pa. Hist.*
306, 312–13 (1962).
69. See id. at 313.
70. See V. Greene, *The Slavic Community on Strike: Immigrant Labor in Pennsylvania
Anthracite* 132–34 (1968) (citing a contemporary account in the *Wilkes-Barre Times*,
Sept. 4, 1897, at 1).
71. Id. at 135.
72. See id. at 136.

union.''[73] In Duluth, Minnesota, a trade unionist defied an anti-boycott decree to show he was a citizen and not a ''social cipher.''[74]

Anti-Injunction Laws before Norris-LaGuardia

From the beginning, defiance seemed essential, but defiance was always costly. Losing consistently in the courts, labor swiftly turned to the legislatures. From the 1890s through the 1920s trade unionists brought their anti-injunction arguments and stories about ''government by injunction'' to the legislatures. Building on their alternative readings of the common law and the Constitution, labor strove to justify a regime of collective laissez-faire. Organized workers, they argued, were freely associating citizens who ought to enjoy the same freedoms of action and expression that individual workers and citizens enjoyed. To grant them such freedoms was to grant them no more than what ''combinations of capital'' enjoyed as legal persons.[75] Individual workers were powerless in the face of corporate employers; ''true liberty of contract'' required robust trade unions unfettered by an archaic common law of labor relations.

AFL efforts to enlist the legislatures to curb the courts bore fruit even before Congress passed the Clayton Act in 1914. The AFL's model of industrial self-government won favor partly because it harmonized with a more general voluntarist approach toward social reform. In Gompers's hands, the AFL model was a labor version of the kind of business-based associationalism that elite reformers like Herbert Hoover and organizations like the National Civic Federation advocated during the first decades of the new century.[76] In

73. *Justice*, June 8, 1921, at 12.

74. R. Valelly, *Radicalism in the States: The Minnesota Farmer-Labor Party and the American Political Economy* 82 (1989).

75. Cf. *Limiting Federal Injunctions: Hearings on H. R. 23635 before the Subcommittee of the Senate Committee on the Judiciary*, 62d Cong., 2d Sess. 395–96 (1912) (statement of T. C. Spelling).

76. See V. Conner, supra Chap. 4, note 84, at 3–17; M. Green, *The National Civic Federation and the American Labor Movement* 37–89 (1956); B. Ramirez, *When Workers Fight* 66–82 (1978); R. Wiebe, *Business and Reform: A Study of the Progressive Movement* 159–69 (1962); Hawley, ''Three Facets of Hooverian Associationalism: Lumber,

its more democratic variations, the reform ideal also tapped a broad nineteenth-century tradition of anti-statism, self-help, and mutual aid as approaches to social reform.[77] In addition, the growing membership and lobbying capacities of some state federations of labor during the early 1900s encouraged legislative support for anti-injunction measures.[78] So too did the imperial posture of federal and state injunction judges. Congress and state legislatures alike had their popular constitutionalists and civil libertarians, and they were outraged when "government by injunction" undermined trial by jury and trampled on the first amendment.[79]

However, the obstacles facing labor's anti-injunction bills were formidable. The bills' chief adversaries—the National Association of Manufacturers, the American Anti-Boycott Association, and the scores of industry-based employers' associations—were usually more tightly organized and better-heeled than the bills' proponents.[80] The violent tenor of labor conflict also disturbed lawmakers. Labor's advocates and progressive reformers argued that most labor violence originated in employers' intransigence in the face of unions, in the public and private repression that greeted labor protest, and in the legal order's encouragement of this state of affairs. Moreover, they argued, although legal toleration of peaceful labor protest and organizing would strengthen conservative and responsible trade unionism, court-constructed semi-outlawry bred irresponsible and violent

Aviation, and Movies, 1921–1930,'' in *Regulation in Perspective* 95 (T. McCraw, ed., 1981).

77. See C. McWilliams, *The Idea of Fraternity in America* 542–43 (1973); N. Ware, *The Labor Movement in the United States, 1860–1895*, at 320–33 (1929); see also D. DeLeon, *The American as Anarchist: Reflections on Indigenous Radicalism* (1978).

78. See M. Kazin, *Barons of Labor: The San Francisco Building Trades and Union Power in the Progressive Era* (1987); E. Staley, supra Chap. 2, note 32, at 230–37.

79. See "Labor Secures Test Vote," *Ill. State Fed'n Lab. Weekly Newsl.*, Apr. 4, 1925, at 1, col. 1.

80. On the NAM's activities, see *U.S. House of Representatives, Charges against Members of the House and Lobby Activities of the National Association of Manufacturers of the United States and Others before the Select Committee on Lobby Investigations*, 63rd Cong., 1st Sess. (1913); see also C. Bonnett, supra Chap. 3, note 12, at 309–15; E. Staley, supra Chap. 2, note 32, at 353–60; R. Zieger, *Republicans and Labor, 1919–1929*, at 72–73 (1969).

elements within the labor movement.[81] But politicians often failed to take full account of this argument, allowing judicial intemperance, political considerations,[82] and perhaps the judiciary's view of the stakes of lessening restrictions to cloud their views.[83] Notwithstanding these obstacles, organized labor won more than fifty anti-injunction laws from state legislatures during the first two decades of the century.[84]

Labor's first state and federal anti-injunction bills appeared in the late 1890s and early 1900s. At the state level, some bills tracked labor's earlier efforts to draw the sting from criminal conspiracy doctrine by focusing now on the doctrine of *civil* conspiracy.[85] Others sought to exempt unions from antitrust or restraint of trade doctrines.[86] In Congress, several early bills sought both objectives.[87]

81. See, e.g., J. Fitch, *The Causes of Industrial Unrest* 324–33 (1924); J. Hardman, *American Labor Dynamics* 349–56 (1928); *Final Report*, supra Chap. 2, note 33, at 38–79; *Civil Liberties in the Coal Fields*, supra Chap. 4, note 36, at 175–80.

82. See F. Frankfurter and N. Greene, supra Intro, note 9, at 198.

83. See supra pp. 64–66, 83–88 (discussing the judiciary's perception of the result of allowing unrestricted labor activity).

84. F. Frankfurter and N. Greene, supra Intro., note 9, at 136–98.

85. Examples of such earlier statutes aimed at repealing criminal conspiracy doctrine affecting labor protest include: 1873 Ill. Laws 76; *Me. Rev. Stat.* tit. 11, ch. 126, §18 (1883); 1 *Md. Code Pub. Gen. Laws* art. 27, §31 (1888); 1884 Md. Laws 366, ch. 266; *Minn. Penal Code* §138 (1886); 1883 N.J. Laws 36, ch. 28; *N.J. Rev. Stat.* 1296 (1877); 1882 N.Y. Laws 540, ch. 384; 1870 N.Y. Laws 30, ch. 19 (1870); *N.Y. Penal Code* §170 (1881) (declaring that peaceful assembly or cooperation by employees to obtain an advance in their wage rate is not a criminal conspiracy); 1885 Pa. Laws 300. The New York penal code example is instructive. Section 170 was construed in light of a prior section 168, which criminalized, inter alia, the prevention of another from exercising a lawful trade and the use of "force, threats, [or] intimidation" to effect a lawful end. As a result, the unions gained little, if anything. For example, the court in *People v. McFarlin*, 43 Misc. 591, 89 N.Y.S. 527 (1904), stated that a union may lawfully: "use fair argument and persuasion to influence their friends to withdraw their patronage from the manufacturers in order to bring them to terms. But to go further and threaten the manufacturers with business annihilation, with the waging of a war of destruction against them by the malicious use of the boycott . . . such action has never been called legal by a court . . . but . . . was condemned at common law . . ." Id. at 599, 89 N.Y.S. at 531; see People ex rel. Gill v. Walsh, 110 N.Y. 633 (1888).

86. See, e.g., Nebraska Anti-Injunction Act of 1897, *Neb. Compiled Stat.* §5343(a) (Brown and Wheeler 1897). This act was invalidated by a federal district court in Niagara Fire Ins. Co. v. Cornell, 110 F. 816, 825 (D. Neb. 1901). It was upheld, however, by the state supreme court in Cleland v. Anderson, 66 Neb. 252, 260, 92 N.W. 306, 308

None of these early national efforts succeeded, but several states, such as California, responded generously to labor's early entreaties for relief from the new uses of civil conspiracy and restraint of trade doctrines against strikes and boycotts. These states passed far-reaching "anti-conspiracy laws" that sought to immunize from civil liability any activity that would not be actionable if done by an individual in the absence of a strike, and went on to bar injunctions against such activities.[88]

In responding to labor's first anti-conspiracy law and anti-injunction victories, courts set a pattern from which they rarely departed until the New Deal. They swept the laws aside as irresponsible and ill-considered legislative tinkering with a realm of law that belonged by right to the judiciary. California's high court, for example, noted sternly that the California legislature's "anti-conspiracy law" seemed to contemplate a drastic hemming-in of the common law of industrial conflict. But such a hemming-in would run afoul of an industrial employer's "constitutional right to acquire, possess, enjoy, and protect property.[89] To avoid that result the court read the statute in a way that respected the rights of property but left the state's labor law unaltered.[90] Also around the turn of the century, Illinois, Nebraska, and Minnesota joined California in passing pi-

(1902), *aff'd,* 66 Neb. 273, 96 N.W. 212 (1903), *rev'd,* 66 Neb. 276, 98 N.W. 1075 (1904), *rev'd on rehearing,* 76 Neb. 273, 105 N.W. 1092 (1905).

87. The first such bill was H.R. 8917, 56th Cong., 1st Sess. (1901). In 1902 an identical bill passed the House. In the next two years like measures were proposed but never emerged from committee. See F. Frankfurter and N. Greene, supra Intro., note 9, at 154 and nn81–83.

88. See, e.g., *Cal. Gen. Laws Ann.* act 1605, §1 (Deering 1931); 1914 Mass. Acts ch. 778, §2; *Minn. Stat.* §4258 (1927).

89. Goldberg, Bowen and Co. v. Stablemen's Union, 149 Cal. 429, 434, 86 P. 806, 808 (1906) (enjoining the union from parading in front of plaintiff's place of business with "unfair" and "don't patronize" placards, to deter employees and patrons from entering). The court stated that the statute "cannot . . . be construed as undertaking to prohibit a court from enjoining the main wrongful acts charged in the complaint [parading in front of plaintiff's place of business with 'unfair' and 'don't patronize' placards, to deter employees and patrons from entering] . . ., and, . . . if it could be so construed, it would to that extent be void, because violative of plaintiff's constitutional right to acquire, possess, enjoy and protect property." Id. at 434, 86 P. at 808.

90. See id. at 434–35, 86 P. at 808–09.

oneering measures exempting unions from antitrust and restraint of trade suits.[91] All four were struck down by federal courts as "class legislation" trenching on the fourteenth amendment:

> On one side, by this legislation, we have organized labor. Those men are not amenable to the [antitrust] statute. On the other side we have men who do not belong to organized labor . . . They are amenable [to the statute] . . . Dozens of statutes have been held invalid by appellate courts which sought to make it invalid for one class of men to do one thing and lawful for other men, practically under the same circumstances, to do another, but like, thing.[92]

Over the next quarter-century, states enacted at least forty more reforms, attacking portions of the substantive law (by legalizing activities such as peaceful picketing or persuasion, for example, or condemning yellow-dog contracts and other forms of anti-union discrimination), seeking procedural changes (such as jury trials for criminal contempt charges in labor disputes), or repealing or narrowing equity jurisdiction over labor controversies.[93] Ambivalent legislatures sometimes produced anti-injunction statues that were deliberately ambiguous in their reach.[94] Many statutes, however, clearly were aimed at erecting significant barriers to judicial intervention. At least twenty-five of these anti-injunction statutes were struck down on constitutional grounds,[95] surrounding employers'

91. See *Cal. Gen. Laws Ann.* act 1605, §1 (Deering 1931); 1898 Ill. Laws 76; *Minn. Stat.* §4255 (1900); Nebraska Anti-Injunction Act of 1897, *Neb. Compiled Stat.* §5343(a) (Brown and Wheeler 1897).

92. Niagara Fire Ins. Co. v. Cornell, 110, F. 816, 825 (D. Neb. 1901); see also Connolly v. Union Sewer Pipe Co., 184 U.S. 540 (1902) (striking down the cognate Illinois statute).

93. See F. Frankfurter and N. Greene, supra Intro., note 9, at 136–98. For a list of the appellate decisions considering the constitutionality of these reforms, see infra Appendix C.

94. Section 20 of the Clayton Act is an outstanding example. See infra pp. 0000–00.

95. One approach used in striking down anti-injunction measures was to attack substantive judge-made limits on collective action. See, e.g., Truax v. Corrigan, 257 U.S. 312 (1921) (striking down an Arizona statute prohibiting injunctions against a range of peaceful protest activities); Coppage v. Kansas, 236 U.S. 1 (1915) (striking down a state statute proscribing yellow-dog contracts); Adair v. United States, 208 U.S. 161 (1908) (striking down §10 of the Erdman Act, which made it a crime for an interstate carrier to

sometimes fragile hold over workers and the workplace with con-
stitutionalized rights of property, and constitutionalizing the availability of injunctions to protect those rights.[96] Most of the measures
that were not invalidated were vitiated by narrow construction.[97]

discharge an employee for union membership); Montgomery v. Pacific Elec. Ry., 293
F. 680 (9th Cir. 1923) (striking down a California statute proscribing yellow-dog con-
tracts), *cert. denied*, 264 U.S. 586 (1924); People v. Western Union Telegraph Co., 70
Colo. 90, 198 P. 146 (1921) (same regarding a Colorado statute); Gillespie v. People,
188 Ill. 176, 58 N.E. 1007 (1900) (same regarding an Illinois statute); Coffeyville Brick
& Tile Co. v. Perry, 69 Kan. 297, 76 P. 848 (1904) (same regarding a Kansas statute);
Opinion of the Justices, 211 Mass. 618, 98 N.E. 337 (1912) (advisory opinion holding
unconstitutional a bill to immunize workers from tort liability arising out of union activities); State v. Daniels, 118 Minn. 155, 136 N.W. 584 (1912) (same regarding a Minnesota
statute); People v. Marcus, 185 N.Y. 257, 77 N.E. 1073 (1906) (same regarding a New
York statute); Jackson v. Berger, 92 Ohio St. 130, 110 N.E. 732 (1915) (same regarding
an Ohio statute). Examples of cases striking down anti-injunction measures aimed at
procedural reforms include Michaelson v. United States, 291 F. 940 (7th Cir. 1923),
rev'd, 266 U.S. 42 (1924), which invalidated a Clayton Act provision providing for a
jury trial for contempt violations; In re Atchison, 284 F. 604 (S.D. Fla. 1922), which
invalidated a state law provision similar to that struck down in *Michaelson*; and Walton
Lunch Co. v. Kearney, 236 Mass. 310, 128 N.E. 429 (1920), which held unconstitutional
a statute providing for a jury trial in contempt proceedings as applied in a labor dispute.
    96. For examples of cases invalidating statutes that sought to limit equity's jurisdiction
over labor disputes, see Truax v. Corrigan, 257 U.S. 312 (1921), which held that the
equal protection clause prohibits the legislature from denying equitable relief in labor
disputes while retaining the power for other types of cases; and Bogni v. Perotti, 224
Mass. 152, 158, 112 N.E. 853, 856 (1916), which stated that: ''it is enough to say that
the power of the courts to afford injunctive relief cannot be impaired by the Legislature
in such a way as to prevent its use in favor of one property owner, when it is preserved
for the benefit of other property owners.''
    97. See, e.g., Pierce v. Stablemen's Union, 156 Cal. 70, 103 P. 324 (1909) (construing
a state statute, which prohibited injunctions against actions to further trade disputes, to
allow enjoining of picketing to avoid holding the law an unconstitutional violation of
employer's ''property rights''); Goldberg, Bowen & Co. v. Stablemen's Union, 149 Cal.
429, 86 P. 806 (1906) (same). Other cases narrowing the reach of anti-conspiracy laws
include: Gevas v. Greek Restaurant Workers' Club, 99 N.J. Eq. 770, 134 A. 309 (1927),
which conditioned statutory immunity to an injunction on the existence of a ''legitimate''
dispute; Grassi Contracting Co. v. Bennett, 174 A.D. 244, 160 N.Y.S. 279 (1916); and
Auburn Draying Co. v. Wardell, 89 Misc. 501, 152 N.Y.S. 475 (1915), which held that
a statute decriminalizing peaceable assembly to maintain or advance wage rates did not
apply to ''immediate purpose'' of striking for a closed shop, *aff'd*, 178 A.D. 270, 165
N.Y.S. 469 (1917), *aff'd*, 227 N.Y. 1, 124 N.E. 97 (1919). Courts usually read ambiguous
anti-injunction or anti-conspiracy laws so crabbedly they rendered them null. See, e.g.,
Vonnegut Mach. Co. v. Toledo Mach. & Tool Co., 263 F. 192 (N.D. Ohio 1920)

In 1896, one year after the Supreme Court's *Debs* decision,[98] Gompers campaigned for the Democratic presidential candidate, William Jennings Bryan. Bryan's candidacy issued from a fusion of the People's Party and the Democrats, and thus enjoyed the support of labor Populists in the AFL. Bryan was an outspoken critic of the *Debs* decision, of the labor injunction, and of the federal judiciary. In addition, he favored immigration restriction. For both reasons, he won the staunch backing of Gompers and his AFL followers.[99] After 1896 Gompers led the AFL toward a thorough aloofness from political engagement. Not surprisingly, then, Congress spurned the AFL's efforts in the late 1890s and early 1900s to win federal anti-injunction laws.

Meanwhile, however, the federal courts continued to extend their prohibitions on collective action. After a decade, in 1906, judicial hostility finally goaded Gompers and the AFL to abandon their aloofness from national politics in favor of vigorous—albeit anti-statist—involvement.[100] The AFL published *Labor's Bill of Grievances,* in-

(authorizing a temporary injunction to stop picketing because section 20 of the Clayton Act was held not to sanction secondary boycotts), *rev'd on jurisdictional grounds sub. nom.* Gable v. Vonnegut Mach. Co., 274 F. 66 (6th Cir. 1921); Bull of Theatrical Stage Employees v. International Alliance, 119 Kan. 713, 241 P. 459 (1925) (holding an act forbidding issuance of injunctions between employers and employees inapplicable when the parties were not technically employed); Folsom Engraving Co. v. McNeil, 235 Mass. 269, 126 N.E. 479 (1920) (stating that a statute proscribing injunctions against "peaceful persuasion" did not protect strikers engaged in an "illegal purpose"—to "coerce" employer into accepting a new contract); Greenfield v. Central Lab. Council, 104 Or. 236, 192 P. 783 (1920) (stating that the statute at issue did not legalize picketing merely to procure recognition of a union), *modified,* 104 Or. 259, 207 P. 168 (1922); Pacific Typesetting Co. v. I.T.U., 125 Wash. 273, 216 P. 358 (1923) (holding that urging refusal to work on "unfair" materials was not protected under statute); see also F. Frankfurter and N. Greene, supra Intro., note 9, at 137 and n7. For a more complete list, see infra Appendix C.

98. *In re* Debs, 158 U.S. 564 (1895).

99. Immigration restriction and anti-court legislation became the AFL's chief political desiderata as, under Gompers's leadership, it abandoned the labor movement's earlier and wider class-based politics in favor of a voluntarist and interest-group approach. For a brief discussion, see supra pp. 16–17; and see generally G. Mink, supra Chap. 2, note 20.

100. The *Bucks Stove* injunction and *Danbury Hatters* trial were the immediate occasions prompting the AFL for the first time to turn in earnest to congressional lobbying

dicting the courts, the injunction, and judge-made law, and seeking pro-labor commitments from congressional candidates around the country.[101] It also sought to unseat a handful of labor's most vigorous foes.

At the same time as it launched this campaign of rewarding labor's friends and punishing its enemies, the AFL altered the form of its anti-injunction bills. Frustrated by the seeming futility of seeking legislative revision of judge-made substantive law, it attacked the scope of equity jurisdiction. The first such bill was introduced in Congress by Representative Pearre.[102] Like many of the anti-injunction bills sponsored by labor over the next two decades, the Pearre Bill focused on the definition of "property." Forbidding any federal judge to issue an injunction in any labor dispute, except to prevent irreparable injury to property, the Pearre Bill provided:

> [F]or the purposes of this Act, no right to continue the relation of employer and employee or to assume or create such relation with any particular person or persons, or at all, or to carry on business of any particular kind, or at any particular place, or at all, shall be construed, held, considered or treated as property or as constituting a property right.[103]

Chief among those who testified before the House Judiciary Committee in support of the bill was Andrew Furuseth, the leader of the Seaman's Union, and the AFL's principal lobbyist and most impressive jurist.[104] No one better exemplified the labor movement's

and campaigning. See Gompers v. Bucks Stove and Range Co., 221 U.S. 418 (1911); Loewe v. Lawlor, 208 U.S. 274 (1908); see also M. Karson, supra Chap. 5, note 22, at 50–66.

101. See "Labor's Bill of Grievances," 13 *Am. Federationist* 293, 294–96 (1906). The other main grievance was unrestricted immigration. See id. at 294; supra Chap. 5, note 99.

102. H.R. 94, 60th Cong., 1st Sess. 13 (1907).

103. F. Frankfurter and N. Greene, supra Intro., note 9, at 155 (quoting H.R. 94, 60th Cong., 1st Sess. 13 (1907)).

104. Into the twentieth century, admiralty law entitled shipmasters to flog seamen, to use other forms of corporal punishment, to arrest forcibly or have arrested seamen who jumped ship, and to hold such sailors in irons. The law's condoning of state and private violence to enforce labor contracts and labor discipline smacked of slavery. In the federal courts, Furuseth and his union unsuccessfully challenged the power to arrest sailors who

bitter and paradoxical immersion in legal culture. Over the years of anti-injunction campaigning Furuseth had delved into the history of equity. With T. C. Spelling, the AFL's counsel on injunction matters, Furuseth drafted the Pearre Bill and defended it with considerable eloquence. Rehearsing the history of chancery in England, Furuseth contended that the principle limiting equity to the protection of property was embedded in English jurisprudence at the time the federal judiciary was founded and the boundaries of federal equity power set. "[A]ny extension in jurisdiction," Furuseth claimed, "must come from the people through an amendment to the Constitution or there is judicial usurpation."[105]

Then Furuseth turned to his thirteenth amendment claim. In the typical labor strike or boycott, he observed, the workers "have not destroyed any tangible property; . . . nor threatened to interfere with any property."[106] Yet the employer typically succeeds in enlisting the court's equity power to protect "what it calls its property."[107]

> [A business] sets forth that it has the land, the appliances, the raw material, and contracts to deliver goods; but, owing to a "conspiracy" on the part of labor, it is unable to get workmen, and its property— that is, its business—is being destroyed. The judge takes the statement

---

quit their vessel under the thirteenth amendment. See Robertson v. Baldwin, 165 U.S. 275 (1896); H. Weintraub, *Andrew Furuseth, Emancipator of the Seamen* 35–36 (1959). They then turned to Congress. Shipping-industry spokesmen argued to the House Committee on Merchant Marine that Furuseth's bill was unthinkable. Giving sailors the right to desert would destroy the industry. See id. at 39. "Why?" Furuseth demanded: "When a vessel is delayed, it may mean 24 hours demurrage—possibly $100 or $150, but what will the owner of a glass factory lose by having its furnaces go cold; half a million dollars. What will a cotton planter lose by not being able to pick his cotton when it is ripe? Is there any good reason why, because I am a sailor, I should have shackles put upon my hands and made to feel that I, of all men, am the one upon whom the United States is putting the stamp of servitude?" *Id.* (quoting *Coast Seaman's Journal*, Aug. 12, 1896, at 1).

Finally, during the Progressive era, Furuseth's lobbying secured passage of the Seamen's Act of 1915. See id. at 108–32. No doubt this struggle to abolish legalized compulsion against seamen informed Furuseth's passionate part in the anti-injunction campaign.

105. 48 *Cong. Rec.* H3650 (daily ed., 1912) (statement of Andrew Furuseth).

106. Id. at 3651.

107. Id.

and issues an order forbidding the workmen "to interfere with the business" of the firm.[108]

The corporate bar, in other words, has "set[] up the idea that the earning power of property is property," and because "the earning power of a plant depends upon labor," owners of factories somehow possess a property right "to so much labor . . . as will make [their factories] profitable."[109] This reasoning succeeds in bringing strike activities within the reach of equity only by violating the "fundamental principle of American law . . . that there shall be no property rights in man."[110]

The representatives of capital at the hearing also appealed to history. Since time immemorial, declared attorney Daniel Davenport, the General Counsel of the American Antiboycott Association, "the common sense of mankind [has] recognize[d] [a man's enterprise to be his] property." "To say that Congress can declare by statute that not to be property which the uniform decisions of innumerable courts have declared to be property . . . is simple nonsense."[111]

The Republican leaders of the House allowed labor's bill to languish in committee, but in 1912 Democrats took over for the first time in the new century. In that year, Democrats on the Judiciary Committee offered legislation that eventually became part of the Clayton Act, passed in 1914 after years of AFL lobbying.[112] Borrowing language from another labor-sponsored measure, section 6 of the Clayton Act declared simply that "the labor of a human being is not a commodity."[113] Section 20 of the Act provided, in its first paragraph, "That no restraining order or injunction shall be granted by any court of the United States . . . in any case between an employer and employees, or between employers and employees, . . .

---

108. Id.

109. Id.

110. Id. at 3650.

111. *Injunctions: Hearings on Injunctions before the House Committee on the Judiciary*, 62d Cong., 2d Sess. 294–95 (1912) (statement of Daniel Davenport).

112. See F. Frankfurter and N. Greene, supra Intro., note 9, at 155–63 (tracing the legislative path of the labor injunction provisions of the Clayton Act).

113. H.R. 15657, 63d Cong., 2d Sess. 16756 (1913–1914).

involving or growing out of a dispute concerning terms or conditions of employment . . . "[114]

The second paragraph of section 20 catalogued specific acts against which no injunction could issue: communicating peacefully, "ceasing to patronize" or persuading others to do so, paying strike benefits, assembling peaceably, "doing any act or thing which might lawfully be done in the absence of such dispute by any party thereto."[115]

Gompers read this language as giving the AFL all that it had demanded.[116] He greeted the Act as labor's "Magna Carta."[117] But the first paragraph of section 20 had a final qualifying clause. No injunctions were to be issued, it concluded, "unless necessary to prevent irreparable injury to property, or to a property right, of the party making the application."[118] The "unless" helped undo what the previous language had seemed to accomplish. Courts continued to find that employers had a property right in the ongoing labor of their employees, and anti-strike injunctions continued to be granted. The statute was held inapplicable when a strike was to unionize a factory or, generally, for any purpose other than immediate betterment of working conditions. The Act could not be invoked once the employer had refilled vacancies: persons who continued to strike and picket thereafter were no longer employees under the Act. Nor

114. Id.

115. Id.

116. Many of labor's friends in Congress and elsewhere looked at the language and made gloomier, and more accurate, prophecies. See F. Frankfurter and N. Greene, supra Intro., note 9, at 159–61 (discussing the debate among congressmen whether the Act wrought broad changes in existing law or would merely ratify the judicial status quo); see also "Labor Is Not a Commodity," *New Republic*, Dec. 3, 1916, at 112 (stating that "the rallying cry that labor is not a commodity . . . has been attached, whether by design or by accident we do not know, to a legislative program which does not give labor what it wants, or what it thinks it is getting"). Historians have documented the sharp divisions, uncertainty, and ambivalence about the scope of the Act's labor provisions among the congressmen who drafted and adopted them. See Kutler, "Labor, the Clayton Act, and the Supreme Court," 3 *Lab. Hist.* 19 (1962); Jones, "The Enigma of the Clayton Act," 10 *Indus. and Lab. Rel. Rev.* 200 (1957).

117. Gompers, "The Charter of Industrial Freedom," 21 *Am. Federationist* 971, 972 (1914).

118. H.R. 1567, 63d Cong., 2d Sess. 16756 (1913–1914).

did judicial attitudes toward picketing change: "practical people," wrote one federal judge construing section 20, "question the possibility of peaceful persuasion through the practice of picketing."[119] In ten of the thirteen decisions reported between 1916 and 1920 in which lower federal courts applied section 20, the Act was held not to impede the granting of an injunction.[120] Moreover, in 1921 the Supreme Court announced that section 20 codified the common law of the injunction as it already had existed.[121] Another decade of broad injunctions and broken strikes followed before Congress again considered the matter.

The Norris-LaGuardia Act

Beleaguered by hostile federal administrations and ruthless open-shop drives, as well as by rank-and-file restiveness and internal dissent, the AFL leadership grew ever more cautious and conservative during the 1920s. The AFL's bitterness toward the courts, however, remained constant. It united Gompers and the rest of the leadership with the Federation's most radical dissenters and rank-and-file militants.[122] The 1920s saw the widespread use of "yellow-dog" injunctions against organizing campaigns in the southern coal fields; injunctions also hindered garment workers' efforts to hold on to wartime gains. During the 1920s, courts issued more than 2,100 anti-strike decrees, and the proportion of strikes met by injunctions to the total number of strikes reached an extraordinary 25 percent.[123] The proliferation of injunctions prompted articulate disobedience on

119. Vonnegut Mach. Co. v. Toledo Mach. and Tool Co., 263 F. 192, 199 (N.D. Ohio 1920).

120. See F. Frankfurter and N. Greene, supra Intro., note 9, at 165.

121. See Duplex Co. v. Deering, 254 U.S. 443 (1921). See generally F. Frankfurter and N. Greene, supra Intro., note 9, at 161–76 (detailing the history of section 20 from its passage through the *Duplex* decision). Canvassing this history, Frankfurter and Greene conclude: "The Clayton Act was the product of twenty years of voluminous agitation. It came as clay into the hands of the federal courts . . . The result justifies an application of a familiar bit of French cynicism: the more things are legislatively changed, the more they remain the same judicially." Id. at 176.

122. See R. Zieger, *Republicans and Labor, 1919–1929* 259 (1969).

123. See infra Appendix B.

an unprecedented scale. Never before was the labor movement so riveted upon the rights and liberties denied by the legal order.

So much protest and defiance directed at the legal order disturbed many middle-class "experts" and reformers, many elite lawyers, academics, and politicians.[124] Increasingly, studies and commission reports concluded that "government by injunction" was among the prime "causes of industrial unrest."[125] The government could not keep industrial peace, they warned, if one side thought the rules laid down were fundamentally unfair. No "efficient" industrial order could rely too heavily on coercion; a minimum of consent was essential. Workers seemed to be withdrawing that minimum of consent; the judge-made rules of the game had begun to seem untenable.[126] Even "leaders of the Bar" were alarmed: the courts were squandering their own legitimacy.[127]

Amid these events, in February 1928, Senator George Norris, chair of the Senate Judiciary Committee, opened hearings on a new anti-injunction bill,[128] and labor's representatives brought to Con-

124. See, e.g., Pepper, "Injunctions in Labor Disputes," reprinted in G. Pepper, *Men and Issues* 61–63 (1924) (former senator decrying injunctions); Baker, "Labor Relations and the Law" 8 *A.B.A. J.* 731 (1922) (reprinting an address delivered before the Cleveland Bar Association, Oct. 1922); see also I. Bernstein, *The Lean Years*, supra Intro., note 9, at 394–95 (describing the efforts of legal scholars and reform politicians to draft anti-injunction legislation).

125. J. Fitch, *The Causes of Industrial Unrest* 1 (1924).

126. See, e.g., id. at 324–54; R. Hoxie, supra Chap. 4, note 3, at 237–39; E. Witte, supra Intro., note 9, at 132, 298; "Injunctions in Labor Disputes," 13 *Proc. Acad. Pol. Sci.* 37–92 (1928) (discussing academics and other "experts" who agreed with the AFL that "industrial peace" and "efficiency" require broad legal toleration of labor organizing and peaceful strikes and protests).

127. See, e.g., Pepper, supra Chap. 5, note 124, at 163 ("Under such a system of government as ours the maintenance of well-nigh universal confidence in the judiciary is pretty nearly essential to national safety"); Baker, supra Chap. 5, note 124, at 733 ("[T]here is no field of legal administration which has so absolutely failed to secure public confidence and respect as the law in labor disputes. Nor is this lack of respect limited to the workers").

128. See G. Norris, *Fighting Liberal* 310–17 (1945). During the 1926 election campaigns, Norris, a Progressive from Nebraska, had stumped Pennsylvania on an ally's behalf. He had visited coal towns and spoken with miners about life in the towns and conditions in the mines, about efforts at union organizing, and about the yellow-dog contract and the courts. His sympathy for their plight grew, prompting him to fight for passage of an anti-injunction act abolishing yellow-dog contracts. See id. at 234–43.

gress their common law arguments, their exiled constitutional claims, and their stories of judicial repression of worker-citizens in the country's coal fields and manufacturing districts.[129] The bill, sponsored by the AFL, had been introduced by Senator Henrik Shipstead. It was not lengthy. Like previous bills over the past decades it was drafted by Furuseth and turned on the definition of property. The bill provided that "for the purposes of determining" equity courts' jurisdiction to protect property "nothing shall be held to be property unless it is tangible and transferable."[130]

The hearings, originally scheduled for three days, lasted from February 8 through March 10. At the hearings' opening Furuseth tersely announced the AFL's perception of the issue. "Now we, therefore, come to you to ask you to determine what is property . . . That is the pith and essence of this question."[131] By treating people as a form of property, the labor injunction broke the promise of the thirteenth amendment. "If they go on making human relations into property relations," Furuseth told the committee, "the Thirteenth Amendment to the Constitution will be evaded, circumvented and dead."[132] Senator Shipstead embraced labor's constitutional framework when he concluded that the hearing had revealed a distinct conflict between the fifth and fourteenth amendments on one side and the first and thirteenth on the other.[133] So too would Senator

---

129. See id.

130. I. Bernstein, *The Lean Years*, supra Intro., note 9, at 395.

131. *Limiting Scope of Injunctions in Labor Disputes: Hearings before the Subcommittee of the Senate Committee on the Judiciary*, 70th Cong., 1st Sess. 24 (1928) [hereinafter *Limiting Scope of Injunctions*].

132. Id. at 148.

133. See *Senate Committee on Judiciary, Hearings on the Shipstead Bill, S. 1482*, 70th Cong., 1st Sess. (1928). Similarly, Justice Brandeis adopted this perspective in his dissent in Bedford Cut Stone Co. v. Journeymen Stone Cutters Ass'n, 274 U.S. 37 (1927), when he declared: "If on the undisputed facts of this case [involving stonecutters' peaceful refusal to work on 'unfair' stone] refusal to work can be enjoined," then Congress in establishing the antitrust laws had fashioned "an instrument for imposing restraints upon labor which reminds of involuntary servitude." Id. at 54, 65 (Brandeis, J., dissenting); see also Kemp v. Div. No. 241, Amalgamated Ass'n of St. and Elec. Ry. Employees, 255 Ill. 213, 227, 99 N.E. 389, 394–95 (1912) (invalidating an anti-strike decree under the thirteenth amendment). Justice Brandeis never fully embraced consti-

Norris in telling the Senate that the labor injunctions' "effect has often been involuntary servitude on the part of those who must toil in order that they and their families may live."[134]

The law of the labor injunction had so fitted itself to the logic and demands of capital that the Constitution itself had been deformed. From the perspective of AFL spokesmen the injunction signified the ultimate, legal alienation of labor, and indeed, the vocabulary of Marx's *Capital* finds a strange echo in the words of "pure and simple trade unionist" Furuseth:

> Now, if you are going to permit this kind of expansion of the word "property" to cover every human relation, you set up a condition, gentlemen, under which the creator, the human being who through his creative power . . . has created certain property, you make that man fall down on his knees and worship what he himself has produced.[135]

As the hearings unfolded, the AFL-sponsored bill with its evocative narrowing of "property" to "things" and its wholesale eviction of courts from industrial disputes was assailed not only by employers' representatives but also by legal academics and progressives who objected that it swept too broadly outside the domain of industrial strife, and in any event, would never pass constitutional muster. Senator Norris enlisted Felix Frankfurter and a number of other progressive legal reformers to draft a substitute bill.[136] Their draft made no mention of the definition of "property," but it was a

tutionalizing the right to strike. His vision of industrial democracy was not of a laissez-faire regime like the AFL's. His was rather a more statist and republican, progressive outlook. He envisioned a democratic state regulating labor disputes for the common good. He endorsed incorporating unions and state-enforced arbitration. See P. Strum, *Louis D. Brandeis: Justice for the People* 104–06, 177–79 (1984).

134. 75 *Cong. Rec.* 4502 (1932).

135. *Limiting Scope of Injunctions*, supra Chap. 5, note 131, at 20.

136. The other principal draftsmen were Donald Richberg, counsel to the railway brotherhoods; Edwin Witte, chief of the Wisconsin Legislative Library and the era's most perspicacious chronicler of the labor injunction; Herman Oliphant of Columbia Law School; and Frances Sayre, a colleague of Frankfurter's at Harvard. See I. Bernstein, *The Lean Years*, supra Intro., note 9, at 397; G. Norris, supra Chap. 5, note 128, at 312; T. Vadney, *The Wayward Liberal* 85–87 (1970).

thorough and well-crafted set of hedges against labor injunctions.[137] In its preamble it sounded some of the themes of labor's Constitution.[138] Four years later, in 1932, a barely altered version of that substitute bill passed Congress as the Norris-LaGuardia Act.[139]

Already in 1928 the Senate had revealed its readiness to indict "government by injunction" when it rejected Hoover's Supreme Court nomination of federal circuit judge John Parker, author of the notorious *Red Jacket* opinion[140] that upheld the blanket anti-strike injunctions gained by 316 coal operators against striking Southern miners in 1923.[141] Parker's opinion did not stray greatly from the lines laid out by the Supreme Court in *Hitchman*, but by the mid-1920s a widening spectrum of the nation's political elites was growing disenchanted with the courts.[142] The repressiveness of the old judge-made order disturbed liberal consciences, sapped the courts' legitimacy among the working classes, and seemed to increase, not diminish, industrial unrest.[143] Labor's exiled Constitution deserved

137. For a detailed description of the substitute Shipstead bill, see I. Bernstein, *The Lean Years*, supra Intro., note 9, at 397–403, and F. Frankfurter and N. Greene, supra Intro., note 9, at 207–28.

138. See 69 *Cong. Rec.* 10050 (1928). "[T]he individual unorganized worker is commonly helpless to exercise actual liberty of contract and to protect his freedom of labor . . . wherefore it is necessary that he have full freedom of association, self-organization, and designation of representatives of his own choosing . . . and . . . be free from the interference, restraint, or coercion . . . in self-organization . . . concerted activities . . . or other mutual aid . . ." Id.

139. See I. Bernstein, *The Lean Years*, supra Intro., note 9, at 403, 412–14.

140. United Mine Workers of Am. v. Red Jacket Consol. Coal and Coke Co., 18 F.2d 839, 840 (4th Cir.), *cert. denied*, 275 U.S. 536 (1927).

141. See I. Bernstein, *The Lean Years*, supra Intro., note 9, at 406–09; Fish, "*Red Jacket* Revisited: The Case That Unraveled John J. Parker's Supreme Court Appointment," 5 *Law and Hist. Rev.* 51, 102–03 (1987).

142. The AFL and its progressive allies in the Senate, Norris, LaFollette, and Borah, succeeded in transforming the Parker nomination into a Senate vote on the *Hitchman* and *Red Jacket* decisions and the use of labor injunctions and yellow-dog contracts in the nation's nonunion coal fields. As UMW president John Lewis posed the question to Congress: "Why lay another lash across the tortured shoulders of the struggling mine workers, by placing in a position of vastly increased power a man who regards them as industrial bondsmen?" I. Bernstein, *The Lean Years*, supra Intro, note 9, at 408–09. The Senate rejected Parker 41–39, the first time in 36 years it had turned down a Supreme Court nominee. See id. at 407–09.

143. See R. Zieger, supra Chap. 5, note 122, at 260–77.

more respectful attention. Yet in spite of these considerations and in spite of congressional reproaches over the courts' role in the 1922 Railway Shopmen's Strike, the courts seemed to be expanding, not tempering, "government by injunction."[144]

Also in spite of these considerations, a Republican-dominated Senate Judiciary Committee blocked Norris's efforts to have his new bill reported out until after the 1930 elections.[145] Throughout the 1920s Gompers's AFL campaigned vigorously to reward congressional friends and punish congressional enemies. By the end of the decade, the "Al Smith Revolution" in the Democratic Party of 1928 also had mobilized for the first time a national immigrant working-class constituency for the Democrats. Moreover, the early 1930s saw a crisis of business and Republican legitimacy prompted by the Great Depression. These broader changes combined with the more specific disrepute of the old labor law regime to produce the remarkably broad support the Norris and LaGuardia anti-injunction bills enjoyed when they finally reached the Senate and House floors in January 1932. The House bill passed by 362 to 14; the Senate bill by 75 to 5.[146] In signing the bill, Hoover quoted his Attorney General's view that the matters raised by the bill "can only be set at rest by judicial decision,"[147] and Norris and other supporters of the legislation feared he was right.[148] However, the new anti-injunction law did not undergo Supreme Court scrutiny until 1938.[149] By then a Constitutional revolution had occurred, and New Deal judges and jurisprudence had begun to vanquish the old order.

Frankfurter and the other lawyers and academics who drafted the Norris-LaGuardia Act were typical of the close-knit professional community of labor law reformers in rejecting the laissez-faire ideals and old-fashioned rights talk of a Gompers, Furuseth, or Frey.[150]

---

144. Of the roughly 4,300 injunctions against union activities between 1880 and 1930, 2,100, or nearly half, were issued in the 1920s alone. See infra Appendix B.

145. See I. Bernstein, *The Lean Years*, supra Intro., note 9, at 409–10.

146. See id. at 413.

147. Id. at 414 (citation omitted).

148. See id.

149. See Lauf v. E. G. Shinner and Co., 303 U.S. 323, 330 (1938).

150. See Ernst, "The Yellow Dog Contract and Liberal Reform, 1917–1932," supra

Both Frankfurter and Donald Richberg, who did the bulk of the actual drafting, had their strongest links with unions and labor leaders with a more statist outlook than the AFL mainstream. We have already seen Frankfurter's close ties with Sidney Hillman of the Amalgamated Clothing Workers.[151] Similarly, Richberg was counsel to some of the railway brotherhoods whose politics had taken a more "progressive," statist turn. The brotherhoods sought nationalization of the railways in the 1920s; they succeeded in passing through Congress the Railway Labor Act of 1926. This Act, which Richberg also drafted, included a national administrative structure and provisions condemning anti-union discrimination by employers and protecting workers' rights to organize and freely elect bargaining representatives. These would serve as models for parts of both the Norris-LaGuardia and Wagner Acts.[152]

Frankfurter, Richberg, and the other legal reformers believed that simply ousting courts from regulating industrial relations, as the AFL hoped to do, would not stand up to constitutional attack.[153] Nor did they think that gaining the collective laissez-faire regime that the AFL envisioned was an adequate goal. Like Hillman and UMW president John Lewis (the chief champion of industrial unionism and chief rival of the old guard within the AFL), they wanted more positive help for labor organizing from the national government.[154]

Chap. 4, note 64, at 263–65 (contrasting the "public policy" rhetoric of the reformers with the rights talk of the trade unionists).

151. See supra pp. 119–21; supra Chap. 4, note 81. In addition to litigating, Frankfurter and Hillman collaborated during the 1920s with other future New Dealers to fashion proposals for a vastly expanded national administrative role in economic development generally and labor relations in particular. See Fraser, supra Chap. 4, note 74, at 241. Under Roosevelt, Hillman would become the labor movement's most powerful representative in the White House, see 3 A. Schlesinger, Jr., *The Age of Roosevelt: The Politics of Upheaval* 442, 600 (1960), whereas Frankfurter was among Roosevelt's "ministers without portfolio" until FDR appointed him to the Court in 1937. See Fraser, supra Chap. 4, note 74, at 223–25.

152. See I. Bernstein, *The New Deal Collective Bargaining Policy* 42, 57–75 (1950) [hereinafter I. Bernstein, *New Deal Policy*]; T. Vadney, supra Chap. 5, note 136, at 51–65.

153. See F. Frankfurter and N. Greene, supra Intro., note 9, at 207.

154. See I. Bernstein, *New Deal Policy*, supra Chap. 5, note 152, at 18–28; C. Tomlins, supra Intro., note 9, at 189–96.

Laissez-faire might suffice for the already established craft unions, but more affirmative forms of legal protection and state enforcement of labor's rights seemed necessary to help organize the unorganized in the mass-production industries like auto, rubber, and steel, which had been overwhelmingly open shop since their creation. That was the general view on labor matters of the men and women who after 1932 became "New Deal attorneys" and the builders of a new American state. A group of these attorneys, several of them students of Frankfurter and inspired by the industrial-union vision of Hillman and Lewis, created an administrative alternative to the AFL's vision—the National Labor Relations Act and Board.[155] They envisioned it as a vastly more even-handed and efficient guarantor of industrial peace than "government by injunction," and a more active guardian of labor's liberties than the courts could be, even if the courts were filled with judges like the one who had decided *Quinto*.[156]

Thus, the Wagner Act contained the associational liberties and freedom of collective action that the old AFL warhorses championed. But, as Furuseth, Frey, and other AFL anti-injunction-campaign veterans darkly prophesied, the Act inaugurated a regulatory regime that, in administering the new liberties, might resurrect many of the old restraints.[157] If the old guard grossly underestimated the good that would flow from the new order, they were not wrong about the possibility that within it many of the old common law restraints on collective action might reassert themselves.[158] The federal courts have interpreted the NLRA to prohibit virtually all forms of secondary strikes and boycotts, and the Supreme Court has upheld this bar against constitutional challenges.[159] Even peaceful picketing urg-

155. See I. Bernstein, *New Deal Policy*, supra Chap. 5, note 152, at 57–75; C. Tomlins, supra Intro, note 9, at 132–40; and see generally J. Gross, *The Making of the National Labor Relations Board* (1974).

156. See supra pp. 122–24.

157. See C. Tomlins, supra Intro., note 9, at 140–45; Jaffe, "Law Making by Private Groups," 51 *Harv. L. Rev.* 201 (1937).

158. See J. Atleson, *Values and Assumptions in American Labor Law*, 19–34, 67–107 (1983) (detailing contemporary courts' preservation of old injunction-era common-law values and assumptions across a broad array of labor-law issues).

159. Pope, "Labor and the Constitution: From Abolition to Deindustrialization," 65 *Tex. L. Rev.* 1071, 1079 and n65 (1987). But see Edward J. DeBartolo Corp. v. Florida

ing the public to boycott unfair goods is routinely enjoined, and first amendment challenges are routinely rebuffed.[160] The persistence of these old restraints on labor protest seems anomalous today, when outside the labor context, both boycotting and peaceful picketing enjoy substantial constitutional protection.[161] On its face, the refusal of constitutional protection for workers' boycotts and other protest activities would appear hard to defend. But labor protest occupies what one observer has called a constitutional "black hole."[162] Courts continue to treat labor and labor protest on marketplace terms. The Gompers era idea that they had a distinctive place in the Constitution has left few traces.[163] The old common law concepts rule from the grave. Labor remains a commodity in contemporary constitutional law.[164]

Gulf Coast Bldg. and Constr. Trades Council, 108 S. Ct. 1392 (1988) (holding, in order to avoid serious constitutional problems, that peaceful and orderly distribution of handbills asking consumers not to patronize anti-union employers was not banned by Congress).

160. See Pope, supra Chap. 5, note 159, at 1116 and n286 (citing NLRB v. Retail Store Employees Union, Local 1001, 447 U.S. 607, 616 (1980)).

161. See NAACP v. Claiborne Hardware Co., 458 U.S. 886 (1982); see also Pope, supra Chap. 5, note 159, at 1080–96; Harper, "The Consumer's Emerging Right to Boycott: *NAACP v. Claiborne Hardware* and Its Implications for American Labor Law," 93 *Yale L. J.* 409 (1984).

162. See Pope, supra Chap. 5, note 159, at 1073; see id. at 1074–82 (arguing that labor is denied constitutional protections routinely extended to other groups because the courts treat workers as commodity sellers, regulation of whose activities is subject to rational basis review).

163. The idea gained some ground in the 1930s and 1940s. See id. at 1076, 1089–94; *see also* Thornhill v. Alabama, 310 U.S. 88 (1940) (holding that labor picketing had an affirmative value in the constitutional scheme). In subsequent years, however, the constitutional protections of labor eroded and the Court issued a series of opinions affirming labor as a commodity and labor relations as purely commercial activity. See Pope, supra chap. 5, note 159, at 1091–96.

164. See Pope, supra Chap. 5, note 159, at 1091–96.

Conclusion

Responding to the Shipstead Bill, Felix Frankfurter politely ridiculed the AFL leaders' "gallant" attempts to narrow the law's definition of property.[1] Edwin Witte was similarly quizzical about labor-drafted section 6 of the Clayton Act, which provides that "the labor of a human being is not a commodity."[2] The provision, he observed, had no bite, for no antitrust holding against workers' collective action turned on the proposition that they were monopolizing or restraining trade in their own labor.[3] But the Shipstead Bill and section 6, like union leaders' speeches attacking the courts' "expansion of . . . property," all had meaning, legal meaning, that eluded the progressive lawyers. They embodied a search within liberal legal and constitutional discourse for a critique of the "commodification" of labor—and for the authority to curb it. The search was not only "gallant"[4] but also shrewd and wise in light of the courts' repeated propensity to revert to a commodified view of labor.

1. See F. Frankfurter and N. Greene, supra Intro., note 9, at 207. Frankfurter wrote about Furuseth: "Of a studious nature, he delved into the history of chancery, and from his conclusions . . . formulated a remedy which became the Shipstead Bill. With indomitable tenacity, Mr. Furuseth has persisted in his own conception of legal history and in the espousal of a reform deemed by him the correct legal tradition. There is much that is gallant in the picture of this self-taught seaman challenging the power and skill of an entire learned profession. For, almost without exception, the informed opinion of lawyers . . . regards his proposals as an attempt to throw out the baby with the bath." Id.

2. 15 U.S.C. §17 (1982).

3. See Witte, "The Doctrine That Labor Is a Commodity," 69 *Am. Acad. Pol. and Soc. Sci. Ann.* 133 (1917).

4. See F. Frankfurter and N. Greene, supra Intro., note 9, at 207.

The discourse within which the search was conducted, however, was not ideal for the purpose, for it could not comprehend a critical aspect of workers' predicament: workers could be treated like commodities, or like property at someone else's disposal, not only because of the law of the labor injunction (and the anti-union violence it encouraged), but also because of many other social and economic inequalities. Remedying those inequalities—making every worker a citizen and not a cipher of the industrial world—not only required an arena for union organizing and collective action freed from harsh legal restraints; it also required a broader redistributive politics and public reconstruction and regulation of the emerging corporate economy. The Gilded Age labor movement had begun to develop this type of broad vision of the uses of law and state power. But such a vision ran afoul of turn-of-the-century AFL voluntarism, which embraced the sanctity of the "private" economic sphere. As we have seen, the AFL's spokesmen fashioned their case against the labor injunction and their trade union philosophy within this restricted voluntarist discourse. Accordingly, when they spoke on behalf of "all the nation's toilers"—unorganized as well as organized, unskilled as well as skilled—they spoke with a constricted voice.

Gompers elevated voluntarism into a matter of principle. But historically the rise of voluntarism as the movement's dominant collective outlook was a matter of necessity and grudging accommodation. Scholars generally have assumed that the judiciary's role in the making of the labor movement and its voluntarist philosophy was a slight and derivative one. This book has shown that view to be wrong. Voluntarism's victory resulted from many highly constrained and divisive collective choices that were imposed upon the American labor movement, largely by the nation's obdurate state of courts and parties. This book has detailed how judge-made law and legal violence limited, demeaned, and demoralized workers' capacities for class-based social and political action. Between the 1880s and the early 1900s, courts' sway over labor laws helped make the broad reformism and lawmaking ambitions of the Gilded Age labor movement bootless. The courts' implacable hostility to big strikes and broad mutual aid over the same decades made the earlier movement's more inclusive union vision seem too costly.

If in the mid-1880s most trade unionists agreed that the ballot and the legislature contained "all the enginery of power" to remake industry, by the early 1900s many had concluded that legislation was a distressingly unreliable engine. It was folly to try to remake industry by legislation; the most significant thing one could seek from lawmakers was simply repeal of the old common law restraints on collective action. Indeed, from 1900 until 1930 the growing number of anti-strike decrees and the mounting burdens and indignities of outlawry riveted labor's political energies on attaining just that reform. The goal of repealing the judge-made law of labor conflicts became the central theme of an anti-statist politics. Ironically, the very intensity of judicial repression, combined with courts' broader institutional and ideological authority, made the language of the law beckon as a framework within which to contend for relief. During these decades, labor relinquished a republican vocabulary of protest and reform for a liberal, law-inspired language of rights.

The legal order's part in the formation of American labor politics confirms Tocqueville's prophetic insight, too often truncated in quotation:

> The more we reflect upon all that occurs in the United States, the more we shall be persuaded that the lawyers . . . form the most powerful . . . counterpoise to the democratic element . . . The courts of justice are the visible organs by which the legal profession is enabled to control the democracy . . . Scarcely any political question arises in the United States that is not resolved . . . into a judicial question. Hence all parties are obliged to borrow, in their daily controversies, the ideas, and even the language, peculiar to judicial proceedings . . . The language of the law thus becomes, in some measure, a vulgar tongue. And the spirit of the law penetrates into the bosom of society, even into the lower classes.[5]

This book not only confirms Tocqueville's emphasis on the powers of the American legal and judicial elite over against society's "democratic element[s]"; it also confirms his insights into the subtler sway of the "language of the law." Lately, the influence of the language of the law on American social movements has become a

---

5. 1 A. de Tocqueville, *Democracy in America*, supra Chap. 1, note 73, at 288–90.

topic of increasing interest and debate among legal scholars and activists. One reason for this recent concern is a disillusionment, shared by many of these scholars and practitioners, respecting the new legal rights that were won by movements of black, poor, and other subordinate Americans during the 1960s and 1970s. As the courts have become increasingly unfriendly arenas for these groups, some of their advocates have come to regard their earlier victories as counterfeit, as inspiring but ultimately hollow changes in the *status quo ante*. In retrospect, these lawyers and legal scholars have concluded, the movements' reliance on "rights talk" and "rights-based strategies" set significant limits on the kinds of reform the movements could achieve, limits in addition to those imposed by other social and political forces. Hoping to use legal and constitutional rights to overcome subordination was a case of trying to dismantle the master's house with the master's own tools.[6] It cannot be done, they say.

This view harmonizes with some other trends in recent legal scholarship, especially in the study of law as ideology or "discourse." Inspired variously by feminist, post-structuralist, and neo-Marxist theory, this work has a common theme: that "rights talk" and "legal consciousness" sharply delimit the political imaginations of the downtrodden. The language of the law, along with other discourses of the powerful, lays down the very terms within which subordinate groups are able to experience the world and articulate their aspirations. Thus these recent schools of legal theory echo Tocqueville in underscoring the ideological hindrances law can impose on democratic movements.

Although Tocqueville praises the process and the radical scholars bemoan it, for both of them the language of the law works as a subtle web of constraints in the consciousness of the "lower classes." It enmeshes them in a world view that is not theirs, limiting their social visions, silencing many of their aspirations, and eliciting their consent to the dominant groups' versions of the natural and good. The story I have told supplies rich examples of these ruses

6. The metaphor is Audre Lorde's in *Sister Outsider* 110 (1984).

of legal language, or, rather, of how legal language and legal coercion collaborated to produce such conformity. But the story also shows the transformability of the language of law and its emancipatory uses.

Labor's law-inspired laissez-faire rights rhetoric imported some of the liberal legal order's key assumptions about the uses and limits of state power. Thus it helped to recast many of labor's aspirations for reform and redistribution as not fit to be addressed to the state and polity; in so doing, it pushed to the margins a competing language of labor protest that treated the law and the state as vehicles of social transformation. But it bears remembering that this competing language, with its roots in an earlier labor republicanism, was itself a rhetoric of rights, a subversive reworking of an inherited tradition. Moreover, while the newer, narrower rights talk was a reaction and an accommodation to the harshness and violence of the late-nineteenth-century legal order, it also helped labor greatly in assailing that order. The tradition of liberal legal discourse proved plural and open-textured enough to enable labor to reinterpret its doctrines to support broad-based collective action, broad freedoms of expression and association, and even defiance of the courts.

Thus the language of the law in America is best conceived as a tradition of discourse with divergent and conflicting strands. Radical analyses of law and subaltern social consciousness cannot ignore the open-endedness and mutability of legal discourse. The language of law, like other languages about the social world, does not possess such immutable or intrinsic meanings that the mere act of speaking or thinking in it automatically binds the speaker or thinker to a web of fixed associations, meanings, and values. It can often have this effect. But the discourse cannot always keep its terms frozen in place. As language, it is capable of transformations of meanings, of metaphorical extensions into new realms of social experience: as state-enforced debt peonage becomes "involuntary servitude," so too do state-enforced strike-prevention and strike-breaking. Just so, the arrest of pickets becomes the repression of citizens "associating to redress wrongs." In an era when courts were a hostile place for them, trade unionists still managed to seize on the common law's

to seize on the common law's ambiguities and the Constitution's recessive radical strains to enact a process of revision and reform.

This historical account makes another, simpler present point. Organized labor is in the worst trouble it has seen since the era this book recounts. Union leaders and activists are debating anew the role that law and government should play in American industry. Nor are they alone in pondering fundamental revision; many management and government leaders as well as policy intellectuals are deeply disaffected with the present labor law regime and have begun to articulate sweeping alternatives.

From the labor movement's perspective, the nation's labor law has largely failed over the past two decades to protect union organizing or to defend existing unions from a new open shop movement on the part of employers in many unionized sectors. So great is organized labor's discontent that one has begun to hear labor leaders mooting, half-seriously, the desirability of a "deregulation" of labor relations. One hears, in other words, strong echoes of the anti-statism of the Gompers era.

The appeal of this anti-statist outlook is clear enough. Today, as in Gompers's day, a legal order that, through "deregulation," allowed broad freedoms of collective action could contribute to a vastly stronger labor movement. Moreover, events abroad, as well as the deregulation movement at home, have given the rhetoric of anti-statism an amazing vigor. Yet this history forcefully demonstrates the deceptive side of that rhetoric: it was this history, after all, that motivated the Realists' famous lesson: "There is no such thing as a free market."[7] There are only competing regimes of regulation.

Now, as then, it seems doubtful that a laissez-faire regime, even a pro-labor laissez-faire regime, would suffice to meet the aspirations of a great many American workers. There would remain desirable kinds of regulation and redistributions of power that such laissez-faire measures could not accomplish. Policy prescriptions, however, are not this historian's stock in trade. Only this emerges clearly: In the past, the institutional framework and policies of labor law played

7. I am told that Professor Gerald Frug coined this formulation of the Realist insight.

a substantial part in shaping the character of the labor movement. We deceive ourselves if we attribute too much of that character to "deeper" forces. Thus the imagining and scrutinizing of possible new institutions and new laws should be done with all the canniness labor and its friends can muster; for these institutions and laws may go a long way toward shaping the identity and the capacities for collective action of the labor movement of the future.

Appendixes

Index

Appendix A: Labor Legislation in the Courts, 1885–1930

I. GILDED AGE LABOR'S CORE LEGISLATIVE GOALS

A. Discrimination against Union Members

Struck Down:

State ex rel. Zillmer v. Kreutzberg, 114 Wis. 530, 90 N.W. 1098 (1902) (overturning an act prohibiting employers from discouraging union membership and from discharging employees because of union membership).

Gillespie v. People, 188 Ill. 176, 58 N.E. 1007 (1900) (overturning an 1893 act prohibiting employers from discouraging union membership and from discharging employees because of union membership).

State v. Bateman, 10 Ohio Dec. 68 (Ohio C.P. 1900) (same).

Commonwealth v. Clark, 14 Pa. Super. 435 (1900) (same).

State v. Julow, 129 Mo. 163, 31 S.W. 781 (1895) (same).

Davis v. State, 30 Ohio Wkly. Law Bull. 342 (Ohio C.P. 1893) (upholding an Ohio anti-discrimination statute, but on a ground so narrow as to vitiate the law: the employer could fire an employee for any reason; he violated the law only by coercing, or attempting to coerce, the employee into quitting).

Upheld:

Curran v. Galen, 2 Misc. 553, 22 N.Y.S. 826, *aff'd*, 152 N.Y. 33 (1893). (Not reaching the constitutional question in light of Penal Code sections 170 and 171—misdemeanor to coerce workers not to join union—the court denied an injunction and equitable damages where the union struck to persuade nonunion employees to resign).

B. Weighing Coal at Mines

Struck Down:

In re Preston, 63 Ohio St. 428, 59 N.E. 101 (1900) (invalidating a statute that demanded that coal not be screened until it had been weighed and credit had been given to the miner for the full amount he mined).

Commonwealth v. Brown, 8 Pa. Super. 339 (1898) (same).

In re House Bill No. 203, 21 Colo. 27, 39 P. 431 (1895) (same).

Harding v. People, 160 Ill. 459, 43 N.E. 624 (1896) (similar).

Ramsey v. People, 142 Ill. 380, 32 N.E. 364 (1892) (similar).

Millett v. People, 117 Ill. 294, 7 N.E. 631 (1886) (similar).

Upheld:

Wilson v. State, 7 Kan. App. 428, 53 P. 371 (1898), *aff'd*, 61 Kan. 32, 58 P. 981 (1899).

Martin v. State, 143 Ind. 545, 42 N.E. 911 (1896) (failing to reach constitutional question because the evidence showed that the nature of the coal made screening necessary before an accurate weight could be determined).

Peel Splint Coal Co. v. State, 36 W. Va. 802, 15 S.E. 1000 (1892).

C. Requiring Regular (Weekly, Monthly) Payment of Wages

Struck Down:

Johnson v. Goodyear Mining Co., 127 Cal. 4, 59 P. 304 (1899) (statute required monthly payment, and gave employees a lien if employer failed to so provide).

State v. Lake Erie Iron Co., 1 Ohio Dec. 254 (same, but applied to only certain types of employment), *aff'd mem.*, 55 Ohio St. 423, 442, 45 N.E. 313, 315 (1896).

Commonwealth v. Isenberg & Rowland, 4 Pa. D. 579 (1895) (statute required semimonthly payment for employees in mining and manufacturing).

Leep v. Railway Co., 58 Ark. 407, 25 S.W. 75 (1894) (statute requiring full payment of accrued wages at time of discharge and an assessment of continuing wages against an employer as penalty for non-payment was held an unconstitutional invasion of personal rights but a constitutional use of police power against corporations).

Braceville Coal Co. v. People, 147 Ill. 66, 35 N.E. 62 (1893) (weekly payment law).

San Antonio & A.P.R.R. v. Wilson, 4 Tex. Civ. Cas. 565, 19 S.W. 910 (Tex. Civ. App. 1892) (payment upon discharge for railroad employees).

Godcharles v. Wigeman, 113 Pa. 431, 6 A. 354 (1886) (Pennsylvania statute regulating time of payment and outlawing use of scrip).

Upheld:

Skinner v. Garnett Gold-Mining Co., 96 F. 735 (C.C.N.D. Cal. 1899) (same statute as in *Johnson v. Goodyear Mining*, supra).

Slocum v. Bear Valley Irrigation Co., 122 Cal. 555, 55 P. 403 (1898) (statute granting a preferred lien to mechanics and laborers who were employed by the week or month struck down as unconstitutional "special legislation").

Hancock v. Yaden, 121 Ind. 366, 23 N.E. 253 (1889) (statute upheld as constitutional).

In re House Bill No. 1230, 163 Mass. 589, 40 N.E. 713 (1895) (weekly wage payment).

D. Payment in Scrip/Regulation of Company Stores

Struck Down:

Luman v. Hitchens Bros. Co., 90 Md. 14, 44 A. 1051 (1899) (statute prohibiting railroad or mining companies from selling goods to employees, and prohibiting officers or directors of such companies from acquiring an interest in general stores).

In re House Bill No. 147, 23 Colo. 504, 48 P. 512, (1897) (payment in legal tender).

Marsh v. Poston & Co., 35 Ohio Law Bull. 327 (payment in scrip), *aff'd mem.*, 54 Ohio St. 681, 47 N.E. 1114 (1896).

State v. Loomis, 115 Mo. 307, 22 S.W. 350 (1893) (invalidating statute requiring payment in legal tender).

State v. Paint Rock Coal Co., 92 Tenn. 81, 20 S.W. 499 (1892) (misdemeanor to refuse to redeem scrip in lawful currency constitutes unconstitutional indirect imprisonment for debt).

Frorer v. People, 141 Ill. 171, 31 N.E. 395 (1892) (invalidating statute requiring payment in legal tender and prohibiting "Truck Stores").

State v. Goodwill, 33 W. Va. 179, 10 S.E. 285 (1889) (statute requiring payment in legal tender invalid under the fourteenth amendment).

State v. Fire Creek Coal & Coke Co., 33 W. Va. 188, 10 S.E. 288 (1889) (another provision of the statute in *Goodwill*, prohibiting employers from charging employees more than others for goods at company stores).

State v. Haun, 61 Kan. 146, 59 P. 340 (1899) (payment in legal tender).

Upheld:

Harbison v. Knoxville Iron Co., 103 Tenn. 421, 53 S.W. 955 (1899) (payment in legal tender).

Avent Beattyville Coal Co. v. Commonwealth, 96 Ky. 218, 28 S.W. 502 (1894) (same).

State v. Peel Splint Coal Co., 36 W. Va. 802, 15 S.E. 1000 (1892) (same).

E. Hours Laws

1. Public Works

Struck Down:

Fiske v. People, 188 Ill. 206, 58 N.E. 985 (1900).

Seattle v. Smyth, 22 Wash. 327, 60 P. 1120 (1900).

State v. McNally, 48 La. Ann. 1450, 21 So. 27 (1896).
Ex parte Kubach, 85 Cal. 274, 24 P. 737 (1890).

Upheld:

People ex rel. Warren v. Beck, 144 N.Y. 225, 39 N.E. 80 (1894) (eight hour statute upheld, but merely directory as to certain provisions to be inserted in the labor contract).
People v. Phyfe, 136 N.Y. 554, 32 N.E. 978 (1893) (ten-hour statute upheld, but held merely advisory and unenforceable).

2. Private Employment

Struck Down:

In re Morgan, 26 Colo. 415, 58 P. 1971 (1899) (rejecting *Holden v. Hardy*, 169 U.S. 366 (1898)).
In re Eight-Hour Law, 21 Colo. 29, 39 P. 328 (1895).
Low v. Rees Printing Co., 41 Neb. 127, 59 N.W. 362 (1894).
Wheeling Bridge & Terminal Ry. v. Gilmore, 8 Ohio C.C. 658 (1894).

Upheld:
Holden v. Hardy, 169 U.S. 366 (1898).

3. Women

Struck Down:
Ritchie v. People, 155 Ill. 98, 40 N.E. 454 (1895).

Upheld:
Commonwealth v. Hamilton Mfg. Co., 120 Mass. 383 (1876).

4. Sunday Work

Struck Down:
Ex parte Jentzsch, 112 Cal. 468, 44 P. 803 (1896).
State v. Southern Ry., 119 N.C. 814, 25 S.E. 862 (1896).
Eden v. People, 161 Ill. 296, 43 N.E. 1108 (1896).
State v. Granneman, 132 Mo. 326, 33 S.W. 784 (1895).
Ragio v. State, 86 Tenn. 292, 6 S.W. 401 (1888).

Ex parte Westerfield, 55 Cal. 550 (1880).

Ex parte Newman, 9 Cal. 502 (1858) (invalidating statute on first amendment grounds), *overruled by Ex parte Andrews*, 18 Cal. 678 (1861).

Upheld:

Petit v. Minnesota, 177 U.S. 164 (1900).

Breyer v. State, 102 Tenn. 103, 50 S.W. 769 (1899).

Nesbit v. State, 8 Kan. App. 104, 54 P. 326 (1898).

People v. Havnor, 149 N.Y. 195, 43 N.E. 541 (1896), *appeal dismissed*, 170 U.S. 408 (1898).

Ex parte Andrews, 18 Cal. 678 (1861).

F. Tenement Labor

Struck Down:

In re Jacobs, 98 N.Y. 98 (1885) (striking down a law prohibiting the manufacture of cigars in tenement houses).

G. Labor Injunction Reforms

Struck Down:

Bradley v. State, 111 Ga. 168, 36 S.E. 630 (1900) (nonlabor case with act similarly narrowed as in *Hale*).

Hale v. State, 55 Ohio St. 210, 45 N.E. 199 (1896) (holding that, in a nonlabor case involving a statute that redefined the crime of contempt and made it an ''offense against public justice,'' the act could not be interpreted so as to limit the court's power to punish contempt).

Cheadle v. State, 110 Ind. 301, 11 N.E. 426 (1886) (holding that, in a nonlabor case involving an 1881 statute, which provided for a jury trial for indirect contempt, the legislature cannot limit contempt power).

H. Statutes Seeking to Reform
Criminal Conspiracy Doctrine as Applied to Labor

1. New York

Cases Vitiating, Narrowing, or Ignoring Statutory Reforms:

People v. McFarlin, 43 Misc. 591, 89 N.Y.S. 527 (Monroe County Ct. 1904) (section 170 construed in light of section 168 as not protecting union members engaged in boycotts from criminal conspiracy indictments).

People ex rel. Gill v. Walsh, 15 N.Y. St. Rptr. 17 (holding it a criminal conspiracy for union to label someone a "scab" and seek to prevent his being hired—section 170 not mentioned in court's decision), *aff'd mem.*, 110 N.Y. 633, 17 N.E. 871 (1888).

People ex rel. Gill v. Smith, 10 N.Y. St. Rptr. 730 (1887) (holding that section 170 of the Penal Code, which sanctions peaceable assembly by workers to maintain or raise wages, does not protect strikers when their object is not directly related to wage rates).

People v. Kostka, 4 N.Y. Crim. Rptr. 429 (1886) (secondary boycott violates criminal conspiracy statute, Penal Code section 168, without mentioning labor in section 170 of the Penal Code).

Cases Applying Statutory Reforms:

People v. Radt, 71 N.Y.S. 846 (1900) (holding that under section 168 distribution of leaflets did not constitute a criminal conspiracy).

Reynolds v. Everett, 22 N.Y.S. 826 (1892) (in light of sections 170 and 171—misdemeanor to coerce workers not to join union—court denies injunction and equitable damages where union struck to persuade nonunion employees to resign).

2. Pennsylvania

Cases Vitiating, Narrowing, or Ignoring Statutory Reforms:

Erdmann v. Mitchell, 10 Pa. D. 701, *aff'd*, 207 Pa. 79, 56 A. 327 (1903) (equity court will enjoin union from striking to force employer to fire workers of another union. While 1872, 1876, and 1891 acts decriminalized peaceable labor activities to raise wages and better working conditions, the acts did not make such actions lawful. Such conduct may still be enjoined and punished by the contempt power. Indeed, if the statutes did legalize the union conduct, they would violate the state Bill of Rights, which guarantees a remedy for any injury to person or property).

Flaccus v. Smith, 199 Pa. 128, 48 A. 894 (1901) (construing the act of 1872 as not protecting an organizer's persuasion of apprentices to join union in contravention of employment contract, the court did not mention the amendments of 1876 and 1891, which extended protection to acts with a lawful purpose and strikes for better conditions).

The Conspiracy Trials of 1875 (unreported). *See The Railway World*, Oct. 16, 1875, at 672; *New York Sun*, Oct. 7, 1875, at 1; *Miners' National Record*, Oct. 1875, at 195. The case arose out of anthracite field strikes deliberately provoked by the coal operators. Judge Orvis charged the jury "that any agreement, combination, or confederation, to increase or depress the prices of any vendible commodity, whether labor, merchandise, or anything else, is indictable as a conspiracy under the laws of Pennsylvania." The 1872 act protected only the union's decision not to work for an employer, but any hindering of other workers constituted a criminal combination.

Case Applying Statutory Reforms:

Commonwealth ex rel. Vallette v. Sheriff, 15 Phil. Rpts. 393 (1881) (holding that agreement to strike not a conspiracy in light of acts of 1872 and 1876).

3. New Jersey

Cases Vitiating, Narrowing, or Ignoring Statutory Reforms:

Connett v. United Hatters of N. Am., 76 N.J. Eq. 202, 74 A. 188 (1909) (noting that the 1883 act does not apply to civil suits to enjoin labor unions from violent acts intended to intimidate and interfere with owner's employees pending a strike).

Frank & Dugan v. Herold, 63 N.J. Eq. 443, 52 A. 152 (1902) (holding that despite the 1883 act, employers have the right to restrain third parties from interfering with their employees by persuading them to break their contracts).

Cumberland Glass Mfg. Co. v. Glass Bottle Blowers' Ass'n, 59 N.J. Eq. 49, 46 A. 208 (1899) (holding that although the purpose of the 1883 act was "to legalize strikes," "the means adopted must be persuasive and not coercive"—under these circumstances the injunction is valid against those who physically or verbally intimidated nonstriking workers).

II. SECONDARY LEGISLATIVE DEMANDS

A. Protection of Employees as Voters

Struck Down:

United States v. Amsden, 6 F. 819 (1881) (federal statute penalized employers who threatened to fire or refuse to renew employment contracts in order to intimidate employees not to vote).

B. Child Labor

Upheld:

People v. Ewer, 8 N.Y. Crim. Rptr. 383 (1892) (upholding the state's police power over the rights of parents to prohibit exhibition of children under age sixteen as dancers).

C. Statement of Cause of Discharge

Struck Down:

Wallace v. G.C. & N.R.R., 94 Ga. 732, 22 S.E. 579 (1894) (holding unconstitutional an act requiring certain corporations to tell discharged employees the cause of their discharge).

D. Convict-Made Goods

Struck Down:

People v. Hawkins, 157 N.Y. 1, 51 N.E. 257 (1898) (striking down a statute requiring labeling of in-state prison-made goods).

Arnold v. Yanders, 56 Ohio St. 417, 47 N.E. 50 (1897) (striking down a statute of 1894 requiring a license and the posting of a bond to sell convict-made goods).

People v. Hawkins, 32 N.Y.S. 524 (1895) (striking down 1894 statute requiring labeling of all prison goods imported from other states).

In re Yanders, 1 Ohio N.P. 190, (1892) (holding unconstitutional a statute regulating the selling of out-of-state convict-made goods).

E. Emigrant Agents

Struck Down:

State v. Moore, 113 N.C. 697, 18 S.E. 342 (1893) (tax on persons who recruit laborers to go outside their state to work).

Joseph v. Randolph, 71 Ala. 499 (1882) (same).

F. Mechanics' Liens

Struck Down:

Palmer v. Tingle, 55 Ohio St. 423, 45 N.E. 313 (1896). This statute was upheld in *Jones v. Great S. Fireproof Hotel Co.*, 86 F. 370 (6th Cir. 1898) and *Great S. Fireproof Hotel Co. v. Jones*, 193 U.S. 532 (1904).

Waters v. Wolf, 162 Pa. 153, 29 A. 646 (1894).

John Spry Lumber Co. v. Sault Savings Bank, Loan & Trust Co., 77 Mich. 199, 43 N.W. 778 (1889).

G. Lien and Wage Suits—Attorneys' Fees

Struck Down:

Davidson v. Jennings, 27 Colo. 187, 60 P. 354 (1900) (enforcement of mechanics' liens).

Gulf, Colo. & Santa Fe Ry. v. Ellis, 165 U.S. 150 (1897) (reversing Texas statute allowing for attorneys' fees).

Randolph v. Builders' & Painters' Supply Co., 106 Ala. 501, 17 So. 721 (1895) (enforcement of mechanics' liens).

Hocking Valley Coal Co. v. Rosser, 53 Ohio St. 12, 41 N.E. 263 (1895) (same).

Grand Rapids Chair Co. v. Runnels, 77 Mich. 104, 43 N.W. 1006 (1889) (general wage claims).

Upheld:

Title Guarantee & Trust Co. v. Wrenn, 35 Or. 62, 56 P. 271 (1899) (wage claim).

Singer Mfg. Co. v. Fleming, 39 Neb. 679, 58 N.W. 226 (1894) (same).

H. Union Labor on Public Works

Struck Down:

Fiske v. People ex rel. Raymond, 188 Ill. 206, 58 N.E. 985 (1900) (statute mandating union-only work on public projects).

Adams v. Brenan, 177 Ill. 194, 52 N.E. 314 (1898) (same).

III. TWENTIETH-CENTURY LABOR LAWS STRUCK DOWN

This list compiles a selection of the most significant categories of labor laws struck down during the first two decades of the century. Far more labor laws were passed as well as struck down during those decades than during the two preceding ones, for which I have supplied a comprehensive list. A complete list of labor laws invalidated from the 1880s through 1922 would run to roughly "300 separate statutes, bills, and ordinances whose constitutionality [was] successfully challenged in the courts." See L. Clark, "Labor Laws That Have Been Declared Unconstitutional," *Bulletin of the U.S. Bureau of Labor Statistics* 2, no. 10 (November 1922). This BLS report contains citations to all the laws, bills, and ordinances struck down. See id. at 85–90 (listing "Cases Cited.")

A. Statement of Cause of Discharge

In re Opinion of the Justices, 220 Mass. 627, 108 N.E. 807 (1915).

St. Louis Southwest Ry. v. Griffin, 106 Tex. 477, 171 S.W. 703 (1914).
Atchison, Topeka & Santa Fe Ry. v. Brown, 80 Kan. 312, 102 P. 459 (1909).

B. Blacklisting
Wabash R.R. v. Young, 162 Ind. 102, 69 N.E. 1003 (1904).

C. Employment of Women
People v. Williams, 189 N.Y. 131, 81 N.E. 778 (1907).
Burcher v. People, 41 Colo. 495, 93 P. 14 (1907).

D. Protection of Local Labor
City of Chicago v. Hulbert, 205 Ill. 346, 68 N.E. 786 (1903).
People v. Warren, 13 Misc. 615, 34 N.Y.S. 942 (1895).

E. Tax on Alien Employees
Ex parte Kotta, 187 Cal. 27, 200 P. 957 (1921).
Truax v. Raich, 239 U.S. 33 (1915).
Ex parte Case, 20 Idaho 128, 116 P. 1037 (1911).

F. Wages—Rates on Public Work
Wagner v. Milwaukee, 177 Wis. 410, 188 N.W. 487 (1922).
Wright v. Hoctor, 95 Neb. 342, 145 N.W. 704 (1914).
Ryan v. New York, 177 N.Y. 271, 69 N.E. 599 (1904).
Street v. Varney Elec. Supply Co., 160 Ind. 338, 66 N.E. 895 (1903).
People ex rel. Rodgers v. Coler, 166 N.Y. 1, 59 N.E. 716 (1901).
Frame v. Felix, 167 Pa. 47, 31 A. 375 (1895).

G. Mechanics' Liens
Rittenhouse & Embree Co. v. William Wrigley, Jr., Co., 264 Ill. 40, 105 N.E. 743 (1914).

Kelly v. Johnson, 251 Ill. 135, 95 N.E. 1068 (1911).

Page v. Carr, 232 Pa. 371, 81 A. 430 (1911).

Sterling Bronze Co. v. Syria Improvement Ass'n, 226 Pa. 475, 75 A. 668 (1910).

Henry Taylor Lumber Co. v. Carnegie Inst., 225 Pa. 486, 74 A. 357 (1909).

Vulcanite Portland Cement Co. v. John W. Allison Co., 220 Pa. 382, 69 A. 855 (1908).

Vulcanite Paving Co. v. Philadelphia Rapid Transit Co., 220 Pa. 603, 69 A. 1117 (1908).

Gibbs v. Tally, 133 Cal. 373, 65 P. 970 (1901).

Meyer v. Berlandi, 39 Minn. 438, 40 N.W. 513 (1888), *overruled by State v. Anderson*, 159 Minn. 245, 199 N.W. 6 (1924).

H. Attorneys' Fees for Suits to Foreclose upon Mechanics' Liens

Union Terminal Co. v. Turner Constr. Co., 247 F. 727 (5th Cir. 1918).

Becker v. Hopper, 22 Wyo. 237, 138 P. 179 (1914), *aff'd*, 23 Wyo. 209, 147 P. 1085 (1915).

Mills v. Olsen, 43 Mont. 129, 115 P. 33 (1911).

Fort Worth & D.C. Ry. v. Loyd, 63 Tex. Civ. App. 47, 132 S.W. 899 (1910), *overruled by Missouri, K. & T. Ry. v. Mahaffey*, 105 Tex. 394, 150 S.W. 881 (1912) (statute does not allow for payment of attorneys' fees).

Manowsky v. Stephan, 233 Ill. 409, 84 N.E. 365 (1908).

Builders' Supply Depot v. O'Connor, 150 Cal. 265, 88 P. 982 (1907).

Atkinson v. Woodmansee, 68 Kan. 71, 74 P. 640 (1903).

I. Time Payment of Wages

Davidow v. Wadsworth Mfg. Co., 211 Mich. 90, 178 N.W. 776 (1920).

Brannon v. Parsons, 144 La. 295, 80 So. 542 (1919).

Bofferding v. Mengelkoch, 129 Minn. 184, 152 N.W. 135 (1915).

State v. Prudential Coal Co., 130 Tenn. 275, 170 S.W. 56 (1914).

Cleveland C.C. & St. L. Ry. v. Schuler, 182 Ind. 57, 105 N.E. 567 (1914).

Ex parte Crane, 26 Cal. App. 22, 145 P. 733 (1914).

Missouri, K. & T. Ry. v. Braddy, 135 S.W. 1059 (Tex. Civ. App. 1911).

State v. Potomac Valley Coal Co., 116 Md. 380, 81 A. 686 (1911).

Toledo, St. L. & W.R.R. v. Long, 169 Ind. 316, 82 N.E. 757 (1907).

Republic Iron & Steel Co. v. State, 160 Ind. 379, 66 N.E. 1005 (1903).

J. Payment in Scrip/Regulation of Company Stores

State v. Nashville, C. & St. L. Ry., 124 Tenn. 1, 135 S.W. 773 (1911).

Union Sawmill Co. v. Felsenthal Land & Townsite Co., 84 Ark. 494, 106 S.W. 676 (1907).

Jordan v. State, 51 Tex. Crim. 531, 103 S.W. 633 (1907).

Leach v. Missouri Tie & Timber Co., 111 Mo. App. 650, 86 S.W. 579 (1905).

State v. Missouri Tie & Timber Co., 181 Mo. 536, 80 S.W. 933 (1904).

Kellyville Coal Co. v. Harrier, 207 Ill. 624, 69 N.E. 927 (1904).

Dixon v. Poe, 159 Ind. 492, 65 N.E. 518 (1902).

K. Hours—Public Works

People ex rel. Cossey v. Grout, 179 N.Y. 417, 72 N.E. 464 (1904).

People v. Orange County Rd. Constr. Co., 175 N.Y. 84, 67 N.E. 129 (1903).

City of Cleveland v. Clements Bros. Constr. Co., 67 Ohio St. 197, 65 N.E. 885 (1902).

L. Hours—Private Employment

Chan Sing v. City of Astoria, 79 Or. 411, 155 P. 378 (1916).

Yee Gee v. San Francisco, 235 F. 757 (N.D. Cal. 1916).

United States v. Howell, 5 Alaska 578 (1916).

Commonwealth v. Boston & M.R.R., 222 Mass. 206, 110 N.E. 264 (1915).

Saville v. Corless, 46 Utah 495, 151 P. 51 (1915).

State v. Legendre, 138 La. 154, 70 So. 70 (1915).

Ex parte Wong Wing, 167 Cal. 109, 138 P. 695 (1914).

Erie R.R. v. New York, 233 U.S. 671 (1914) (commerce clause).

State v. Barba, 132 La. 768, 61 So. 784 (1913).

North Pac. R.R. v. Washington, 222 U.S. 370 (1912) (commerce clause).

State v. Miksicek, 225 Mo. 561, 125 S.W. 507 (1910).

State v. Missouri Pac. Ry., 212 Mo. 658, 111 S.W. 500 (1908).

State v. Chicago, M. & St. P. Ry., 136 Wis. 407, 117 N.W. 686 (1908).

M. Inspection and Regulation of Workplaces

Chicago & N.W. Ry. v. Railroad & W. Comm'n, 280 F. 387 (C.A. Minn.) (invalidating, on statutory grounds as well as for being too vague and indefinite for criminal prosecution, a statute requiring an employer to build repair sheds), *aff'd*, 260 U.S. 697 (1922).

Commonwealth v. Beaver Dam Coal Co., 194 Ky. 34, 237 S.W. 1086 (1922) (mine regulations invalidated on delegation grounds).

People v. Schenck, 257 Ill. 384, 100 N.E. 994 (1913) (noting that the prohibition of the use of emery wheels in basements is not a proper classification, due to a lack of an exception for properly ventilated areas).

State v. Miksicek, 225 Mo. 561, 125 S.W. 507 (1910) (bakery regulations violated equal protection by not attaching to all types of bakeries and similar workplaces).

Beaumont Traction Co. v. State, 122 S.W. 615 (Tex. Civ. App. 1909) (motorman protection measure).

Starne v. People, 222 Ill. 189, 78 N.E. 61 (1906) (statute providing for washing facilities at mines held "special legislation").

Schaezlein v. Cabaniss, 135 Cal. 466, 67 P. 755 (1902) (unconstitutional delegation of legislative authority to executive officer, the factory inspector).

N. Union Labor on Public Works

Wright v. Hoctor, 95 Neb. 342, 145 N.W. 704 (1914).
Lewis v. Board of Educ., 139 Mich. 306, 102 N.W. 756 (1905).
State v. Toole, 26 Mont. 22, 66 P. 496 (1901).

Appendix B: Approximating the Numbers of Labor Injunctions and Their Relation to Other Strike Statistics, 1880–1930

An accurate tally of the total number of injunctions issued in labor disputes in the fifty years following 1880 is impossible.[1] Most labor injunctions were temporary or preliminary decrees, and the truncated nature of the proceedings from which they issued resulted in few reported opinions.[2] Many researchers with many lifetimes would be required to sift through the relevant court records of the industrial states where injunctions bulked largest, and even then the search would not yield more than a fraction of the total number of unreported labor injunction cases. Many court records have disappeared, especially in the lower state courts where most anti-strike decrees originated. Moreover, ex parte orders frequently issued, even from metropolitan courts, without leaving a trace on dockets or in files.[3]

I estimate that roughly 105 labor injunctions issued in the 1880s, 410 in the 1890s, 850 in the 1900s, 835 in the 1910s, and 2130 in the 1920s. My estimates include both temporary and permanent decrees, but count only one when a permanent decree followed a temporary one in the same case. I base these very rough but, I will argue, conservative estimates on the only two reasonably systematic

1. In 1932 Congress passed the Norris-LaGuardia Act. The major industrial states passed "little Norris-LaGuardia Acts" shortly thereafter, and together these statutes ended the era of the labor injunction and the old labor law regime. See C. Gregory, supra Chap. 3, note 2, at 191–93.

2. See F. Frankfurter and N. Greene, supra Intro., note 9, at 49–51; E. Witte, supra Intro., note 9, at 84.

3. See F. Frankfurter and N. Greene, supra Intro., note 9, at 49n8.

efforts undertaken during the injunction era to record or retrieve a state's unreported labor injunction cases.

First, the Massachusetts Bureau of Labor Statistics collected statistics based upon union reports of labor injunctions issued by state and federal courts in that state between 1898 and 1916.[4] In all, the Bureau compiled a list of 260 injunctions issued in that state between 1898 and 1916.[5] During the same period there were 31 reported injunction cases in Massachusetts, 8 from the federal courts and 23 ordered by state courts. Thus, putting aside the incompleteness of the Bureau's list,[6] the ratio of unreported to reported labor injunction cases for Massachusetts in the period was roughly 8.5:1.

Second, in the late 1920s and early 1930s two Cornell University labor economists, Paul Brissenden and his student Cleon Swayzee, undertook an extensive study of labor injunctions issued by New York courts.[7] Relying chiefly on Swayzee's research in the court's records of New York, Kings, Queens, Bronx (i.e., New York City) and Westchester Counties, they concluded that "no less than nine

---

4. See Commonwealth of Mass. Bureau of Statistics, *Labor Injunctions in Massachusetts* (Labor Bulletin no. 70) (1909) (covering cases from 1898 to 1908); Commonwealth of Mass. Bureau of Statistics, *Labor Injunctions in Massachusetts* (Labor Bulletin no. 117) (1917) (covering cases from 1910 to 1916).

5. See id. Even this figure doubtless falls short of the actual number. Edwin Witte, who collected information on unreported injunction suits throughout the country, wrote in his report to the Industrial Commission: "It is doubtful whether for the first few years of this period . . . all injunctions issued by Massachusetts courts in labor disputes are included in this list." Quoted in F. Frankfurter and N. Greene, supra Intro., note 9, at 51n13. As evidence Witte pointed to the omission of an injunction issued by an equity judge in Suffolk County on July 7, 1899, against a machinists' union and reported in some detail in the *Machinists' Monthly Journal* for August 1899, at page 464. Witte also noted that the "Committee on 'Relations between Employers and Employees' [of the Massachusetts state legislature] made a report . . . in Jan., 1904, stat[ing] that 57 injunctions had been issued by Massachusetts courts in connection with labor disputes in the six years 1897–1902. [Yet,] Labor Bulletin No. 70 lists only 29 injunction actions in the five years 1898–1902 . . ." Id.

6. See supra Appendix B., note 5.

7. See Brissenden and Swayzee, "The Use of the Labor Injunction in the New York Needle Trades, II," 45 *Pol. Sci. Q.* 87 (1930); Brissenden and Swayzee, "The Use of the Labor Injunction in the New York Needle Trades, I," 44 *Pol. Sci. Q.* 548 (1929); C. Swayzee, supra Chap. 4, note 38. The files of these studies, including lists of cases and copies of records, are held in the Cornell University Library.

hundred and one injunctions, either preliminary, temporary or permanent [counting only one for each case in which a permanent decree followed a temporary or preliminary order] were granted in the New York state courts'' between 1904 and 1932.[8] The same period saw 149 reported (state court) cases, yielding a 6:1 ratio of unreported to reported labor injunction cases in state courts. Once again, I have not tried to guess and factor into this ratio how many *more* unreported injunctions issued but were not uncovered by the study. Because the authors only examined court records for New York City,[9] and not those of other important centers of union activity in New York such as Buffalo and Troy, the number of unreported injunctions left out was, again, surely substantial.

The average of these two states' ratios of unreported to reported injunctions is 7.25:1, which means that we must multiply the number of reported cases for the nation as a whole by 8.25 to arrive at rough national totals of all (reported and unreported) labor injunctions for these decades.[10] I am confident that this multiplier rests on a conservative estimate of the actual ratio for several reasons. In addition

8. C. Swayzee, supra Chap. 4, note 38, at 41–42. Brissenden and Swayzee did not consider federal cases.

9. Besides those records, the authors relied on the published State Reports and on the *New York Daily Law Journal*, which, again, reported primarily on New York City cases. Id. at 41.

10. For the national total of *reported* injunction suits, as well as for the New York and Massachusetts totals of reported cases, I have relied on the compilation of all reported state and federal labor injunctions carried out by Petro, "Injunctions and Labor Disputes, 1880–1932," 14 *Wake Forest L. Rev.* 341 (1978). Petro found 182 federal and 342 state court cases. See id. at 547–69. Although I have used Petro for this purpose, his polemical intent and his somewhat skewed methodology limit his study's general usefulness. Petro seeks to exonerate the courts of the injunction era by showing that the judges of the time were not "anti-labor" but rather stalwart foes of those "lawless men lusting for power and influence" who sought to infuse a "profoundly destructive strain of criminal syndicalism" into American trade unions. Id. at 342–43. The burden of Petro's article is to demonstrate that virtually no injunctions issued against peaceful labor protest; rather, all but a tiny handful were directed against union violence. Petro fails to analyze critically the evidence upon which he bases many conclusions. He relies on court findings that rested on affidavits submitted by employers' attorneys—affidavits that were, in turn, frequently sworn out by company-hired private detectives or "sluggers." Even more dismaying is the vague and misleading fashion in which he categorizes and classifies the opinions and decrees themselves. Petro calculates the proportion of reported cases re-

to the significant number of unreported decrees probably overlooked in both studies, both New York and Massachusetts were among the states with the most thorough official reporting of cases. Thus, the ratios were probably smaller than those of other states.[11] That my ratio of unreported to reported decrees is a conservative one also finds corroboration in the ratios of unreported to reported injunction suits that have been found for a number of individual strikes. The 1894 Pullman Strike gave rise to five reported court orders but at least 95 unreported decrees.[12] The Chicago Teamsters Strike of 1905 saw nine injunctions, but only one of these was reported.[13] Similarly, the Illinois Central Strike of 1913–1915 prompted at least eleven injunctions, but only one was reported.[14]

straining picketing to include only those that do so expressly and ignores the substantial number of reported blanket decrees restraining all "interference."

Finally, Petro makes the astonishing assertion that 1,500 is the "outside figure" for the total number of labor injunctions *sought* in the decades from 1880 to 1930. See id. at 361. This assertion flies in the face of Witte's collection of records for 531 unreported cases (of injunctions granted) for the Commission on Industrial Relations. The records are available today at the Wisconsin Historical Society together with Witte's list of references—in newspapers chiefly—to 1,364 state and 508 federal injunction cases (again, decrees granted). See E. Witte, supra Intro., note 9, at 84. Petro does note Witte's work, but he ignores the Massachusetts Bureau of Labor Statistics report listing 231 unreported injunctions (compared to 30 reported) for the years 1898–1916, as well as Brissenden and Swayzee's work on unreported New York cases. The latter found 620 injunction cases in New York state, only 103 of which find their way onto Petro's lists. Petro sensibly chooses not to use Witte's collection of unreported cases for his analyses of kinds of conduct and strikes enjoined, because Witte's records are far too fragmentary, usually recording nothing more than the issuing of decrees. However, Petro does not explain how his "outside figure" on the total number of injunctions, reported and unreported, can be reconciled with Witte's research. Indeed, Petro does not explain how he arrived at his "outside figure" at all.

11. More difficult to assess is the possible impact of variations in labor law doctrine from state to state. But New York stood at the liberal end of the spectrum and Massachusetts toward the conservative end. So insofar as those variations had any impact, one might expect that they would not greatly affect these estimates. On New York doctrine, see supra Chap. 3, note 3; on Massachusetts, see Kelman, "American Labor Law and Legal Formalism: How "Legal Logic" Shaped and Vitiated the Rights of American Workers," 58 *St. John's L. Rev.* 1 (1983).

12. See Allen, supra Chap. 3, note 8, at 847.

13. See F. Frankfurter and N. Greene, supra Intro., note 9, at 50.

14. See id.

In 1937, the United States Bureau of Labor Statistics (BLS) published a compilation of strikes per year for the years 1881 to 1936, excepting 1906 through 1913.[15] Labor historians have relied on this compilation for national strike statistics for the period.[16] Using the BLS statistics and my approximations of the numbers of injunctions per decade, we can, roughly but conservatively, reckon the percentage of all strikes in each decade that were attended by injunctions. The BLS statistics also record the numbers of sympathetic and other secondary actions per year. So, we can also roughly estimate the proportion of such actions met with injunctions.

Looking first at the percentages of all strikes enjoined in each decade, there were 10 per every thousand strikes or 1 percent for the 1880s; 31 per thousand strikes or 3 percent for the 1890s; 29 per thousand strikes from 1900 to 1905 or, again, 3 percent; 47 per thousand or 5 percent for 1914 through 1919; and 251 per thousand or 25 percent for the 1920s. The dramatic increase in the percentage of strikes enjoined in the 1920s is partly a reflection of the sharp decline in the total number of strikes that occurred in that decade. The increased percentage also reflects the increased proportion of large strikes,[17] most notably the railway shopmen's strike of 1922–1923 and the miners' strikes in the early and latter parts of the decade, all of which met with scores of injunctions.[18]

What proportion of sympathetic or secondary strikes and boycotts saw court intervention?[19] At least 10 percent of the sympathetic

15. See Peterson, supra Chap. 3, note 10.

16. See, e.g., P. Edwards, *Strikes in the United States, 1881–1974* (1981); Montgomery, supra Chap. 3, note 9.

17. See Peterson, supra Chap. 3, note 10, at 26.

18. Indeed, the railway shopmen's strike by itself may have accounted for more than 200 injunctions in 1924. See Sen. G. Pepper, "Address to American Bar Association, 1924," reprinted in Ill. *State Fed'n Lab. Newsl.*, Apr. 24, 1924, at 2, col. 2; see also Petro, supra Concl., note 10, at 351n12.

19. Here I have relied on Petro's reckoning of which reported injunction decisions barred secondary actions and used his reckoning as a proxy for the proportion of the total number of injunctions that were directed at such strikes or boycotts. This figure almost certainly undercounts the actual number of reported cases in which secondary actions were enjoined for the simple reason that many case reports do not reveal the nature of the underlying strike's objectives. I have derived the total numbers of secondary actions from the BLS statistics. See Peterson, supra Chap. 3, note 10, at 33, 39.

actions undertaken by workers in the 1880s were greeted by the new equitable device. In the 1890s—a decade that saw the greatest number of sympathy strikes of any decade in the country's history—the proportion of such strikes enjoined was at least 15 percent, which almost surely amounted to more than 90 strikes. As the number of sympathetic and secondary actions diminished the number attended by injunctions increased: at least 29 percent in the 1900s; 23 percent in the 1910s, and 46 percent in the 1920s.

Appendix C: Judicial Treatment of Statutes Seeking to Protect Union Organizing and Action by Revising Equity and Common Law Doctrine

A. Protection of Workers against Discharge for Union Membership

Struck Down:

Coppage v. Kansas, 236 U.S. 1 (1915) (in striking down the statute, the Court reversed the state court's narrowing construction, which allowed the employer to discharge for any reason, but prohibited actual coercion of employees into quitting), *rev'g*, State v. Coppage, 87 Kan. 752, 125 P. 8 (1912).

Adair v. United States, 208 U.S. 161, 172 (1908) (striking down section 10 of the first Erdman Act, making it a crime for an interstate carrier to discharge an employee for union membership).

Montgomery v. Pacific Elec. Ry., 293 F. 680 (9th Cir. 1923), *cert. denied*, 264 U.S. 586 (1924) (California statute prohibiting yellow-dog contracts).

Goldfield Consol. Mines v. Goldfield Miners' Union, 159 F. 500, 515–17 (D.N.Y. 1908) (Nevada statute prohibiting yellow-dog contracts).

People v. Western Union Tel. Co., 70 Colo. 90, 93, 198 P. 146, 149 (1921) (yellow-dog contracts).

Jackson v. Berger, 92 Ohio St. 130, 133, 110 N.E. 732, 733 (1915).

Bemis v. State, 12 Okla. Crim. 114, 152 P. 456 (1915).

State ex rel. Smith v. Daniels, 118 Minn. 155, 160–61, 136 N.W. 584, 586 (1912).

People v. Marcus, 185 N.Y. 257, 264, 77 N.E. 1073, 1075 (1906) (yellow-dog contracts).
Coffeyville Vitifried Brick & Tile Co. v. Perry, 69 Kan. 297, 76 P. 848 (1904) (same).
State ex rel. Zillmer v. Kreutzberg, 114 Wis. 530, 90 N.W. 1098 (1902) (same).

B. Antitrust Exemptions for Union Activity

Struck Down:

People ex rel. Akin v. Butler Street Foundry & Iron Co., 201 Ill. 236, 66 N.E. 349 (1903).
Niagara Fire Ins. Co. v. Cornell, 110 F. 816 (C.C.D. Neb. 1901).

Upheld:

Cleland v. Anderson, 66 Neb. 252, 92 N.W. 306 (1902).

C. Anti-Injunction Legislation

Struck Down:

Truax v. Corrigan, 257 U.S. 312 (1921) (Supreme Court invalidated state version of section 20 of the Clayton Act—prohibiting the issuance of restraining orders or injunctions in cases arising out of a labor dispute unless necessary to prevent irreparable injury to property, and protecting actions such as peaceful assembly and persuasion and the paying or witholding of strike benefits—after the Arizona Supreme Court had construed the statute to protect union picketing), *rev'g*, 20 Ariz. 7, 176 P. 570 (1918).
Bogni v. Perotti, 224 Mass. 152, 112 N.E. 853 (1916) (invalidating state version of section 20 of the Clayton Act in action between two unions; law preventing restraining orders or injunctions against peaceful picketing violative of plaintiff union's equal protection and due process rights).

Narrowed or Vitiated:

Duplex Printing Press Co. v. Deering, 254 U.S. 443 (1921) (section 20 of the Clayton Act did not prevent an injunction against workers

who refuse to work on nonunion materials—the federal statute
did not change preexisting law).

Vonnegut Mach. Co. v. Toledo Mach. & Tool Co., 263 F. 192, 200
(N.D. Ohio 1920) (state version of section 20 of the Clayton Act
must be narrowly construed so as not to violate Constitution. As
such, the statute allows temporary injunction to issue against workers engaged in a secondary boycott).

Ossey v. Retail Clerks Union, 326 Ill. App. 405 (1927) (state version
of section 20 of the Clayton Act did not protect mass picketing).

United Shoe Mach. Corp. v. Fitzgerald, 237 Mass. 537, 130 N.E.
89 (1921) (statute legalizing peaceful persuasion held not to prevent injunctions against picketing where the strikes were undertaken for an ''illegal purpose'').

Folsom Engraving Co. v. McNeil, 235 Mass. 269, 126 N.E. 479
(1920) (same).

Pierce v. Stablemen's Union, Local No. 876, 156 Cal. 70, 103 P.
324 (1909) (statute prohibiting injunctions against and contempt
citations for union activity construed not to prohibit injunctions
against ''wrongful acts,'' and held to violate substantive due process rights if not read in this narrow fashion).

Goldberg, Bowen & Co. v. Stablemen's Union, 149 Cal. 429, 86
P. 806 (1906) (same).

D. Cases Construing Anti-Injunction Laws to
Restate Previous Law as in Duplex

Bull v. International Alliance, 119 Kan. 713, 241 P. 459 (1925).

Pacific Typesetting Co. v. Int'l Typographical Union, 125 Wash.
273, 216 P. 358 (1923).

Crane & Co. v. Snowden, 112 Kan. 217, 210 P. 475 (1922).

Greenfield v. Central Labor Council, 104 Or. 236, 207 P. 168
(1922).

Pacific Coast Coal Co. v. Dist. 10, United Mine Workers of Am.,
122 Wash. 423, 210 P. 953 (1922).

Heitkemper v. Central Labor Council of Portland, 99 Or. 1, 192 P.
765 (1920).

A.J. Monday Co. v. Automobile, Aircraft & Vehicle Workers, 171 Wis. 532, 177 N.W. 867 (1920).

E. Cases Narrowing Anti-Conspiracy Laws

Ossey v. Retail Clerks' Union, 326 Ill. 405, 158 N.E. 162 (1927) (state version of section 20 of the Clayton Act did not protect mass picketing).

Gevas v. Greek Restaurant Workers' Club, 99 N.J. Eq. 770, 134 A. 304 (1926) (statute prohibiting contempt citations and injunctions in labor disputes did not sanction unlawful activity, and did not apply to strikes with illegal purpose).

Vonnegut Mach. Co. v. Toledo Mach. & Tool Co., 263 F. 192, 200 (N.D. Ohio 1920) (state version of section 20 of the Clayton Act must be narrowly construed so as not to violate Constitution. As such, the statute allows temporary injunction to issue against workers engaged in a secondary boycott).

Folsom Engraving Co. v. McNeil, 235 Mass. 269, 126 N.E. 479 (1920) (statute legalizing peaceful persuasion held not to prevent injunctions against picketing where the strikes were undertaken for an "illegal purpose").

United Shoe Mach. Corp. v. Fitzgerald, 237 Mass. 537, 130 N.E. 89 (1921) (same).

Grassi Contracting Co. v. Bennett, 174 A.D. 244, 160 N.Y.S. 279 (1916) (holding statute construed in *Auburn Draying* and *Davis Machine* does not proscribe injunctive relief when union threatens to strike in violation of employment contract over hiring of a foreman).

Auburn Draying Co. v. Wardell, 89 Misc. 501, 152 N.Y.S. 475 (1915) (holding statute legalizing peaceable assembly to advance wage rates does not protect workers striking for an open shop), *aff'd*, 178 A.D. 270, 165 N.Y.S. 469 (1917), *aff'd*, 227 N.Y. 1 (1919).

W. P. Davis Mach. Co. v. Robinson, 41 Misc. 329, 84 N.Y.S. 837 (1903) (holding statute legalizing peaceable assembly to advance wage rates does not protect workers who acted ''merely'' to harm employer's interests by a secondary boycott).

F. Procedural Reform of Conspiracy Law

Struck Down:

Walton Lunch Co. v. Kearney, 236 Mass. 310, 128 N.E. 429 (1920) (statute that provided for jury trial in contempt cases where criminal punishment possible violated ''fundamental law of the land'').

G. Nonlabor Cases Striking Down Statutes Providing for Juries in Contempt Proceedings

Ex parte McCown, 139 N.C. 95, 51 S.E. 957 (1905) (contempt regulation unconstitutionally violated inherent power of judiciary).

State ex rel. Boston & Maine Consol. Copper and Silver Mine Co. v. Clancy, 30 Mont. 193, 76 P. 10 (1904) (same).

Burdett v. Commonwealth, 103 Va. 838, 48 S.E. 878 (1904).

State ex rel. Crow v. Shepherd, 177 Mo. 205, 76 S.W. 79 (1903) (contempt regulation unconstitutionally violated inherent power of judiciary).

Smith v. Speed, 11 Okla. 95, 66 P. 511 (1901) (same).

Index